THE POETICS OF
SUPPLICATION

A volume in the series

MYTH AND POETICS

edited by Gregory Nagy

A full list of titles in the series appears at the end of the book.

THE POETICS OF SUPPLICATION

Homer's *Iliad* and *Odyssey*

KEVIN CROTTY

CORNELL UNIVERSITY PRESS

ITHACA AND LONDON

30511050

Copyright © 1994 by Cornell University

First published 1994 by Cornell University Press

Printed in the United States of America

♾ The paper in this book meets the minimum requirements
of the American National Standard for Information Sciences—
Permanence of Paper for Printed Library Materials, ANSI Z39.48-1984.

Library of Congress Cataloging-in-Publication Data

Crotty, Kevin, 1948–
    The poetics of supplication : Homer's Iliad and Odyssey / Kevin Crotty.
      p.   cm. — (Myth and poetics)
    Includes bibliographical references and index.
    ISBN 0-8014-2998-6
    1. Homer—Criticism and interpretation.   2. Epic poetry, Greek—History and
criticism.   3. Rites and ceremonies in literature.   4. Rites and ceremonies—
Greece.   5. Sympathy in literature.   6. Oral tradition—Greece.   7. Grief in
literature.   8. War in literature.   I. Title.   II. Series.
PA4037.C685   1994
883'.01—dc20   94-20261

For Anna Brodsky

Contents

Foreword

Gregory Nagy

The Homeric *Iliad* cannot give us the last word on Achilles. Despite the claims of various recent studies, including an influential commentary on the last of the twenty-four books of the *Iliad,* the hero of this epic does not come to terms with our own expectations of his humanity when he encounters face to face, in the epic's near-final scene of vicarious grief, the mourning father of his deadliest enemy. The ceremony of supplication that takes place at this moment in the *Iliad* creates an emotional effect so powerful—and so troubling—that it will take another epic, this time, the *Odyssey,* to follow up on its resonances.

This insight into the interplay of the *Iliad* and *Odyssey* becomes a central achievement of Kevin Crotty's *Poetics of Supplication,* which explores how the emotion of *eleos* forces the main hero of each of these two epics to reengage his whole life experience. This emotion, which we translate as "pity" and which the ancient Greeks publicly enacted in ceremonies of supplication, is the driving force behind the poetics of heroic redefinition in these epics. Moreover, this distinctly Greek idea of pity becomes the rationale for epic's own continuing self-redefinition. For Crotty, supplication thus serves as a model for the poetics of the *Iliad* and the *Odyssey.* The suppliant's message of grief must turn things around: the winner's perspective must be reshaped by that of the loser.

The myth of the hero—and thereby the poetic form of epic itself—is being shaped by the ceremony of supplication, since the pity that is generated by this ceremony will radically affect the hero's outlook on his own identity. Thus this book amounts to a defense of pity, following a line Aristotle himself had taken in rehabilitating *eleos* after Plato's attack.

In doing so, it also amounts to a declaration of emancipation from the confines of a special kind of Homeric criticism that insists on thinking of the hero as the creature of a specious reality called "Homeric warrior society." As Crotty argues, a hero such as Achilles experiences a kind of pity that is unique not only to his Iliadic situation but also to the passionate and uncompromising self that keeps on asserting itself within this situation.

The key to the role of pity as a shaper of both plot and character in Homeric narrative is Crotty's model of supplication as a *ceremony*. This book makes a hermeneutic distinction between ritual and ceremony, in that the second of the two is concerned specifically with *individual* responses to traditional situations. Thus the ceremony of supplication serves to individualize the epic, even the myth of the hero. The poetics of supplication become the poetics of individuality.

Preface

In *The Poetics of Supplication,* I explore the connections between a particular ceremony and the poetics of the *Iliad* and the *Odyssey.* I present the Homeric epics as tales of griefs, intended—like the suppliant's plea—to rouse memories of mortal vulnerability and to excite the emotion of pity. The title of this book carries two senses. On the one hand, I argue that the ceremony of supplication, as presented in the *Iliad,* has a complex internal structure, like that of a poem or a fictional narrative. As a ceremony, supplication has both traditional and expressive aspects. It consists of a traditional form that bundles together many of the constituent values of the warrior society, but also affords the individual within that society a means of articulating his or her particular distress. Supplication also has a moral dimension, for it provides the one supplicated with an occasion for insight into the contours of mortal life—its vulnerability to circumstance, and the seriousness of the claim another's suffering has to one's attention. As a ceremonial imitation of the child's utter dependence on the parent, supplication becomes in the *Iliad* an expression of the inevitable rift between the generations and the tragic absence of a benevolent and powerful father. For all these reasons, supplication is poemlike, and the kind of thing that may be said to have an implicit "poetic."

The second sense in which I intend the title of this work is that scenes of supplication are vital for understanding the poetics imbuing both the *Iliad* and the *Odyssey.* I believe that an adequate poetics of the Homeric epics must be, at least in part, a "poetics of supplication." "Remember your father," Priam says, when he begs Achilles to return Hector's body. The memory that Priam seeks to evoke, I will contend, is suggestive for—indeed, is a model for—the kind of memory that guides the poet of the Homeric epics, and, by extension, the kind of memory the poet seeks to awaken in his listeners. The memory called up by the poems is less a historical recollection or preservation of past events than a recreating, in emotional terms, of what griefs are like.

Because supplication is in large part a ceremony crystallizing the emotion of *eleos,* I begin with a discussion of that emotion—which I will here provisionally translate as "pity." I explain that the warrior society in the *Iliad* cannot be adequately understood wholly within the terms of the model of a "shame society." *Eleos* is a powerful, spontaneous, and unpredictable emotion that the warrior society simultaneously suppresses and invokes. By describing in some detail the complex place of *eleos* within and, so to speak, underneath that society, I seek to bring out the full implications of supplication as portrayed in the *Iliad*.

In the second part of this book, I show that the *Odyssey* uses supplication to elaborate a poetics of Homeric epic, for example, by self-consciously placing supplication scenes in contexts that are inevitably suggestive of poetics. The poetics I develop here differs from that often associated with the Homeric epics, which seem to present themselves as reliable accounts handed down by the Muses. I trace a poetics that is resolutely and unavoidably mortal. Such "authority" as the Homeric poems possess, I argue, is like that paradoxical kind of authority that suppliants exert over those who have conquered them. That supplication affords an expressive vehicle able to carry the person's tragic sense of loss is the feature that perhaps most likens it to poetry and best enables it to provide a model for the epic poem and the relationship between the poet and his listeners. Like supplication, the poem represents a kind of mastering of mortal experience, a transformation of private suffering into a public statement capable of conveying to others a vivid sense and deepened comprehension of grief.

In citing the *Iliad* and the *Odyssey,* I have used the Oxford Classical Text editions. Translations from the Greek are my own. This book was largely written during 1990–91, when I was a Visiting Fellow at the Classics Department at Yale University. I thank the Yale Classics Department for its hospitality, and, in particular, for the opportunity to read to the members of the department an earlier version of part of the section on the *Iliad*. The questions and comments on that occasion were a great help to me in formulating my thoughts. I also thank Gregory Nagy for his suggestions and encouragement, as well as for the vivacity of his own writings, all of which have contributed to this work. I owe a debt of thanks, as well, to Marylin Katz, whose book on Penelope proved to be a valuable stimulus to my own thinking and who read and commented on the final chapter. Finally, my deepest gratitude is to Anna Brodsky, to whom I dedicate this book.

KEVIN CROTTY

New York City

PART I

PITY AND SUPPLICATION IN THE *ILIAD*

CHAPTER I

Eleos and Book 24 of the *Iliad*

Book 24 of the *Iliad* has seemed to many commentators to evince a spirit different from the rest of the poem.[1] The "new spirit" of the book is due in large part to the sense of pity that imbues its action. Thus, the book opens with the gods looking upon Hector's corpse and feeling pity (*eleaireskon*, 24.23). Apollo angrily criticizes Achilles for his hard-heartedness toward Hector's corpse: "Achilles has destroyed pity (*eleon*), nor has he any shame," he tells the assembled gods (24.44). Achilles himself is presented not at all as a triumphant warrior, but as a mourner bewildered by the lack of means to express his grief:

> Nor did sleep
> That subdues all take him, but he wandered here and there. . . .
> [R]emembering these things, he wept a round tear,
> Lying now on his side, now
> On his back, now on his belly, until he stood
> And wandered aimlessly by the sea's edge.
>
> (24.4–5, 9–12)

Priam, too, is presented pathetically. Iris, rushing to tell Priam of the gods' decision concerning Hector's body, discovers him rolling in dung, surrounded by his weeping children (24.160–65). Most impor-

---

[1] The history of scholarship concerning Book 24 and its relation to the rest of the *Iliad* is set forth in C. W. Macleod, *Homer: "Iliad," Book XXIV* (Cambridge: Cambridge University Press, 1982), pp. 8–35. See also Seth L. Schein, *The Mortal Hero: An Introduction to Homer's Iliad* (Berkeley: University of California Press, 1984), p. 153; Götz Beck "*Die Stellung des 24. Buches der Ilias in der Alten Epentradition*" (Inaugural diss., Tübingen, 1964); and Walter Burkert, "Zum Altgriechischen Mitleidsbegriff" (Inaugural Diss., Erlangen, 1955), pp. 99–100, n. 3.

tant, for our sense of a new spirit animating the last book, Priam appeals to Achilles' pity, and Achilles in fact feels pity and, under its sway, does what the old king asks.

How to relate the humane kindness that seems to prevail in the final book to the savagery of the books preceding it has posed a problem in Homeric scholarship.[2] Analytic critics saw in Book 24 the product of a later, more humane age, which took offense at the unreconstructed fierceness and cruelty of the vengeance that Achilles exacts.[3] Even critics inclined to treat the *Iliad* as a unity nonetheless see a sharp disparity between Achilles' behavior in Book 22, when he brutally rejects Hector's plea, and in Book 24, when he finally grants it. Such critics tend to speak of Achilles' "return" to "humanity" in the last book, and to explain the disparity between Achilles' savagery and humanity in terms of his complexity. So, for example, Charles Segal, in a well-known study, writes: "Unquestionably, Homer's joy in the violent passions of his heroes and in the vital energies of nature glimpsed in the similes taps the deepest springs of his creative powers. Homer does not moralize and does not gloze over or flinch from the grimmest truths. But he need not openly censure his heroes for their more extreme acts of cruelty in order to indicate that barbarity is taking place and that something valuable in human life is being outraged."[4] Achilles' behavior on the battlefield constitutes, Segal writes, a "falling off from a higher level of humanity."[5] Such failures of humanity are to some extent themselves pitiable, in light of the distress that gives rise to them. For Segal and for others, Book 24 resolves the action of the poem by restoring Achilles to his humanity.[6] The *Iliad* emerges as a

---

[2] See, e.g., Charles Segal, *The Theme of the Mutilation of the Corpse in the "Iliad"* (Leiden: Brill, 1971), pp. 11, 15–16; and James M. Redfield, *Nature and Culture in the "Iliad"* (Chicago: University of Chicago Press, 1975), pp. 183–86, 203–4. See also Katherine Callen King, *Achilles: Paradigms of the War Hero from Homer to the Middle Ages* (Berkeley: University of California Press, 1987), pp. 13–28; Jasper Griffin, *Homer on Life and Death* (Oxford: Clarendon Press, 1980), pp. 20–21, 33–39, and 54–56; and Cedric H. Whitman, *Homer and the Heroic Tradition* (Cambridge: Harvard University Press, 1958), p. 206. On battle scenes in general see Bernard Fenik, *Typical Battle Scenes in the "Iliad": Studies in the Narrative Techniques of Homeric Battle Descriptions* (Wiesbaden: Steiner, 1968).

[3] See, e.g., Ulrich von Wilamowitz-Moellendorff, *Die "Ilias" und Homer,* 2nd ed. (Berlin: Weidmann, 1920), pp. 70–79; and Peter von der Mühll, *Kritisches Hypomnema zur Ilias* (Basel: Reinhardt, 1952), pp. 369–71.

[4] Segal, *Mutilation,* p. 11.

[5] Ibid., p. 16.

[6] See ibid., p. 60 ("The god's civilized behavior prefigures the calmer, more resumable attitude in the human realm."); King, *Achilles,* pp. 42–45; Schein, *Mortal Hero,* pp. 99, 162; and Bennett Simon, *Mind and Madness in Ancient Greece* (Ithaca: Cornell University Press, 1978), pp. 72–77.

poem celebrating the humane and civilized values of consideration, gentleness, and pity.

Yet, as Segal recognizes, Achilles' gentleness exists simultaneously with his violence.[7] Achilles offers Priam a seat and seeks to comfort him, but then threatens to kill him when the old man shows signs of rejecting Achilles' kindness (see 24.552–70). The passions that brought Achilles to the verge of feeding on Hector's flesh are in evidence in this last scene as well. Thus, Achilles' companions take care to keep Hector's body out of Priam's sight, for fear the old man might say something that could provoke Achilles to slay him (24.583–86). Nor does Achilles act solely out of disinterested, "humane" motives like pity: he is attracted, too, by the sizable ransom Priam brings. Achilles asks the shade of Patroclus not to be angry, since the ransom was "not to be despised" (*ou . . . aeikea*, 24.594), and promises that Patroclus, too, will have his share (595). Indeed, it was to honor Achilles (and, incidentally, to avoid trouble with Thetis) that Zeus decreed that Priam must supplicate Achilles for the return of Hector's body (24.71–76, 110–19).[8]

Moreover, it is not immediately clear why Achilles is prompted by pity in the first place, to the extent that he is. True, his continued abuse of Hector's body has grown increasingly tedious and pointless (see 24.4–21). The frustration of his repetitious efforts to abuse Hector's corpse may explain why Achilles would finally just as soon give the body back—especially when he stands to obtain a large ransom. His frustration alone, however, can scarcely explain Achilles' extraordinary offer of hospitality and friendship to the father of his worst enemy.

Segal's reading, therefore, while sensitive to the nuances of Achilles' feelings, leaves unexplained what Achilles' gentleness and his violence have to do with each other. They appear to be contradictory attitudes—restraint exerting only a precarious control over Achilles' more savage instincts. This "tension" within Achilles, however, merely restates the problem of how—and, indeed, whether—the final scenes of compassion grow from the violence that preceded them.

Moreover, while Segal speaks of the "stabilizing return of a larger order," it is important to be precise about the order that returns.[9] Although Achilles is finally reconciled to the leaders of his society, he

---

[7] Segal, *Mutilation*, p. 65.

[8] See Mary Scott, "Pity and Pathos in Homer," *Acta Classica* 22 (1979): 1–14, who rightly emphasizes that details that may strike a modern audience as purely pathetic redound to the hero's greater honor. Scott's reading, however, is essentially based on Adkins' view of the ethics (or lack of it) in heroic society—a view I consider inadequate to the complexity of the *Iliad*. See below, Chapter 2.

[9] Segal, *Mutilation*, p. 60.

can hardly be said, at the close, to embrace its values wholeheartedly or to dedicate himself to its goals. The death of Patroclus has estranged Achilles forever from the belief that the honors bestowed by society truly compensate for the loss of life. His return of Hector's body and his bestowal of friendship on Priam take place outside the warrior society. Indeed, Achilles is at pains to keep the meeting secret lest the other Achaeans take the enemy king prisoner (24.650–55). Because the civilization described in the *Iliad* is inadequate to contain the act of pity that climaxes the poem, a complete understanding of the final book requires a closer look at the distinctive relationship between Achilles and Priam, which seems to displace, albeit only temporarily, the kinds of social ties binding members of the warrior society. While I agree with Segal that the conflicts of the *Iliad* are finally resolved, the repose achieved by the conclusion is nonetheless a troubling one, for it seems possible only outside the boundaries of the warrior society. Order does not "return," then, so much as a new kind of order is discovered.

James Redfield, in his *Nature and Culture in the "Iliad,"* presents a different reading of *Iliad* 24.[10] The warrior, as Redfield writes, perpetually verges on the wild and frenzied: the tendency of the soldier in battle is toward becoming a *berserker*.[11] To use Redfield's terms, the warrior ceases to be a part of culture and becomes a part, rather, of nature. Rites of purification are necessary to reassimilate the warrior to the community. One of these rites is the funeral, in which the "impure" corpses are definitively consigned to a realm of the dead and so attain a kind of purity. The community of the living meanwhile reasserts itself and reaffirms the ties binding its members. Culture thus again assimilates the warriors who had in battle slipped into the realm of nature.

The funeral rites for Patroclus in Book 23 represent an attempt by the Achaeans to reaffirm their community, and, indeed, these rites and the funeral games that follow are the first time that we see Achilles actively and deliberately participating in the life and concerns of the Achaean society. Yet the funeral rites and games are insufficient to reassimilate Achilles, whose grief for Patroclus remains unassuaged.

Redfield distinguishes between the form of an action and its resolution. "An action is resolved," he writes, "when the needs and demands of the actors are either met or crushed out. Such an outcome is *for the actors* and concludes the action on the ethical level. Form, on the other

---

[10] Redfield, *Nature and Culture*, pp. 183–203.

[11] On this term, see Mircea Eliade, *Zalmoxis: The Vanishing God,* trans. by Willard R. Trask (Chicago: University of Chicago Press, 1972), pp. 6–7, 16–20.

hand, is *for us;* an action is formed when it reveals a lucid meaning to the contemplative eye of the poet and his audience."[12] Redfield then argues that the conflicts inherent in the warrior society are incapable of resolution. When Achilles comes to understand the kinship of mortals as sharing a common nature and common fate, this does not "resolve" the contradiction of combat,[13] but gives artistic "form" to the action, by lending it an intelligibility and lucidity that it would otherwise lack. This is the distinctive purity of art, which finds meaningful form in situations that are unresolved and unresolvable. Homer transfers the characters to an "Archimedean point" outside the warrior society where hero and poet "stand aside from the human world and judge it."[14] Achilles' vision of mortals and meaninglessness is intolerable within society but is an appropriate poetic vision of what underlies this society.

Art, for Redfield, repairs the insufficiencies of culture; it does artificially what culture itself cannot do. Book 24 occupies a plane different from that of the rest of the poem. In it, we see the artist's self-conscious magic at work. For Redfield, the purification worked by art replaces or supplements the purification attempted by ritual. Poetry, as it emerges from Redfield's book, is tragic at its core, for not only is it spawned by culture's inability to secure a conflict-free world for humans, but it is essentially a meditation on the insufficiency of culture. Culture, so to speak, attempts finally to resolve its conflicts by dwelling in song and story on its inability to do so.[15]

Redfield offers a moving and deeply interesting description of Book 24 as embodying, finally, a reflection on the tragedy of culture (mortals' effort to repair the insufficiencies of nature) and on the relation between art and culture. He does so, however, at considerable cost to the coherence of the poem. Rather than growing out of the preceding action, Priam's visit to Achilles and Achilles' response appear to be simply imposed on it. Redfield seems to take the gods' orchestration of Priam's supplication as a reflex of the poet's unilateral ordaining of the conclusion. Yet, as Colin Macleod has shown, Book 24 is tied to what

---

[12] Redfield, *Nature and Culture*, p. 219.

[13] Ibid., p. 221.

[14] Ibid., p. 221.

[15] See Redfield, *Nature and Culture*, pp. 218–23. See also Redfield's article, "The Economic Man," in *Approaches to Homer*, ed. Carl A. Rubino and Cynthia W. Schelmerdine (Austin: University of Texas Press, 1983), pp. 218–47, and, in particular, p. 239, where Redfield suggestively contrasts the *Iliad* (in which culture raises problems which are resolved only in poetry) and the *Odyssey* (in which culture successfully mediates between the primitive and the decadent, or between what Redfield calls "hypo-entertainment" and "hyper-entertainment").

precedes it by several narrative strands.[16] So, for example, when in Book 22, Priam conceives the desperate idea of going to Achilles in person to plead for the return of Hector's body, it seems clear that the poet is already looking forward to the action in Book 24, when what had seemed a wildly unrealistic plan becomes, under the gods' supervision, a reality.

Notwithstanding the richness of Redfield's reading, I believe he unduly simplifies the concluding supplication, when he describes it as a "ceremony founded on a universal concept of man *qua* man."[17] This ceremony is not simply the occasion for reflections on the mortal condition; it also honors Achilles for his military prowess. Nor does Achilles perceive Priam so abstractly as "man *qua* man," since Priam powerfully evokes Peleus and stirs up in Achilles his yearnings for his own father. That Redfield treats the conclusion as beyond the scope of the warrior society (and possible only by artistic fiat) grows from his view of Achilles as essentially a passive character. For Redfield, Achilles, like the Iliadic warriors in general, is to be construed in terms of his society. Because the warrior's values are essentially those of his community, Achilles' personal complexity and depth reflect unresolved conflicts in the warrior society and are, really, microcosms of it.[18]

Any view of Achilles as essentially passive, and as a reflection of the society that created him and that seeks to contain him, makes implausible a reading that would attribute to him an ability to synthesize and articulate his experience—to come to grips with his sorrows and to resolve them. Yet in Book 24, Achilles displays an ability actively to engage his experience and to find novel expressions adequate to his understanding. He takes the unprecedented step of joining with the enemy king in a common meal; this is not the sort of gesture within the competence of an essentially passive character. Book 24 thus challenges the conception of the Homeric individual as such a creature. It challenges, too, the idea of ceremony as something wholly outside the individual's control. Rather, Achilles puts the traditional meal of *philotēs* to a new use and endows it with a powerful new significance.

A full appreciation of the relation between Book 24 and the rest of the *Iliad* requires a closer look at pity, for as it functions in this final scene, it scarcely seems the kind and humane compassion we generally understand it to be. I begin by considering Hector's dying plea, in

---

[16] See Macleod, *Iliad XXIV*, pp. 16–35.
[17] See Redfield, *Nature and Culture*, p. 219.
[18] Ibid., pp. 103–9. See Fränkel, *Early Greek Poetry*, pp. 79–83.

which he begs Achilles to remember and do the same things that Priam asks in the final book.

> I beg you by your life, your knees, your parents—
> Do not let the dogs devour me by the Achaeans' ships.
> Accept the bronze and gold in heaps,
> The gifts my father and lady mother will give,
> And give my body back, so that
> The Trojans and their wives give me my portion of fire.
>
> (22.338–43)

Hector's supplication is marked by its deep pathos. Although it shares several elements with other scenes of warriors supplicating, the elements take on a new significance here. Other warriors, too, in begging for their lives, propose an exchange of wealth in return (see 6.46–50; 11.131–35), but they seem to look upon supplication almost as a commercial transaction—a specially urgent one, to be sure, but nonetheless essentially a question of exchange. For example, in 11.131–35, the sons of Antimachus supplicate Agamemnon:

> Take us alive, son of Atreus, and accept worthy ransom.
> Many treasures lie in the house of Antimachus,
> Bronze and gold and much-worked iron.
> From these, our father would bestow boundless ransom on you
> If he should hear that we are alive by the Achaeans' ships.
>
> (11.131–35)

The sons of Antimachus refer to their father, and do so largely in terms of his wealth and willingness to pay.[19] Hector does so, too, but refers to *Achilles'* father as well: he begs Achilles "by your parents" (XXII.338). The father is not merely a source of wealth, but one uniquely and tenderly devoted to the son: Hector implicitly pleads with Achilles to attribute to Priam (and his feelings for Hector) the feelings that Peleus has for Achilles.

Again, the sons of Antimachus speak of their own lives, and assure their victors of their father's generosity should he hear that his sons are alive (11.135; cf. 6.50). Hector, in contrast, refers to *Achilles'* life, begging him "by your *psukhē*" (22.338). In Homer, *psukhē* is not "life" in some abstract sense, but a thing—the departing life-spirit, whose absence renders the body a corpse. It is sometimes like breath; thus, Achilles at one point says that the *psukhē* of a man cannot be retrieved

---

[19] See also the speech of Adrestus, 6.46–50.

once it has crossed the "fence of teeth" (*herkos odontōn,* 9.408–9). Sometimes it is like blood, as when the *psukhē* is said to "rush out by the gaping wound" (14.518).[20] Hector, in other words, pleads in the name of an intimate part of Achilles himself—his life, construed concretely as a quasi-organ.[21]

Hector deliberately appeals to matters about which Achilles may be expected to have the strongest feelings. Indeed, Achilles' feelings about his father and his own life are at their most intense during his encounter with Hector: it is precisely because of them that he spurns Hector's anxious plea. Achilles' love for Patroclus and his anger at himself for failing to save his friend both inflame his hatred for Hector. Moreover, Achilles' mourning for Patroclus is imbued with his longing for Peleus (see 19.321–24). When Achilles conjures up the memory of his father, he pictures him as grieving for his son (19.323–24): Achilles' grief for his father is, in part, a reflection of his feelings for himself.[22] Thus, Achilles is indeed mindful, as Hector prays, of "his parents and his life." Yet this very mindfulness makes it unthinkable that he should do what Hector asks. Hector couches his plea to Achilles in the name of the very ties that Hector has most outraged.

That Achilles rejects Hector's supplication, however, cannot disguise the fact that pity, or *eleos,* as Achilles feels it in Book 24, flows from the same springs as does his earlier killing-frenzy. In feeling pity for Priam—just as in refusing it to Hector—Achilles is mindful of his grief not only for Patroclus, but for his father and himself as well (24.511–12, 534–42). Quite apart from the question why his responses to Hector and to Priam are so different, we should appreciate the common source of *eleos* and of savage hatred in Achilles' distress for himself and those he most deeply loves. Whatever the precise connections between Books 22 and 24, it is clear that the pity Achilles ulti-

---

[20] See David B. Claus, *Toward the Soul* (New Haven: Yale University Press, 1981), pp. 61–63. For more on *psukhē* in Homer, see Jan Bremmer, *The Early Greek Concept of the Soul* (Princeton: Princeton University Press, 1983); Bruno Snell, *The Discovery of the Mind* (New York: Dover, 1982), pp. 1–22; R. B. Onians, *The Origins of European Thought* (Cambridge: Cambridge University Press, 1988), pp. 93–122; and Joachim Böhme, *Die Seele und das Ich im Homerischen Epos* (Leipzig: Teubner, 1929), pp. 97–105.

[21] In other solemn moments of oath taking or supplication in Homer, the person regularly refers to persons or things intimately related to the one being supplicated: for example, parents (15.660), mother, father, and child (24.466–67), or knees (9.451). See Claus, *Toward the Soul,* p. 61 n. 6, who argues, partly on the basis of these passages, that *psukhē,* as invoked by Hector at 22.338, is a concrete thing, and not an abstraction.

[22] I discuss in more detail the relation between Achilles' grief for Patroclus and his memories of his father in Chapter 3.

mately comes to experience cannot be understood apart from the savagery which at first glance seems so alien to it.

Such a concept of pity is initially strange to modern audiences, for the English word "pity" seems to name the humane emotion par excellence, a far cry from the violent *eleos* Achilles feels for Priam in the *Iliad*. The modern concept of pity and the kindred notions of compassion or sympathy are felt to express an ethical ideal: the ability to imagine and be moved by the suffering of one's fellow creatures. It is through sympathy, Edmund Burke writes, "that we enter into the concerns of others; that we are moved as they are moved, and are never suffered to be indifferent spectators of almost any thing which men can do or suffer."[23] Indeed, pity—in Adam Smith's words, "the emotion which we feel for the misery of others, when we either see it, or are made to conceive it in a very lively manner"[24]—is felt to lie at the very heart of moral judgments and to be the basis on which they are made. For Rousseau, pity is a "natural sentiment, which, by moderating in every individual the activity of self-love, contributes to the mutual preservation of the whole species." The several virtues are, for Rousseau, but different formations or developments of the natural impulse of pity. "In fact, what is generosity, what clemency, what humanity, but pity applied to the weak, to the guilty, or to the human species in general?"[25]

Notwithstanding the central place that pity has occupied in Western ethical thought, it has had some powerful enemies: a consideration of these will enable us to sharpen the picture of *eleos* as presented in *Iliad* 24. The most forceful modern adversary of pity is Nietzsche, who criticized it essentially as a refusal to acknowledge the importance of suffering. For Nietzsche, pity (or *Mitleid*) was a pleasurable sop, whose

[23] Edmund Burke, *A Philosophical Enquiry into the Origin of Our Ideas of the Sublime and Beautiful* (Oxford: Oxford University Press, 1990), p. 41.

[24] See Adam Smith, *The Theory of Moral Sentiments* (New York: Augustus M. Kelley, 1966), p. 3: "However selfish soever man may be supposed, there are evidently some principles in his nature, which interest him in the fortune of others, and render their happiness necessary to him, though he derives nothing from it, except the pleasure of seeing it. Of this kind is pity or compassion, the emotion which we feel for the misery of others, when we either see it, or are made to conceive it in a very lively manner."

[25] Jean-Jacques Rousseau, *"The Social Contract" and "Discourse on the Origin of Inequality"* (New York: Washington Square Press, 1967), p. 203. Adam Smith, too, stresses that pity is an "original passion": "This sentiment, like all the other original passions of human nature, is by no means confined to the virtuous and humane, though they perhaps may feel it with the most exquisite sensibility. The greatest ruffian, the most hardened violator of the laws of society, is not altogether without it." See Smith, *Theory of Moral Sentiments*, p. 3.

general effect was to squelch not only suffering, but the powerful acts of self-assertion that necessarily entail suffering and that suffering alone can call forth.[26]

Plato, too, attacked pity on the grounds that it was a pleasurable means of glossing over the person's mistaken fear of death. Because, as Plato insists, no evil can truly befall the good man, the fear of evils is deeply misleading, and the pity that such fear gives rise to is no less so. Thus, in the *Apology,* for example, Socrates steadfastly refuses to make appeal to the jurymen's pity on the grounds that such appeals can only demean the pleader by exposing his craven fear of death. Plato emphasizes the spurious pleasure that the emotion of pity affords the person indulging it. Socrates tells the jurors that, were he to weep and lament, his appeal would be most pleasant for them *(hēdista, Apology* 38d9-e2). The jurors' pleasure rests in part on the sense of power that the defendant's self-abasement gives them—as though, Socrates says, it were in their discretion to give or withhold pardon as a favor *(tōi katakharizesthai ta dikaia, Apology* 35c3). The sense of power is pleasurable at least in part because it enables the jurors to quiet or allay for a while their own fearfulness: among those sitting in judgment of Socrates are those who had had recourse to just such pathetic displays when they were required to stand trial (34c1–7). The counterpart to pity is the resentment or anger that the jurymen feel when an accused refuses to demean himself by appealing to their pity (34b9–c7). Pity and the appeals to it are, for Plato, a baneful distraction from what should be the defendant's effort to persuade by information and rational argument (35c2–5).

The pleasure afforded by pity is nowhere clearer than in the response to epic poetry and to tragedy. The scene of Hector's pathetic supplication of Achilles, for example, is almost certainly one scene that Socrates would have deleted from any version of the Homeric poems that would be acceptable in his ideal state. As Socrates argued, passages from Homer that depict the heroes grovelling in the dust, or miring themselves in dung, or, in general, suggesting by word or deed that

---

[26] See, e.g., Friedrich Nietzsche, *"On the Genealogy of Morals" and "Ecce Homo"* (New York: Vintage, 1969): *Genealogy,* Preface 5 and Second Essay 6; and *Ecce Homo,* Why I Am So Wise 4. See also Nietzsche, *Beyond Good and Evil,* (South Bend, Ind.: Gateway, 1955): Sections 199, 202, 222, and 225. As Nietzsche writes in the Third Essay of the *Genealogy,* Section 14, "What is to be feared, what has a more calamitous effect than any other calamity, is that man should inspire not profound fear but profound nausea; also not great fear but great pity." On pity and its proponents and enemies, see Brian Vickers, *Towards Greek Tragedy* (London: Longman, 1979), chap. 2, especially pp. 64–70.

death is an evil or a dreadful thing must be excised (*Rep.* III.387d–388d). The problem, however, goes deeper than a few objectionable passages, as becomes clear when Socrates returns to Homer in the tenth book of the *Republic*. Socrates argues there that poetry, as a mimetic art, is necessarily drawn to surfaces and will always tend to depict spectacular displays of grief, such as anyone would, and should, be ashamed actually to indulge in. Plato sees in art a certain innate gaudiness. The pity awakened in the audience by poetry is insidious because it is so pleasurable and because, seduced by its pleasure, the person gradually loosens his control over that part of himself that "hungers to weep and lament" (*Rep.*X.606a-b). The unwholesomeness of the pleasure Homer affords makes it necessary, therefore, however regrettable it is, to exclude him altogether from the wisely ruled city (606e–607a).

The pleasurable aspect of pity has consistently provided the starting point for those—beginning with Plato—who denounce the emotion.[27] Yet it is clear that the *eleos* which Achilles feels for Priam in the final book of the *Iliad* is inseparable from events that are grievously *painful* to him—the loss of Patroclus, his own imminent death, and his irreparable separation from his father. *Eleos,* as it emerges from *Iliad* 24, is not at all a pleasurable means of denying one's own mortality. Aristotle's depiction of *eleos* in the *Rhetoric* offers a far more suggestive treatment of that emotion as it functions in the *Iliad,* particularly in the final scenes. Aristotle writes, "Pity (*eleos*) is a painful feeling (*lupē*) brought about by the sight of an evil befalling another that the person can expect might befall himself" (*Rhetoric,* II.8.1385b11). Because Plato criticizes pity as being, essentially, an unwholesome pleasure, Aristotle's assertion that *eleos* is a "painful feeling" may be understood as the first step in his rescue of the emotion of pity from Plato's attack. Pity, says Aristotle, rests on the belief that the person feeling pity is himself vulnerable to the evil he sees befalling another person. As we have

---

[27] See, e.g., Pietro Pucci, *The Violence of Pity in Euripides' "Medea"* (Ithaca: Cornell University Press, 1980), app. 1. Pucci, following the lines laid down by Plato and Nietzsche, argues that pity is a means of turning one's terror of death into a pleasant feeling of one's own nobility. Essentially, Pucci claims that pity enables the person feeling it voluntarily to take on another's grief as his own and, in doing so, to assert his freedom in the face of evil. Evil, Pucci writes, is the "other" in the self—the harms that befall and undo the person and yet seem to be an innate part of what and who he is. Pity is an attempt to deny the other in the self, a way to cast out fear. The tragic catharsis occurs, according to Pucci, because pity purges the spectator's fear of death. In place of the painful emotion of fear, the audience experiences the pleasurable emotion of pity. Pity emerges in Pucci's study as a strategy by which people bind themselves to reality and to the terror of their own inevitable ruin.

seen, Plato said much the same thing: for both Plato and Aristotle, fear and pity are closely linked. For Aristotle, however, a good man may truly, or correctly, fear. Unlike Plato, Aristotle holds that happiness *is* vulnerable to loss: evils truly do befall the good man and do so undeservedly.[28]

Hence, for Aristotle, pity can be a genuinely painful experience, for it rests upon, and is expressive of, the pitier's recognition of his own vulnerability to misfortune. Moreover, it can comport with or express an authentic understanding of the world.[29] Such, I contend, is ultimately the reason why the final book of the *Iliad,* in particular the encounter of Achilles and Priam, is felt to be climatic, and to resolve the action of the poem: in feeling pity for Priam, Achilles attains a kind of insight into the sorrow and anger that have driven him throughout the *Iliad*.

Thus, Achilles' experience of *eleos* for Priam is genuinely painful. Priam elicits this emotion by reminding Achilles of his own father—a memory that is tied for Achilles to thoughts of his own mortality and his best friend's death. The painfulness of this memory is brought out by his enraged response to Hector's supplication, which sought the same benefit Priam seeks and invoked the same thoughts—Achilles' *psukhē,* Achilles' father. Achilles' feeling of *eleos* for Priam signals not a turning away from or denial of the painfulness of such thoughts, however, but an insight into them. The other person, in being pitied, becomes expressive of the pitier's sense of himself as a *kind of being*—specifically, one who is partly constituted by his exposure to serious and unmerited harm. As I shall explain in more detail below, the *eleos* that Achilles ultimately feels for Priam is the emotional expression of his insight that Priam's wretched situation is ultimately his as well.

Pity, as Aristotle presents it, is also associated with pleasure, but the pleasure arises from a genuine understanding of the world and of the mortal's vulnerability which finds expression in it.[30] Because it is a

---

[28] *Nicomachean Ethics* I.8.1099a31–b18 and I.9.1100a4–9. On Aristotle's view of the vulnerability of the good man, see Martha C. Nussbaum, *The Fragility of Goodness* (Cambridge: Cambridge University Press, 1986), pp. 384–85, and the same author's "Tragedy and Self-Sufficiency: Plato and Aristotle on Fear and Pity," in *Essays on Aristotle's "Poetics,"* ed. Amélie Oksenberg Rorty (Princeton: Princeton University Press, 1992), pp. 261–90.

[29] So, for example, praise and blame are appropriate for voluntary actions; in the case of involuntary actions, however, pardon (*suggnomē*) and, occasionally, *eleos,* are appropriate. More specifically, when another acts in ignorance of his actual circumstances, pity and pardon may be the most fitting response. (See *Nicomachean Ethics* III.1 1109b30–32 and 1111a1–2).

[30] On the connection between emotion and understanding in Aristotle's *Poetics,* see, e.g., Stephen Halliwell, "Pleasure, Understanding, and Emotion in Aristotle's *Poetics,"* in Rorty, *Essays on "Poetics,"* pp. 241–60.

characteristic of the virtuous man that he is disposed to be properly affected, an emotion like pity is partly constitutive of virtue. A person of moral excellence takes pleasure in feeling an emotion like pity virtuously—that is, "at the right times, with reference to the right objects, towards the right people, with the right motive, and in the right way."[31]

For Achilles, too, the final scene of the *Iliad* is in a peculiar way one of delight, in which the warrior and the old man not only break their long fast and enjoy the pleasures of the banquet, but experience, as I shall argue, an enlargement of their vision and understanding of the world. Achilles' experience of *eleos* "purifies" his most painful emotions of their brutality, so that they become an occasion, rather, for insight into the quality of his own and others' grief. To invoke Aristotle, Achilles' experience of pity is a *katharsis*—a cleansing or purification of his rage and grief.[32]

I will show that pity, as it is expressed most deeply in the final scene of the *Iliad,* is a key to the poetics of the Homeric poems. On the reading offered here, the Homeric epics aim at arousing in the audience a vivid experience of the griefs endured by the characters. Indeed, as Hermann Fränkel has observed, the name used by characters within the Homeric poems for narratives is "griefs"—*kēdea* or the like.[33]

[31] *Nicomachean Ethics* ll.6.1106b 16–23. On Aristotle's defense of the emotions, see W. W. Fortenbaugh, *Aristotle on Emotion* (London: Duckworth, 1975); on the disposition to be properly affected—to feel emotions appropriately—as a part of virtue, see L. A. Kosman, "Being Properly Affected: Virtues and Feelings in Aristotle's *Ethics,*" in *Essays on Aristotle's "Ethics,"* ed. Amélie Oksenberg Rorty (Berkeley: University of California Press, 1980), pp. 103–16.

[32] A consensus seems to be forming that tragic *katharsis* has to do with the increased understanding, or "clarification," of the emotions brought about by the tragic performance and the experience of emotion in response to it. See, e.g., Stephen Halliwell, *Aristotle's Poetics* (London: Duckworth, 1986), p. 199. Halliwell suggests that "tragic *katharsis* in some ways conduces to an ethical alignment between the emotions and the reason: because tragedy arouses pity and fear by appropriate means, it does not, as Plato alleged, 'water' or feed the emotions, but tends to harmonise them with our perceptions and judgements of the world" (p. 201). See also Nussbaum, *Fragility of Goodness,* pp. 378–95, and more recently her article "Tragedy and Self-Sufficiency," esp. pp. 280–83; Richard Janko, *Aristotle: "Poetics I"* (Indianapolis: Hackett, 1987), pp. xvi–xx, and by the same author, *Aristotle on Comedy: Towards a Reconstruction of "Poetics II"* (London: Duckworth, 1984), pp. 141–42, and "From Catharsis to the Aristotelian Mean," in Rorty, *Essays on "Poetics,"* pp. 341–58; Redfield, *Nature and Culture,* pp. 67–68, and Leon Golden, "Catharsis," *Transactions of the American Philological Association* 93 (1962): 51–60. See, contra, Jonathan Lear, "Katharsis," in Rorty, *Essays on "Poetics,"* pp. 315–40.

[33] See Herman Fränkel, *Early Greek Poetry and Philosophy* (New York: Harcourt Brace Jovanovich, 1973), pp. 14–15. See also Griffin, *Homer on Life and Death,* p. 143. On the connection between the hero and lamentation, see the fundamental discussion in Gregory Nagy, *Best of the Achaeans: Concepts of the Hero in Archaic Greek Poetry* (Baltimore: John Hopkins University Press, 1979), pp. 94–117.

Moreover, characters in the poems understand epic poetry as a necessary part—a flowering or fulfillment—of their griefs.

So, for example, Helen tells Hector, "Zeus has sent an evil fate on [us] so that hereafter we may be the subject of song (*aoidimoi*) for men to come" (6.357–58; cf. Od. 8.579–80). Similarly, when Helen weaves pictures of the war at Troy, she pictures the "ordeals" (*aethlous*) that the Trojans and Argives "were suffering" (*epaskhon*) on her account (3.126–28). The experience of grief—the finality of the loss of something irreplaceable—is made significant, something other than dead loss for the person suffering it, by the thought that others will hear of it and come to know something of its sadness. Epic poetry is essentially a "memory of griefs"; it is the fulfillment to which the characters within the poem look forward.

That Achilles' climactic experience of pity occurs within the context of the ceremony of supplication is crucial for an understanding of *eleos* both as it functions in the final scene of the *Iliad* and as a basis for articulating a poetic of the Homeric epics.[34] Supplication is a formalized kind of pleading and the kind of regular, familiar action to be expected in oral poetry such as the Homeric poems.[35] The formal

[34] The most notable recent study of supplication as it appears in the *Iliad* is Agathe Thornton, *Homer's "Iliad": Its Composition and the Motif of Supplication* (Göttingen: Vandenhoeck & Ruprecht, 1984). The most thorough study of the ceremony of supplication in ancient Greek civilization is John Gould, "Hiketeia," *Journal of Hellenic Studies* 93 (1973): 74–103. I discuss these works in more detail in Chapter 5. As Gould notes, until his article appeared, not much work on supplication was available. See, however, Jean Servais, "Les suppliants dans la 'Loi sacrée' de Cyrène," *Bulletin de Correspondance Hellénique* 84 (1960): 112–47. See also the excellent study of supplication in the *Iliad* by Guy Kevin Whitfield, "The Restored Relation," Ph.D. diss., Columbia University, 1967. Since Gould's article, several studies of supplication in the Homeric poems have appeared, among them, Simon Goldhill, *The Poet's Voice: Essays on Poetics and Greek Literature* (Cambridge: Cambridge University Press, 1991), pp. 73–75; Michael Lynn-George, *Epos: Word, Narrative, and the "Iliad"* (Houndmills, U.K.: Macmillan, 1988), pp. 200–209; Macleod, *Iliad XXIV*, pp. 15–16; Victoria Pedrick, "Supplication in the *Iliad* and the *Odyssey*," *Transactions of the American Philological Association* 112 (1982): 125–40; and Griffin, *Homer on Life and Death*, pp. 53–56. See also the general discussion in Vickers, *Towards Greek Tragedy*, pp. 438–94.

[35] See Walter Arend, *Die Typische Scenen bei Homer* (Berlin: Weidmann, 1975). The significance of Arend's study for the oral nature of the Homeric poems was noted by Milman Parry. See Milman Parry, *The Making of Homeric Verse; The Collected Papers of Milman Parry* (Oxford: Clarendon Press, 1971), pp. 404–7; see also A. B. Lord, *The Singer of Tales* (Cambridge: Harvard University Press, 1960), chap. 4 ("The Theme"). Other studies of the typical scene include Michael Nagler, *Spontaneity and Tradition: A Study in the Oral Art of Homer* (Berkeley: University of California Press, 1974), pp. 131–66; Fenik, *Typical Battle Scenes;* and Mary Louise Lord, "Withdrawal and Return: An Epic Story Pattern in the Homeric Hymn to Demeter and in the Homeric Poems," *Classical Journal* 62 (1966): 241–48.

quality of supplication contributes to its ability, as ceremony, to temper the sufferer's acute and unreflecting experience of grief, and thus to make insight possible—a broadened view of one's own griefs as part of the very shape and fabric of moral life. This claim—that the formal qualities of ceremony enable it to be an enlightening experience for its participants—may seem paradoxical, since the formalism of ceremony may suggest unreflecting, routinized activity, or a social drama that essentially reinforces ideas that are unquestioned and sacrosanct. Because ceremonies are traditional and received by each generation from the preceding one, they lack the idiosyncracy of a particular invention. They are highly regular, and they tend to be associated with certain highly important phases of life. They are also predictable in their sequence; the performance of a ceremony on any given occasion is like its performance on any other occasion.[36] These features ensure that ceremonies constitute a kind of "common knowledge" that helps maintain and partly constitutes the ties binding the community.

The formal properties of ceremony—the rules on which its effectiveness as a ceremony partly depends—are vital to its effect.[37] These formal elements owe their significance in the first instance to their ability to impress a distinctive shapeliness on life and, with it, a greater density of meaning than is possible in the less structured, everyday course of events. A ceremony, as Stanley Tambiah says, is "a culturally constructed system of symbolic communication."[38] A ceremony not only effectuates certain things but represents certain things. It "creates order and is order."[39]

All of these features may seem to militate against the possibility that ceremony could be a clarifying experience. Indeed, as Tambiah notes, ceremony is not designed to express the individual's emotions or states of mind in any direct or spontaneous way, since it consists of highly conventionalized behavior. Thus, Tambiah writes, *"distancing* is the

---

[36] In fact, ceremonies are more responsive to individual circumstances and less uniform in the various performances of them than participants may realize or take into account. See Stanley Jeyaraja Tambiah, *Culture, Thought, and Social Action: An Anthropological Perspective* (Cambridge: Harvard University Press, 1985), chapter 4. Tambiah addresses the problem of the dual aspect of ritual—on the one hand, its invariant and stereotyped features; on the other hand, its openness to context, thanks to which no two performances are exactly the same. One feature of supplication that may render it of particular interest for anthropological studies is that it responds in an especially clear way to context because it has the practical purpose of obtaining something critically important to the suppliant.

[37] See ibid, pp. 127, 131–37. See also Johan Huizinga, *Homo Ludens* (Boston: Beacon, 1950), pp. 11, 19–20.

[38] See Tambiah, *Culture, Thought, and Social Action*, p. 128.

[39] Ibid., p. 127.

other side of the coin of conventionality; distancing separates the private emotions of the actors from their commitments to a public morality."[40] It is a familiar feature of ceremonies—for example, baptism or marriage—that they are effective regardless of the intention or attitude of the participants. "Distancing" may give rise to hypocrisy, or can make a ceremony so rigid or stereotyped as to be essentially meaningless for those who participate in it. Yet, in highly emotional situations (of the kind where supplication is likely to occur), the distancing serves a useful purpose, for it can enable the one afflicted to get out from under the immediate throes of emotion. Ceremony makes available a set of received gestures that express grief, but do so in a formalized way. Suppliants may discover in the traditional embrace of the victor's knees a singularly appropriate gesture that not only expresses their grief but dramatically conveys the kind of thing grief is. To those who are supplicated, as well, the ceremony may prove authentically enlightening. Suppliants' gestures lend their plea the persuasive force of tradition.[41] By means of gestures and words,[42] the suppliants claim that a relationship exists between themselves and the persons supplicated.[43] In supplication, it is not simply a matter of a person describing a desperate need here and now for a particular object: through their formalized gestures suppliants show the perennial contours of the current, fleeting situation, and align their particular demand with a long tradition of urgent needs.

Thus, the participants in a ceremony come to resemble characters in a story, both themselves and more than themselves. By virtue of its ceremonial character, therefore, supplication has a suggestive similarity to a work of art. Indeed, as I shall show, supplication offers a model for understanding the poetics of the *Iliad* and the *Odyssey*. That it can do so owes something to this inherent affinity between ceremony and art.

[40] Ibid., p. 133.

[41] On ritual as a "traditionalizing instrument," see the introduction to Sally F. Moore and Barbara G. Myerhoff, eds., *Secular Ritual* (Assen: van Gorcum, 1977). As Tambiah, *Culture, Thought, and Social Action,* p. 132, writes, the formal features of ritual—repetition, stylization, evocative presentational style—enable it to "attach permanence and legitimacy to what are actually social constructs."

[42] On the suppliant's characteristic gestures, see Thornton, *Homer's "Iliad,"* p. 113; see also Gould, "Hiketeia," although Gould emphasizes gesture and pays less attention to the suppliant's speech. See Lynn-George, *Epos,* p. 201 and the notes thereto for a brief discussion of Gould's article. See also my comments in Chapter 5.

[43] On the self-referentiality of supplication as drawing attention to relative status, see Esther Goody, "'Greeting,' 'Begging,' and the Presentation of Respect," in *The Interpretation of Ritual: Essays in Honor of A. I. Richards,* ed. J. S. LaFontaine (London: Tavistock 1972), pp. 39–71.

From an outsider's perspective, a ritual may seem merely to inculcate what is already known—a society's most unquestionable and im-
mutable beliefs. Tambiah, for example, writes that "cosmological constructs are embedded" in rites, and that rites "in turn enact and
incarnate cosmological conceptions."[44] Tambiah understands by "cosmological conceptions" all those "orienting principles and conceptions
that are held to be sacrosanct, are constantly used as yardsticks, and are
considered worthy of perpetuation relatively unchanged."[45]

Tambiah's description suggests that these principles and conceptions
are in theory capable of clear statement, that they can be at least para-
phrased by anthropologists as propositions that would win the assent
of most members of the society under scrutiny. While it seems clear
that fundamental beliefs and values are embedded in rites, I question
whether they strike "insiders" as straightforward and unproblematic,
as Tambiah's description may suggest. It seems likely that any conflict
among a society's values or commitments finds expression in ceremony, and that the formalized presentation of these conflicts in ceremony
affords participants an opportunity to apprehend these values in a new
and possibly illuminating way. This is how Geertz, for example, presents the Balinese cock-fight in a well-known essay.[46] The cockfight
bundles together a host of sexual, economic, and political values,
which fall short of being a coherent set of principles or conceptions.
The game gives participants the chance to experience these values in all
their unresolved complexity in a heightened and more sharply focused
way than usually possible in everyday life.

Much the same is true of supplication. As I will show in Chapters 2
and 3, Homer's warrior society houses values that exist together only
uneasily. Part of the richness of supplication is that it is expressive of
the competitive excellences that drive the warrior society but views
these values from the distinctive vantage point of the loser. Supplication does not "inculcate" particular ideas; at its deepest, it enables the
participants to experience victory, shame, memory, pity in an especially compelling way and to apprehend and configure them anew. The
form of supplication is better understood as a crystallizing of the emotions of pity and shame and the social or familial values that give rise to
such emotions, than as a program necessary for the supplication to be
efficacious. Supplication is a public enactment of an emotion. The
painful spectacle of abasement before another—the genuflection and

[44] Tambiah, *Culture, Thought, and Social Action,* p. 130.

[45] Ibid.

[46] Clifford Geertz, "Deep Play: Notes on the Balinese Cockfight," in *The Interpretation of Cultures* (New York: Basic Books, 1973), pp. 412–53.

the embracing of the knees—presents a tableau in which the emotions of shame and pity are inherent and find an almost sculptural expression. Yet this form also expresses the individual suppliant's particular sense of the life-or-death importance of what he requests.

On this view, ritual is not so much an "encoding" of unequivocal principles as a concentrated and dramatic encounter with certain pervasive values. Participants do not so much internalize social ideas as they experience them in an especially vivid and at least potentially fresh way. I refer to supplication as a "ceremony," rather than as a "ritual," in order to stress this aspect of it as open to context, drawing significance from the particular occasion, and in turn, capable of shedding light on the participant's personal circumstances. Redfield's distinction between ceremony and ritual is pertinent here. As Redfield writes, "ritual" is felt to have a definite effect on objects—to act upon the world beyond culture—while the power or potency of ceremony is subjective, and limited to the realm of consciousness.[47] It is just this ability to shape consciousness that I intend to convey by using the word "ceremony."

One property of formalized conduct is that it produces an intensified sense of communication among the participants. This property is vital for an understanding of the importance of ceremony at the conclusion of the *Iliad,* where a transient, but profound, "community" arises between Achilles and Priam. Here, too, a distinction between "ritual" and "ceremony" is necessary. Features characteristic of religious rites—dancing, chanting, and formulaic speech—heighten a sense of communion by blurring the contours of the specific persons participating in the rite and fusing all differences into a communal performance.[48] My use of "ceremony" is intended to avoid this suggestion of "community-by-fusion." The community of Achilles and Priam arises from ceremony and reflects a shared sense of mortal life, yet does so in a way that preserves each man's individuality. Achilles' perception of a shared fellowship with the father of his worst enemy, indeed, constitutes not a fading of what is distinctive about Achilles, but a growth of his consciousness.

A distinctive feature of supplication is that unlike many ceremonies, it does not affect status and does not "work" simply by virtue of having been performed.[49] The suppliant strives to achieve a particular

[47] Redfield, *Nature and Culture,* p. 163.

[48] Tambiah, *Culture, Thought, and Social Action,* pp. 145–46.

[49] On ceremonies of initiation or passage, see Victor Turner, *The Ritual Process* (1969; Ithaca: Cornell University Press, 1977); Arnold van Gennep, *Rites of Passage* (Chicago: University of Chicago Press, 1961). The scholarly tradition on initiation ceremonies in

outcome external to the ceremony itself: he may, and in the *Iliad* usually does, fail to secure what he desires. Supplication, then, is a means of *persuading* the other to do as the suppliant wishes. Because of the unique and irreplaceable importance to the suppliant of what he or she seeks, and because supplication is a means of persuading another, the ceremony does not consist of a rigid program that must be carried out with minute attention to each detail if the act is to constitute a supplication. Rather, there is a certain repertory of features, not all of which need appear in every supplication. Supplications can be more or less elaborate.[50]

So, for example, in the opening scene of the *Iliad,* when the old priest Chryses supplicates Agamemnon and the other Achaeans for the return of his daughter, his manner is in keeping with the dignity of his office.[51] Chryses arrives at the Achaeans' camp wearing his official regalia as a priest of Apollo and bringing "boundless ransom" with him (1.12–16). He does not kneel or embrace the knees of Agamemnon, nor does he ask for the Achaeans' pity. In his supplication, Chryses stresses rather that the Achaeans "fear" (*hazomenoi,* 1.21) Apollo, and, indeed, the Achaeans urge Agamemnon to feel shame before or to reverence (*aideisthai,* 1.21) Apollo's priest, rather than to feel pity

---

ancient Greece is very rich. See Walter Burkert, *Greek Religion* (Cambridge: Harvard University Press, 1985), pp. 260–64; Helene P. Foley, *Ritual Irony: Poetry and Sacrifice in Euripides* (Ithaca: Cornell University Press, 1985), pp. 36–39; Pierre Vidal-Naquet, "The Black Hunter and the Origin of the Athenian *Ephebeia,*" in *The Black Hunter: Forms of Thought and Forms of Society in the Greek World* (Baltimore: Johns Hopkins University Press, 1983), pp. 106–28; Claude Calame, *Les choeurs de jeunes filles en Grèce archaïque* (Rome: Ateneo, 1977); Angelo Brelich, *Paides e Parthenoi,* vol. 1 (Rome: Ateneo, 1969); and Henri Jeanmaire, *Couroi et courètes: Essai sur l'education spartiate et les rites d'adolescence dans l'antiquité hellénique* (Lille: Bibliothèque Universitaire, 1939). The very richness of this tradition may tend to obscure the significance of other ceremonies, like supplication, that do not effectuate a change in status.

[50] See Tambiah, *Culture, Thought, and Social Action,* pp. 124–25. Tambiah stresses that the interpretation of rituals or rites of passage must always be open to contextual meanings.

[51] Gould, "Hiketeia," p. 80, n. 39, lists some thirty-five occurrences of supplication in the Homeric poems. As he notes, however, some instances of supplication are "merely reported in the course of a speech or imagined in very general terms." Some of the more elaborate scenes illustrating the typical gestures and appeals of suppliants are: 1.493–510 (Thetis supplicates Zeus, grasping his knees with her left hand, and holding his beard with her right hand); 6.45–50 (Adrestus supplicates Menelaus, grasping his knees and offering him ransom); 11.130–35 (the sons of Antimachus supplicate Agamemnon, offering him ransom); 20.463–71 (Tros supplicates Achilles, attempting to embrace his knees); 21.64–96 (Lycaon supplicates Achilles, embracing his knees and bidding him feel shame and pity); and 24.476–676 (Priam supplicates Achilles, and bids him remember his father and feel pity). In the *Odyssey,* see 5.444–50; 6.141–85; 7.146–52; 9.269–72; 11.66–78; 14.273–84; and 22.312–19, 340–53.

for the old man. Moreover, Chryses is in a position to offer Agamemnon considerable wealth in return for his daughter. Thus, even though Agamemnon has the power to refuse Chryses, and in fact does so, Chryses is hardly abased before the Achaean king: he has the wherewithal to propose a bargain to his enemy. In stark contrast is the supplication of Achilles by Priam at the poem's conclusion. Priam, too, offers "boundless ransom" (24.502) and like Chryses, also bids Achilles to feel shame before the gods (24.503). But Priam's supplication is far more an emotional appeal than Chryses' was, and Priam's appeal is directed more to Achilles' sense of pity than to his sense of shame.[52] As we have already seen, the supplications by young warriors on the battlefield display neither Chryses' august solemnity nor Priam's heart-wrenching pathos. Rather, the young soldiers boast, with perhaps a certain anxious bravura, of their fathers' abundant wealth. If there is any pathos in the young men's supplications, it is in their unsuspecting confidence in that wealth and in their inability to appreciate the full fury of their opponents (see, e.g., 6.53–60). Finally, Thetis' supplication of Zeus in Book 1 is different from all these others. Thetis' gestures are unmistakably those of a suppliant: she embraces Zeus's knees with her left hand and takes hold of his beard with her right (1.500–502). Yet Thetis is, so to speak, a suppliant in gesture only. She uses supplication as a courtly gesture of respect to Zeus and as a formal sign of the importance she attaches to her request. To the extent that supplication is expressive of subjection and domination, however, Thetis' use of it is ironically distanced from the underlying reality that Zeus owes his kingship to her and will seek to avoid her displeasure or distress. Having once rescued Zeus from chains, she is in a position to negotiate with him (1.396–412, 503–4).[53] Her suppliant gestures only show how removed is the gods' unthreatened existence from the anxi-

---

[52] On the connection between Chryses' supplication in Book 1 and Priam's in Book 24, see Macleod, *Iliad XXIV*, pp. 33–34. Cedric Whitman argued that the structure of the *Iliad* as a whole evinced a deliberate symmetry and pointed to the repetition of supplication scenes at the beginning and end of the poem as part of his demonstration. See Whitman, *Homer and the Heroic Tradition*, pp. 249–84, especially pp. 259–60. It is difficult to reconcile Whitman's elaborately symmetrical architecture with conditions of oral performance. Below, in Chapter 4, I suggest a different interpretation of the fact that the *Iliad*'s opening and closing scenes both concern a father's supplication.

[53] See Laura M. Slatkin, "The Wrath of Thetis," *Transactions of the American Philological Association* 116 (1986): 1–24, on the cosmic significance of Thetis as the liberator of Zeus, and the repercussions of her act of liberation for the *Iliad* as a story of her son's *mēnis*, or wrath. See now the same author's *The Power of Thetis: Allusion and Interpretation in the "Iliad"* (Berkeley: University of California Press, 1991). I discuss Thetis' supplication in more detail below in Chapter 5.

eties of human life, which find such vivid and compelling expression in supplication.

Thus, the particular personalities of the participants and the specific circumstances are vital to an understanding of supplication, in a way that they are perhaps not for an understanding of other ceremonies. While supplication possesses a set of gestures or words that persists through the several occurrences of it, yet it is strikingly flexible, drawing a vital part of its meaning from its context: the history, desires, and memories of those who participate in it. In general, therefore, supplication is especially instructive as a corrective to the notion of ceremony as something prior to the individual and as essentially indifferent to the idiosyncratic motivations and wishes of the particular participants. For supplication, to the extent that it seeks to persuade another, and to the extent that it is prompted by the extreme importance the suppliant attaches to his request, necessarily rests upon the distinctive wishes and memories of its participants on any given occasion.

Because supplication, as a ceremony, is responsive to individual contexts, it can be manipulated by individuals to suit the particular circumstances in which they are constrained to plead with another. This, I contend, is precisely what Achilles does in the final book of the *Iliad,* when he enters into a distinctive and novel *philotēs* with his suppliant, in which the two jointly contemplate the mortal condition and the griefs necessarily inhering in it. Supplication affords Achilles a powerful means of expressing his insight into his own situation, and is inseparable from his experience of *eleos* for Priam. Moreover, supplication is a crucial part of my argument that pity is a key to the poetics of the *Iliad* and the *Odyssey*.

In order to show that a poetic is implicit in the climactic supplication of Achilles by Priam, I will first consider some aspects of the relationship between fathers and sons in the *Iliad* (Chapter 2) and then study the roles of shame and pity in the various social structures reflected in the *Iliad* (Chapter 3). I will then consider the action in Book 24 in more detail to show how the last part of the poem grows from and climaxes what has preceded it. I close the first section of this book by considering the significance of the ceremony of supplication in Book 24 and its implications for the poetics of the *Iliad*. In the second section, I will argue that the *Odyssey* works out and elaborates the poetics implicit in Priam's invitation to Achilles to "remember" and to "feel pity."

CHAPTER 2

Fathers and Sons
and the Warrior Society

I

The father looms large in the climatic encounter of Priam and Achilles: Priam is moved to supplicate by his fatherly feelings for Hector, and in appealing to Achilles, he expressly invokes the memory of Peleus, Achilles' father. Indeed, Priam's appeal in the name of Peleus is but a final instance of the role played by the father throughout the supplication scenes in the *Iliad*. As Whitman among others has emphasized, the *Iliad* opens and closes with a father supplicating for the return of his child.[1] The solicitude of fathers is also, as we have seen in Chapter 1, a staple of battlefield rhetoric: captured warriors promise that their fathers will give "boundless ransom" if they should hear that their sons are alive.[2]

Nonetheless, the role of the father in the *Iliad* has not been much studied.[3] Perhaps this is not surprising, for Peleus nowhere appears in person, and Priam has scarcely any interaction with his son. Indeed, Priam addresses Hector but once, when he begs him not to do battle

[1] See Whitman, *Homer and the Heroic Tradition*, pp. 259–60. See also Macleod, *"Iliad" XXIV*, pp. 32–35.

[2] See, e.g., 6.46–50; 11.130–35.

[3] But see W. Thomas MacCary, *Childlike Achilles: Ontogeny and Phylogeny in the Iliad* (New York: Columbia University Press, 1982), p. 216; and Redfield, *Nature and Culture,* pp. 110–12, who offers an ethnographic description of the relative status of fathers and sons as portrayed in the *Iliad* and *Odyssey*. On the importance of Peleus in shaping Achilles' values, see Robert Finley, "Patroklos, Achilleus, and Peleus: Fathers and Sons in the *Iliad*," *Classical World* 73 (1980): 267–73. See also Anthony T. Edwards, *Achilles in the "Odyssey": Ideologies of Heroism in the Homeric Epic* (Königstein/Ts.: Hain, 1985), pp. 53–57.

with Achilles (22.38–76), and even there, a wide gulf separates the two men. It is significant that while Priam addresses Hector in the most poignant terms, the son does not answer a single word to his father's plea.

Nestor, one of the great heroes at Troy, may seem to be the chief exception to the rule that fathers in the *Iliad* are tangential to the ongoing work of the warrior society. Yet not only is Nestor unique among the Iliadic warriors, but his preeminence obscures the prestige of his son Antilochus, who, at least as he appears in the *Iliad,* is no-where near as important a warrior as his father. A kind of inverse ratio exists between the prestige of father and son: important heroes like Achilles and Hector have fathers who are concomitantly weak, while the son of a truly vigorous old man like Nestor is comparatively less prestigious.

If fathers in the poem have not drawn much comment, therefore, that may be because they do not appear to be of much importance for an understanding of the warrior and his values. Indeed, the warriors themselves comment on the relative unimportance of genealogy for the warrior on the battlefield. "Why ask about my family?" Glaucus re-sponds to Diomedes in his famous speech in the sixth book. "Like the race of leaves, so is the race of men" (6.146). Similarly, Aeneas, en-countering Achilles on the battlefield, says, "We know one another's lineage, one another's parents, having heard the famous words of mor-tal men" (20.204). The most striking thing about Aeneas' attitude to the "famous words" is their ultimate irrelevance, in his view, to the fateful conflict of arms. Aeneas recounts his lineage, but he also sug-gests that his ability to do so is a tribute to the "flexible tongues" of mortals and their ability to bandy about "multitudes of words." (See 20.248–49.) Their dueling genealogies liken Achilles and Aeneas, in Aeneas' words, to bickering old women (20.248–55).[4]

Nonetheless, neither Glaucus nor Aeneas is merely uninterested in his family. Glaucus goes on, in fact, to tell Diomedes of his lineage and especially of his ancestor Bellerophon. Aeneas, too, expounds on his descent from Tros and his kinship with the mythic Ganymede, as well as with Priam and Hector. Thus, both Glaucus and Aeneas display a

---

[4] Achilles boasts over a fallen enemy that his lineage, which he traces through Peleus back to Zeus, surpasses that of his enemy, the descendant of a river god (see 21.184–99). Only here does Achilles understand Peleus as giving him a status greater than others; Achilles' boast sounds like hollow bravado, intended to hide the blow to Achilles' ideas of himself. Peleus—as Achilles' mortal parent—is normally an expression of Achilles' mortal self. Thus, Achilles seems to be trying to turn into a boast that which in fact marks out his limits as a mortal man.

considerable ambivalence toward their family background, whose fame is part of their prestige, but nonetheless is ultimately irrelevant to the warrior during the lonely test of arms. The warrior's hesitation about the value of the past implies an ambivalence toward epic poetry as such. Aeneas' reference to "the famous words of mortal men" (*pro-klut' epea thnētōn anthrōpōn,* 20.204) bears a striking resemblance to one of the names for epic song within the Homeric poems—*klea andrōn,* or fames of men. Indeed, Nagy has argued that Aeneas' words reflect a tradition of Aeneas as a master of praise poetry.[5] More generally, I will argue below that the father is an important conduit for transmitting heroic values across the generations. The warrior's feelings for his father, therefore, are important for understanding the poetics of Homeric epic as crowning the warrior's efforts and compensating him for his death. Ultimately, I want to suggest that the poetics of the *Iliad* and *Odyssey* are based on the son's sense of the father's absence, that is, the lack of a beneficent power that reliably shields and supports him.

Thomas MacCary has argued that in the *Iliad* the father is identified with negative qualities, and that fathers tend to be "only words, not action."[6] MacCary believes that the inconsequentiality of the father, as presented in the *Iliad,* partly shapes the character of the warrior. "The son seems almost to pursue death in glorious action simply to escape the fate of the father, as though his attenuation into a speaking shadow were the negative paradeigma held up to him, the very figure of death."[7] While MacCary is right to point out the relative absence and weakness of fathers in the *Iliad,* Peleus and Priam nonetheless both throw long shadows before them. Peleus nowhere appears in the *Iliad,* but he is a recurring presence throughout the poem in Achilles' and others' memories of him. Furthermore, if fathers and sons do not have strong, mutual ties within the *Iliad,* it is nonetheless striking that father- and son-substitutes do: The tender concern Achilles and Phoenix show for each other in *Iliad* 9 is an obvious example. Even more important, the powerful last scene of the *Iliad* is built on Achilles' memories of his father and Priam's complementary memories of his son. Thus, the dearth of scenes between fathers and sons, rather than indicating the unimportance of the ties between the generations, suggests a frustration or yearning at the heart of the warrior's life. As I shall try to show, the warrior seeks the father but is at the same time constrained to be absent from him.

[5] See Nagy, *Best of the Achaeans,* pp. 274–75. See also Andrew Ford, *Homer: The Poetry of the Past* (Ithaca: Cornell University Press, 1992), pp. 64–67, who views Aeneas' speech as reflecting, rather, the frailty of mortals' knowledge of the past.

[6] MacCary, *Childlike Achilles,* p. 216.

[7] Ibid.

The significance of the father in the *Iliad,* notwithstanding his absence or apparent unimportance to the warrior life at Troy, is brought out by three different recollections, recounted at different places in the poem, of Peleus' parting advice to Achilles. Nestor, Odysseus, and Phoenix each recall Achilles' leave-taking on the occasion when Nestor and Odysseus came to fetch Achilles off to the war at Troy. The recollections not only constitute a kind of epitome of the warrior society and its values, but show the importance of the relationship between the father and son for an understanding of the warrior's conduct at Troy.

Nestor recalls how he and Odysseus came to Peleus' house to recruit young men for the war at Troy. There, the two found Peleus offering sacrifice. While the visitors waited at the threshold, the young Achilles leaped up, took them by the hand, and invited them to sit. After they had feasted and Nestor and Odysseus told Peleus of the purpose of their visit, Nestor recalls Peleus advising his son:

> The old man Peleus enjoined his son Achilles
> Always to be best and to be better than others.
>
> (11.783–784)

Odysseus offers his quite different version of the departure during the embassy to Achilles in Book 9:

> Friend, you know your father Peleus enjoined you
> The day he sent you from Phthia to Agamemnon,
> "My son, Athena and Hera will give you
> Strength, if they like, but keep your heart
> Within your breast. Friendly-mindedness is better.
> Leave off evil-planning strife, so that
> Old and young, the Argives will honor you the more."
>
> (9.252–58)

Phoenix, Achilles' tutor, has yet a different recollection of the leave-taking. He recalls Achilles as being, at that time, an "infant" (*nēpios*), literally, "one not able to speak"—as yet ignorant of war and men's councils (9.438–41). Peleus therefore sent Phoenix along with his son to Troy and charged him with teaching Achilles to be a "speaker of words and a doer of deeds" (9.443).

It is immediately apparent that these different recollections of Peleus' last words to Achilles each serves the speaker's immediate rhetorical goals. Nestor is attempting to distinguish Achilles' unsurpassed military prowess from Patroclus' superior talents at giving counsel, by way of urging Patroclus to use his intelligence to break the impasse with Achilles. For the sake of contrast, he presents Peleus as spurring his son on to the competitive excellence of the battlefield. Odysseus, on the other hand, is attempting to win Achilles over to a more forgiving spirit; he therefore recalls Peleus as similarly urging a conciliatory attitude. Phoenix, finally, is above all concerned to assure Achilles of his solicitous regard for him, and his recollections of Peleus reflect that concern. Each one is able to mold Peleus' last words to his own immediate goal.

Yet at the same time the different recollections seem to fit together into a kind of *summa* of the warrior code: in his parting advice to his son, Peleus expresses the importance not only of the competitive excellences ("to be best always and to surpass others") but of the cooperative ones as well ("to be friendly-minded"). "To be a speaker of words and a doer of deeds" completes the portrait of the aristocratic ideal. Peleus emerges, then, as the one who inculcates in his son the leading values of the warrior society.

Peleus' role as inculcator of heroic values is underscored in Book 7, where Nestor refers to him as "the noble speaker and adviser of the Myrmidons" (7.126). Nestor invokes Peleus by way of calling the Achaeans to a sense of shame, after Hector's challenge to a duel has gone unmet.

> Alas! a great sorrow has come to Achaea's land.
> The horsemen Peleus would deeply groan—
> The noble speaker and adviser of the Myrmidons,
> Who once rejoiced to question me in his house,
> Asking the family and parentage of all the Argives.
>
> (7.124–28)

Peleus emerges as a kind of communal conscience, who spurs the Achaeans to live up to their warrior ideals. Before further developing this notion of Peleus as inculcator of heroic values, I must first justify speaking of the "cooperative" excellences as a constituent part of the warrior code, in light of Arthur Adkins' writings on the Homeric warrior ethic. In Homer's warrior society, Adkins writes, "the quieter co-operative excellences must take an inferior position; for it is not evident at this time that the security of the group depends to any large extent upon these excellences."[8] Adkins argues that *agathos,* the strong-

---

[8] See Arthur W. H. Adkins, *Merit and Responsibility: A Study in Greek Values* (Oxford: Oxford University Press, 1960), p. 36. See also Adkins' "'Friendship' and 'Self-Sufficiency' in Homer and Aristotle," *Classical Quarterly* n.s. 13 (1963): 30–45, in which he describes *philos* as referring to a useful and dependable relationship in an otherwise

est term of approbation in the society, characteristically refers to the well-born, propertied, and strong; the *agathos* is the one who evinces those qualities recognized as "essential to the security of society." To treat the injunction "to be always best" as existing in parity, or on a level with the injunction "to be friendly-minded" may seem unwarranted, in light of Adkins' analysis.

Adkins does not, however, do full justice to the complexity of the warrior's motivations. For Adkins, the warrior's life draws its value and prestige from its importance to the security of the larger community. Yet the warriors themselves seem to resist such a notion. When Andromache, for example, presents Hector with a sensible plan to preserve his life and keep Troy safe, Hector rejects the idea as one sure to bring shame upon him. Far more important to the warrior than results is the conspicuousness of his fighting: Hector insists on being seen in the front ranks, whether or not that leads to his death and the downfall of Troy, because that is what the warrior code demands. (See 6.441–46.) The imperative to fight courageously and conspicuously works generally to ensure that a city will be defended when it is attacked, but it requires death-defying behavior even in circumstances where such fighting is likely to prove ruinous. There is a marked anti-utilitarian streak among the warriors that belies Adkins' arguments about their essential motivations at Troy.

Rather than doing what is necessary to secure the safety of others, the warriors fight in order to win a "great renown" (6.446): the fighting at Troy is heavily coded as an effort to win honor and others' recognition. As Hector's response to Andromache suggests, this code of values has a more compelling reality for the warrior than his workaday function of saving lives. Adkins thus overstates his case when he argues that the warrior's excellence depends completely on his success. When Hector faces Achilles in battle, he knows that he will lose, but nonetheless resolves to die "not ingloriously and not without fame" (*mē man aspoudi ge kai akleiōs apoloimēn*) so that future generations will hear of his great deed (22.304). Hector will certainly "fail" in his duel with Achilles; but his certainty that this is so does not prevent him from seeking others' honor for the courage with which he goes down fighting.

Because the warrior seeks honor, it becomes important that others acknowledge it: the warrior who seeks not only "to be always best" but to be recognized as such, needs a society of fellows to extend him

---

indifferent world. As Adkins describes it, *philein* excludes competition, yet is essentially shaped by the competition that by and large governs human relationships.

that recognition. With the need for a society, however, comes the need for cooperation and, as Peleus puts it, "friendly-mindedness" (*philophrosunē*). The society must have a king, and the warrior must be not only loyal to the king but willing to compromise in order to maintain the integrity of the society.

To use Adkins' own utilitarian terms, then, cooperation and a willingness to compromise are valuable because they are essential to what the warrior seeks to achieve: it is only by cooperating with others that he can assure that his deeds do not go unrecognized. When Nestor comments that Achilles, by refusing to fight, will be the only one to benefit from his prowess (11.762–63), it is clear that he thinks Achilles is wasting himself and will live to regret the waste. In order to benefit others, and so receive their recognition, the warrior must cooperate. Thus, Adkins does not capture the complexity of the warrior ethic, which values not only preeminence in battle but the ability to get along with others.[9]

Both the "competitive" and "cooperative" excellences are sustained by social pressures—most especially, shame or *aidōs*—intended to ensure that members of the warrior society behave in accordance with that society's codes.[10] As E. R. Dodds, in particular, has argued, Homeric society is characterized in large part by the importance of shame as a motivating force.[11] The father is instrumental in linking the values of the warrior society to shame. Thus, Glaucus' father, in sending his son off to war, "enjoined" (*epetellen*) him not to "bring shame [*aiskhunein*] upon the family" (6.209):

> He sent me to Troy, and enjoined many things on me,
> Always to be best and to surpass others,
> And not to shame the race of our fathers, who were the best
> In Ephyra and in broad Lycia.
>
> (6.207–10)

[9] For a response to Adkins, see A. A. Long, "Morals and Values in Homer," *Journal of Hellenic Studies* 90 (1970): 121–39. As Long points out at p. 137, the warrior is expected not only to fight commendably, but to show respect for the *timē* of others (see *Od.* 8.396; *Il.* 23.586–611).

[10] For general treatments of *aidōs* in Homer, see Redfield, *Nature and Culture*, pp. 115–19; André Cheyns, "Sens et valeur du mot 'Aidōs' dans les contextes homériques," *Recherches de philologie et de linguistique* 1 (1967): 3–33; Carl Eduard von Erffa, *"Aidōs" und Verwandte Begriffe in Ihrer Entwicklung von Homer bis Demokrit*, Philologus Supplementband 30, part 2 (Leipzig: Dieterich'sche Verlagsbuchhandlung, 1937), pp. 1–33. On the associations between *aidōs* and *philos*, see Emile Benveniste, *Le Vocabulaire des institutions indo-européennes* (Paris: Editions de Minuit, 1969), pp. 335–53.

[11] See E. R. Dodds, *The Greeks and the Irrational* (Berkeley: University of California Press, 1953), pp. 28–63.

In instructing their sons, Glaucus and Peleus fulfill an office that elders typically perform for younger men (see, e.g., 9.438–43, 19.219; and 23.306–18). As Redfield remarks, "In Homeric society, a distinction is made between the young man and the mature man, a distinction correlated with the distinction between council and battle as arenas of excellence and with the contrast between the word and the deed."[12] The elder has a natural authority because he knows more. The youth is typically impetuous and uncalculating. (See 1.259, 9.160–61, 13.355, 21.439–40, and 23.590.)

While the old can in general advise the young on this or that point, the father performs the more profound task of raising his son in the values underlying the warrior society. So, for example, Nestor does not need to instruct his son Antilochus in the practical skill of horsemanship, for—as he says in Book 23 during the funeral games for Patroclus—Zeus and Poseidon have taught Antilochus these arts (23.306–8). It is, however, up to Nestor to instruct his son in "cunning" or *mētis:*

> But come, friend, put in your heart *mētis*
> Of every kind, lest the prizes escape you.
> Cunning, more than strength, makes the superior lumberjack,
> By cunning, the pilot on the wine-dark sea
> Keeps straight the swift ship buffeted by winds;
> By cunning a charioteer surpasses charioteer.
>
> (23.313–18)

Nestor's "track-side" advice illustrates, in a lighter tone,[13] the kind of instruction in heroic values that fathers give their sons. A more somber reflection of the necessity of instructing the child in such values is seen during Hector's visit to Troy in Book 6 and his meeting there with Andromache, who holds their baby son, Astyanax. The description of the young baby's tears at the sight of his father's bronze and his shaking war-plumes is justly famous (6.466–70). One of its implications, however, is that war-regalia, and the heroic values they embody, do not come naturally to the child, but are initially terrifying. Nevertheless, it is Hector's wish for his son that he become a warrior like his father—indeed, an even greater one (see 6.476–81).

---

[12] Redfield, *Nature and Culture*, pp. 110–11. See also Christof Ulf, *Die Homerische Gesellschaft; Materialen zur analytischen Beschreibung und historischen Lokalisierung* (Munich: C. H. Beck, 1990), pp. 51–83.

[13] On Nestor's speech to Antilochus, see Marcel Detienne and Jean-Pierre Vernant, *Les ruses de l'intelligence: La metis des Grecs* (Paris: Flammarion, 1974), pp. 17–31.

That the son learns "shame" from the father helps account for the fact that, as Hector tells Andromache (6.444), he truly wants what, from another point of view, he is constrained to do. *Aidōs* is not simply a fear of others' taunts. The warrior, who has imbibed the emotion from his father, has internalized shame, so that it grows from and reflects his own unwillingness to behave in a manner other than what he and others expect of himself. It is significant that, in refusing to take Andromache's advice, Hector insists that he truly wants to fight in the front lines "winning a great renown for my father and my own self" (6.445–46).

Yet, however much the warrior's own spirit (*thumos,* cf. 6.444) might prompt him to seek renown and others' honor, the society needs to back these values with threats. The values upheld by the warrior society are exacting standards; feelings of shame act partly as an enforcement device, making the warrior unwilling to act in other than prestige-seeking ways, for fear of others' blame and of losing face.[14] This aspect of shame, that it constrains the warrior to meet the exacting standards of the warrior code, seems also to owe something to the relationship between father and son. For Peleus, Priam, and Hippolochus (Glaucus' father) are not presented as warriors. The *Iliad* suppresses any mention, for example, of Peleus' heroic exploits and treats him as one who lived in peace until his wretched old age.[15] Similarly, Glaucus' father Hippolochus seems to be simply a conduit through which Glaucus learns of the family past that he must not shame; in Glaucus' lengthy recital of the family's history of great achievements, Hippolochus stands out by the absence of any exploits of his own.

The father, who is not a warrior, imposes or "enjoins" exacting standards on the son, rather than introducing him to the way of life that seems most natural and pleasant to him. If sons simply followed in their fathers' footsteps, the values animating the warriors might be a description of the only way of life they know or imagine.[16] As it is,

---

[14] *Aidōs* is what makes soldiers unwilling to relax their efforts in battle, for fear of being exposed to others' rebuke and scorn. Thus, *aidōs* is a rallying cry, used to urge the warriors to greater efforts in battle. See 5.787, 8.228, and 13.95–98. *Aidōs* is the unwillingness to expose oneself to *nemesis*—that is, to others' anger or rebuke (see, e.g., 13.121–22; see also 6.441–43; 17.91–101, and 22.104–8).

[15] On Peleus' heroic exploits, see, e.g., Pindar, *Nem.* 3.32–36; *Nem.* 4.54–58; *Isth.* 6.24–25; Pindar fr. 48 (Snell/Maehler).

[16] Even when the father was also a warrior, the son remains sensitive to appeals to his sense of shame. Agamemnon's rebuke of Diomedes and Sthenelus, whose fathers were among the Seven against Thebes, is instructive. Agamemnon uses the exploits of Tydeus (Diomedes' father) to shame the son into action (see 4.370–400). Sthenelus seems to rebuff Agamemnon's invitation to feel shame, by insisting that he and Di-

however, the youths become warriors in order to live up to the demanding standard of preeminence and superiority imposed on them by their fathers. The father thus ensures that shame will be felt as external pressure enforcing the warrior code on the son from without.

II

Shame is associated not only with the competitive excellence of being preeminent but with the other excellence that Peleus "enjoins" on Achilles—the willingness to compromise and to accommodate others. Rather like failures in nerve, refusals to respect claims made on the basis of fellow-feeling, or what Peleus called *philophrosunē,* are met by reminders to "feel shame." Thus, Achilles' intransigence in refusing the compensation Agamemnon offers seems to Ajax a failure in *aidōs.* If Achilles felt shame, Ajax suggests, he would heed his friends' urgent plea that he return (9.639–42). The willingness of the person with a grievance to be propitiated and satisfied is essential to the continued life of a society. Ajax draws the analogy of a man whose brother or child has been killed. A person aggrieved even in this way, Ajax says, will accept what is offered in restitution; similarly, Achilles should, from a sense of *aidōs,* limit his thirst for vengeance and be satisfied with the gifts Agamemnon offers (see 9.632–36).

Insofar as it tends to make the warrior more accommodating to his fellows, shame curbs the individual's egotistic demand that his merit be acknowledged and rewarded. When one's comrades offer restitution for some offense, therefore, it is the part of shame to accept the restitution and be reconciled. In other words, shame leads the person not only to fear others' censure, but to value their praise—to be satisfied with the satisfaction they have to offer.[17]

---

omedes are better warriors than their fathers were (see 4.404–10). Diomedes, on the other hand, feels shame (*aidestheis,* 402), and bids Sthenelus be silent. Sthenelus' response suggests that shame may not be as strong an incentive when the son has followed and surpassed the father, but Diomedes' reaction indicates that, even so, the appeal to shame is appropriate and effective. On the son's boast that he has surpassed his father, see Bernard Schouler, "Dépasser le père," *Revue des etudes grecques* 93 (1980): 1–24.

[17] Whitfield defines supplication as a "ritual plea for *aidōs,* but not *aidōs* as the warrior knows it." Rather, he writes, quoting Santayana, the *aidōs* invoked by the suppliant is a "reverence for the sources of one's being," that is, "the inner restraint that family and society ideally evoke not only for themselves—in the figures of parent, elder and king—but for the weak and helpless whom they sustain and protect." See Whitfield, "Restored Relation," p. 56. I agree with Whitfield that *aidōs,* as invoked by the suppliant, is a sense of inner restraint, and an unwillingness to press one's prerogatives as victor to the hilt. I

Shame, then is an emotion that always tends to make the individual esteem the values of warrior society—not only to fear its blame, but also to value the prestige it has to confer. Not only does shame act as a kind of negative reinforcement for each of these somewhat inconsistent values (the quest for prestige and the willingness to accommodate others), it also serves to soften the inconsistency between them. By the same token, a failure to act in accordance with the dictates of shame threatens to expose these inconsistencies and makes them felt as contradictions that lie at the heart of the warrior society.

So, for example, Agamemnon's refusal to "feel shame before" (*aideisthai*, 1.23) the old priest Chryses and to accept ransom in return for his daughter ironically and appropriately ends with his violating the sense of shame yet further and alienating his greatest warrior. Upon the seer Calchas' prophecy that Agamemnon must return the girl without price or ransom (*apriatēn anapoinon*, 1.99), Agamemnon seeks to arrogate to himself some one else's prize, on the grounds that "it is not seemly" that the king go "without a gift of honor" (*agerastos*, 1.119).

Agamemnon's attempt to maintain conventional decorum, however, is wrong-headed, since he cannot insist on what is "seemly" without violating the sense of shame and restraint that shapes the relations among the warriors. As the leader of the Achaeans, Agamemnon has the power to take whatever he likes,[18] but by exercising that power without regard to the dictates of shame, Agamemnon brings about a violent rupture in the warrior society, and the rejection by his most prestigious warrior of the society's most deeply rooted values. Achilles expressly calls Agamemnon "shameless" (*anaides*, 1.158, cf. 1.149), for in threatening to take someone else's property Agamemnon shows no regard for the service that the Achaeans perform for him at tremendous cost to themselves (see 1.152–60).

Aidōs emerges from the Chryses episode and its consequences as a kind of mutual tact or forebearance. Had Agamemnon heeded the requirements of shame, he would not have insisted on his kingly prerogatives, and so would not have provoked Achilles, in turn, to insist vehemently on the individual warrior's entitlement to the proper recognition of his worth. Before Agamemnon's unwise assertion of power, Achilles had allowed a substantial portion of his spoils to be diverted to Agamemnon; in the spirit of *philophrosunē*, Achilles was content

---

disagree with him, however, that such *aidōs* is wholly different from that the *aidōs* that motivates the warriors on the battlefield. Even within heroic society, *aidōs* implies restraint in exercising one's prerogatives as victor.

[18] See 1.275–84, and 2.196–97, 204–6.

with receiving "a little thing of [his] own" (see 1.166–67; cf. 9.323–33). Agamemnon's breach of *aidōs,* however, destroys the delicate balance between the competitive and cooperative virtues; Achilles brings to the surface all his festering resentment and insists—whatever the cost to others—that he be given his due.

III

Peleus, therefore, in instructing the son both to be preeminent among his comrades and to be cooperative, offers a concise epitome of the warrior society and its values. The "synoptic" view of the warrior society that may be gleaned from the recollections of Peleus by Nestor, Odysseus, and Phoenix suggests the possible existence of a poem, or, at least, a strand within the oral tradition, dealing with Peleus' final words to Achilles and delineating the warriors' aristocratic code. Such a poem, if it existed, may have resembled the "Counsels of Chiron" (*Kheirōnos Hupothēkai*) attributed to Hesiod, which probably dealt with Chiron's advice to his pupil Achilles.[19] However that may be, the very succinctness of Peleus' commands makes clear the troubling contradiction between the imperative to outshine others and the demand that one cooperate with others. The father both upholds the warrior society and shows the instability at its core.

It is not simply *what* Peleus says that is important, however, it is the fact that *he* says it. That the values of the warrior society are truly values—that is, goods genuinely prized by the warrior—flows from the son's regard for the father. The son feels shame before his fellow warriors at least partly because of the respect (*aidōs*) that he felt in the first instance for his father. Hector seeks fame not only for himself but for his father as well (see 6.445–46): the hero's quest for renown is imbued with his relationship to the father. In the *Iliad,* the strength of the tie binding the hero to his father is conveyed above all in the warrior's response to the urgent appeals of the father, when old and frail, to the son's pity or *eleos.* A study of these emotional ties between the father and son will throw light, more generally, on the values of the warrior society and their place in the individual warrior's life.

Throughout the poem, Homer expresses the sadness of a warrior's death by describing its effect on the father (see, e.g., 5.149–58, 11.328–

[19] See Pindar, *Pyth.* 6.22, and the scholiast's annotation (ii.197 Drachmann). The fragments attributed to the "Counsels of Chiron" are set forth in Merkelbach and West's "Fragmenta Selecta," in Friedrich Solmsen, *Hesiodi Theogonia, Opera et Dies, Scutum* (Oxford & Clarendon Press, 1970).

32, 13.658–59, 14.501–02, 20.408–12, and 23.222–24). Indeed, the deaths of his sons can seem Priam's defining characteristic, even to the old man himself (see, e.g., 24.255–56). Achilles too, thinks of death less as an extinguishing of his individual person, and more in terms of its effect on his father: death is conceived as a failure to return home to the fatherland and the father (e.g., 18.324–32, 19.321–33, and 23.144–51).[20] Often a son's death is said to expose the father to loss and danger.[21] (See 4.477–79, 5.22–24, 5.153–58, 22.59–71, and 23.222–25.)

The pathos inherent in the relation between the aged father and his son is perhaps nowhere clearer than in Priam's anguished plea to Hector to return to the safety of Troy, and not to face certain death at Achilles' hands:

> Have pity on my wretchedness while I live,
> And my hard fate, for father Zeus, the son of Cronus, will destroy
>   me
> With a harsh destiny in old age looking upon many evils—
> Sons killed and daughters dragged away.

> (22.59–62)

Priam's appeal to pity (*eleēson*, 59) is intended to awaken in Hector a lively sense of the immediacy of the ties binding father and son and the inextricability of their destinies. For, if Hector dies, Priam says:

> The savage dogs will finally drag me
> To the gates, after an enemy with sharp bronze
> Has beat or struck me and taken life from my limbs.
> Dogs I raised and fed at my table to guard my halls
> Will drink my blood in frenzy
> And lie by the gates. . .
> When the dogs of a slain old man disgrace [*aiskhunōsi*]
> His grey head, his grey beard and his shameful parts [*aidō*]—
> This is the most pitiful thing in our wretchedness.

> (22.66–71; 74–76)

What is most striking here is that Priam seeks, through his emotional and pathetic appeal, to deflect Hector from acting as the warrior

---

[20] On the description of death in terms of its pathetic qualities—and, in particular, in terms of its effect on the father—see Griffin, *Homer on Life and Death*, pp. 103–43, and especially pp. 123–28.

[21] The father's dependence on the son is also a theme in Greek myth. See the examples collected by Edwards, *Achilles in the "Odyssey,"* pp. 54–57.

code dictates—to meet Achilles in battle and to be seen either winning or valorously dying (22.108–10). Priam's appeal cuts through to an instability at the core of the warrior society, for if the father instills *aidōs* in the son, he also pleads with him to feel *eleos,* and to act in a way that would violate *aidōs.* To a substantial degree, therefore, the emotions of *aidōs* and *eleos* are in tension: each flows from and supports values that do not easily coexist with each other. The competitive values of prestige and renown, which are particularly associated with *aidōs,* are to some degree in conflict with the blood ties that the old father piteously invokes.

This is not, however, simply a conflict between two different kinds of commitments (e.g., to honor and to family). Rather, a primary source of the value attached by the warrior to prestige is the son's respect and love for his father—an emotion which can at times tempt the warrior to act in ways that are felt as shameful. *Aidōs,* in other words, has its roots in a relation that, in extreme moments, prompts the warrior to violate the very standards that *aidōs* demands. In his plea, Priam uses for pathetic effect words that elsewhere are associated with shame and the values of the warrior code: *aiskhunein* (here referring to the desecration of the old man's corpse), and most strikingly *aidōs* (here used to refer to the old father's genitals). The density of meaning of *aidōs* and *aiskhunein* in Priam's appeal suggests that the heroic values of prestige and fame (which are normally associated with words for "shame") have their ultimate basis in the ardor of the ties binding father and son (which finds expression here in the emotionally charged use of *aidōs* for the father's genitals).

Hector may sense the wretchedness of Priam's plight and feel pity— as he felt pity for Andromache (6.440–65)—but he cannot act on it, since such conduct would violate the values and imperatives that have been instilled in him. Achilles also felt the strong pull of his father's wretchedness when he thought of Peleus near death and of his mournful grief (*akakhēsthai,* 19.335), but he could not return to Phthia. For if Achilles were to act on the strength of his pity (which his father arouses in him), he would act in such a way as to court shame (which his father has taught him to fear). The father both appeals to a sense of pity in the warrior and, through his inculcation of shame in his son, prevents him from acting on the promptings of pity. This combination of strong emotion and inability to act on it is part of what Achilles ultimately mourns: rather than comforting Peleus in his old age, he fights in a distant land bringing misery to Priam (24.540–42). The imperatives of avoiding shame and seeking individual prestige ensure that the son lives apart from the father, for the son leaves the home to accomplish those feats of valor that will continue the family's illustrious history. The appeals to pity, however, ensure that the separation from the father will be a troubled one and a perennial source of grief for the warrior.

IV

It is sometimes said that Homeric man is characterized by his lack of "innerness": that he exists in his actions and his spoken words. The Iliadic warrior, on this account, can be wholly known through his public conduct, for he is preeminently a social being, to be construed within the fabric of social relationships. As such, the Homeric hero has sometimes been presented as a kind of open field of forces; he is, in his essence, a passive product of the influences of tradition and society.[22] It is no accident, on this view, that *aidōs,* or shame, should be a principal motivation of the warriors in the *Iliad.* For shame seems to be, above all, an emotion that enforces a society's settled notions of appropriate conduct.[23] It is precisely the motivation that one might expect of social and traditional beings like the Homeric warriors.

A disadvantage of this view of "Homeric man," however, is that it tends to give a rather static picture of Homeric society and the individual existing within it. If the warrior simply reflects social codes, then there is little scope for individual spontaneity or inventiveness in the understanding and use of tradition. The values held up by the warrior society seem to have no origin, and it is not clear why these values are *values*—that is, things that people hold dear and that animate their lives.

If we appreciate the origins of the warrior's values in the advice and training he receives from his father, however, it is clear that the warrior's adherence to the exacting standards of the warrior code derives its value in no small part from the strength of the ties binding son to father. Thus, the goods held up by warrior society emerge as *good for* the individual; they have a place in the individual warrior's own sense of what is appropriate and the best course for himself.

Shame, on this view, is not simply the mark of Homeric man's purely traditional and social nature. Rather, it is instilled in the son by the father, and takes root because of the son's respect for his authority.

---

[22] See Fränkel, *Early Greek Poetry,* pp. 79–83; Redfield, *Nature and Culture,* p. 20.

[23] See, e.g., Redfield, *Nature and Culture,* p. 115: "*Aidōs* is the most pervasive ethical emotion in Homeric society; it is basically a responsiveness to social situations and to the judgments of others."

Rather than being a static, culture-wide phenomenon, *aidōs* has its place in the personal histories of those raised within that culture. While Homeric society undoubtedly possesses the characteristics of a "shame culture," it is important to see the origins of that culture in the father's commands to the son. From this familial perspective, it is clear that the shame culture harbors within itself other motivations and values, which are in some ways more compelling than those values upheld by shame. A consideration of fathers and sons in the *Iliad* calls for some modification of the view that Homeric man has no innerness, for prestige and the other values of heroic society are valuable to the warrior in large part because of his intimate ties with his father.

This innerness of Homeric man is most clearly evidenced in the importance of the son's memory of the father. Peleus nowhere appears in the *Iliad,* but, as we have seen, memories of him pervade the poem. Indeed, Achilles conjures up a picture of his father's misery in what is expressly called an act of "remembering" (*mnēsamenos*, 19.314). Similarly, Odysseus reproaches Achilles for "forgetting" what Peleus had "enjoined" upon him when his son left for Troy; Nestor uses identical words when he speaks of the same leave-taking and chides Patroclus for his forgetfulness (9.259 and 11.790).

A striking feature of the several characters' recollections is that the memory never succeeds in reaching back to capture the "real" Peleus. The partial accounts by Odysseus, Nestor, and Phoenix of what Peleus said present different pictures of Peleus and the values he most upheld. Indeed, Achilles' own memories of his father show a similar plasticity. In Book 9, for example, when Achilles threatens to return home, he makes the point that he does not need Agamemnon to give him gifts, for he has an abundant patrimony in Phthia (see 9.364–68). He speaks of Peleus as still thriving and exercising authority in his household: Achilles expects that his father will obtain a wife for him (*Pēleus thēn moi epeita gunaika ge massetai autos*, 9.394).

Far different is Achilles' memory of his father when he grieves over the death of Patroclus and imagines his father as helpless and wretched:

> . . . I could suffer nothing worse,
> Not even should I hear that my father died
> (Who now, I think, sheds round tears in Phthia
> Missing me, his son: I, who amidst an alien people
> Wage war on the Trojans for dread Helen's sake).
>
> (19.321–25)

Although Peleus is not a character in the *Iliad,* he is nonetheless a character in the lives of the characters. He is what the other characters in the poem make of him. As such, he bears an interesting resemblance to that other missing father of Greek epic—Odysseus in the *Odyssey*—who, at least in the Telemachy, is subject to so many different interpretations by the inhabitants of Ithaca.[24] The point here, however, is that none of the characters in the *Iliad*, and least of all Achilles, strives for an objective and reliable representation of Peleus. The "Peleus" of the *Iliad* is partly a reflex of the speaker's immediate rhetorical needs, as in the case of Odysseus' and Nestor's recollections of him. More important, he is also a reflection of Achilles' immediate emotional needs. If others' recollections of Peleus fail to prompt Achilles to act in a particular way, that is partly because Achilles imagines Peleus as an extension of himself.

This emerges most emphatically and movingly in Achilles' lament for Patroclus, where he imagines Peleus grieving for Achilles himself:

> For I think Peleus either is
> Dead or nearly dead from grief
> In hateful old age, and ever awaiting
> Sad news of me, to hear tell of my death.
>
> (19.334–37)

The pathos of the father's wretched old age is a vehicle to express the warrior's feelings about his own life. Achilles is both the rememberer and the remembered; his memory of his father is a refracted mode of *self*-mourning. The paradoxical relationship between fathers and sons in the *Iliad*, therefore, bespeaks a deeper tension within the individual warrior, a tension that may be succinctly described as that between the feelings of shame and pity, and their respective dictates.

The suppliant's invocation of the father, then—and, more particularly, Priam's plea in Book 24 that Achilles remember his father—draws upon a rich and complex relationship between the son and father. This relation calls forth emotions both of pity and shame—the very emotions the suppliant seeks to elicit. As felt in regard to the father, these emotions do not easily coexist with each other, but derive from different aspects of a relationship in which different, and to a troubling extent contradictory, values are upheld. As I shall ultimately argue, Priam, in his climatic supplication, enables Achilles to feel both shame and pity, as innerly consistent emotions, and therefore enables Achilles at last to act on them.

---

[24] See below, Chapter 6.

Before turning to Priam's supplication, however, we must consider *eleos* in more detail. The tension between *aidōs* and *eleos* consists in the fact that shame derives in large part from a relationship whose emotional charge can threaten to overwhelm the warrior-values it once fostered. This tension, and the consequent attempt to discourage or suppress this emotion in the warrior society, have implications for our understanding, more generally, of the warrior society and the poetic animating the poem that celebrates the "unperishing renown" of the heroes in that society. A consideration of these implications will enable us to grasp the climatic power of Priam's supplication—that is, its ability to draw the vast action of the *Iliad* to a satisfying and emotionally profound conclusion.

CHAPTER 3

Eleos and the
Warrior Society

I

In one of the best-known speeches in the *Iliad,* Sarpedon urges his friend Glaucus into battle. Sarpedon reminds Glaucus that they are favored with "pride of place, meats, and full cups" and are looked upon as gods because they are warriors. Their efforts to secure prestige and preeminence would be unnecessary, Sarpedon says, if he and Glaucus were "immortal and unageing." "But, as it is, countless fates of death stand over us, which no man may flee or avoid. Let us go, to see if we afford a boast to another, or another to us" (12.310–28).

The speech owes its fame partly to the way it crystallizes the governing values of the warrior society. As Sarpedon's impromptu words make clear, the worth of prestige as a "good" prized by the warrior society ultimately rests upon the mortality of its participants. It is a good peculiarly appropriate to beings destined to dwindle and pass away.[1] Sarpedon's speech is characteristic, too, in its air of bravura in the face of death: the attitude of the warrior—as a warrior—toward death has a certain insouciance. Thus, Sarpedon presents it as a matter of indifference whether he or his enemy dies—"whether we afford a boast to another, or another to us." Such an attitude is required by the code of the warrior: whether he is to be victorious or defeated must have no effect on the dedication of his fighting or the intensity of his effort. To the extent that the warrior may lose in battle, he must

[1] See the discussions by Redfield, *Nature and Culture,* pp. 99–101; and Jean-Pierre Vernant, "Panta Kala: From Homer to Simonides," in *Mortals and Immortals: Collected Essays* (Princeton: Princeton University Press, 1991), p. 86.

contemplate his life essentially as a commodity—a boast for another. Considered in this way as a form of exchange, death can scarcely be expected to arouse deep emotions.

The heroic indifference Sarpedon articulates is an effort by mortals to look upon their own lives from a divine perspective. For the gods, too, occasionally look upon the mortal's death as merely a biological fact, inevitable for all and befalling now this one, now that. For example, when Hera, fearing Zeus's wrath at her interference, recalls Athena from aiding the Achaeans, she says it is not worth battling with Zeus on account of mortals: "Let one of them die, and another live, as chance may be" (8.429–30). Hera's laissez-faire attitude bespeaks that gap between mortal and immortal that is the hallmark of the post-Promethean age. (See also 1.573–76 and 21.462–67.) Sarpedon attempts to look upon his life with a detachment comparable to Hera's, and with a sense of his own death as but a single event in the continuing order of things.

Yet both heroes and gods also look upon the prospect of the mortal's death in a far more engaged and emotional way as that which frustrates a warrior's deepest aspirations. So, when the same Sarpedon lies wounded, the thought of death is a grievous one whose sadness is captured in terms of his relations to his home and family. "Son of Priam!" he calls to Hector. "Do not let me lie here as prey for the Danaans; defend me!—and then I will die in your city, since it was not my destiny to return to my fatherland to gladden my dear wife and my infant son" (5.684–88).

Sarpedon now speaks of death as a painful and irreversible loss of something beloved, the frustration of his deepest wishes. Sarpedon's response to the threat of death is considerably less lofty, less clearly heroic than in his speech to Glaucus. Rather than channeling his response along the lines laid down by the warrior society and the demands of shame, Sarpedon feels the approach of death in relation to the particulars of his own life—the fatherland he will never see, the wife and baby who will never greet him. He conceives death less in generalized and economic terms, as a form of exchange, and more in terms of its specific and pathetic qualities, that is, the individual consequences that the approach of death will have on him and those he loves.

Similarly, Hera describes death as a sad and painful loss when she urges Athena to action on the Achaeans' behalf:

> Alas! Child of aegis-bearing Zeus, do we no longer
> Have a care finally for the slaughter of the Danaans?
> They meet their evil fate and die

In attacks by one man—Hector, the son of Priam
Who rages unendurably and has done evil deeds.

(8.352–56)

In both Sarpedon's and Hera's pathetic accounts of death, its piteousness is conjured up by the distinctive qualities that it irretrievably destroys. The pathetic disparity that Hera describes between the number of lives lost and the insolence of the one man—Hector—who is responsible contrasts with the unemotional parity of death considered merely as an exchange. Her evocation of the Achaeans' deaths as unbearable and tragic flows from Hera's feelings of *eleos:* "Seeing [the Achaeans], the white-armed goddess Hera felt pity [*eleēse*]" (8.350). Hera's feelings of *eleos* are prompted by the specific qualities of these Achaeans' deaths here and now, and in their immediacy and intensity her feelings are akin to those that mortals experience naturally at the prospect of imminent death. So too, *eleos* moves Zeus at the spectacle of Achilles' unconsolable grief for Patroclus (19.340), and the "blessed gods" feel pity as they look upon (*eisoroōntes*) Hector's body abused by Achilles (24.23).

As all these passages indicate, *eleos* is associated with an emotionally intense, less sublimely heroic response toward death, and one which is at some odds with the dispassionate attitude that shame and the warrior code require. In encouraging a view of mortal life as essentially fungible—("whether we afford a boast to another, or another to us")—shame tends to ignore or deny the importance of the fleeting particulars of the individual's life. In contrast, *eleos* begins with those particulars, and respects the individual's immediate and unreconstructed feelings about his own life, notwithstanding the mortal's distance from or subjection to the gods. In this chapter I will consider those passionate feelings in more detail and show how they underlie the warrior society of the *Iliad*. Although that society suppresses passions like the fear of death and *eleos,* such emotions become ever more overt and significant in the poem. Its climax cannot be understood within the terms and values of the warrior society, but requires that we take into account these compelling urges and fears that lie beneath.

II

It is not clear how best to translate *eleos* in the Homeric poems. As W. B. Stanford points out, the English word "pity" does not convey the visceral character of the Greek *eleos;* Stanford suggests that "compassionate grief" may be closer to the mark.[2] Wolfgang Schadewaldt has argued along similar lines that the German "*Mitleid*" does not convey *eleos,* for it is too imbued with later moral concepts to be an accurate translation of the Greek.[3] *Eleos,* Schadewaldt writes, is characterized by its spontaneity and by its power over the person feeling it. It is a primal or elemental affect (*Elementaraffekt*) that one immediately feels at the sight of a serious harm befalling another and is closely tied to the fear that a similar evil may befall oneself. On this view, *eleos* is to be distinguished from such later Greek words as συναχθέσθαι ("condole with") or συναλγεῖν ("grieve with")—words that convey a genuine "feeling with" (συν-) another's griefs. *Eleos,* in contrast, is an affect of *Jammer* ("misery," "distress") and belongs to the same semantic circle as οἶκτος, οἰκτιρμός, ὀδυρμός, γόος, πένθος, ὀλοφυρμός—all of them words that convey an overwhelming or racking experience of grief. *Eleos,* therefore, is not an emotion based on an awareness of the other's individual importance or the significance of another's distress. Rather, it names feelings that the sight of suffering calls up in the individual—primitive and powerful emotions that are closely related to fear.

In response to Schadewaldt, Max Pohlenz has shown that several aspects of *eleos* as it appears in the Homeric poems accord with more modern conceptions of "*Mitleid*" or "pity" and that *eleos* can be adequately translated by those words.[4] Pohlenz argues that *eleos* is not simply a primal affect, since it is always felt *for* someone. Because it is characteristically transitive, *eleos* is not completely described until we hear of the other person who arouses it; it commonly issues in action intended to relieve or avenge another's distress.[5] Thus, Pohlenz writes, the victor can feel *eleos* for the suppliant. In the final scenes of the poem, Achilles does not "suffer with" Priam, in the sense that he makes the Trojan king's misery his own, but he does allow himself to feel another's grief and to be guided by that feeling: *eleos* is that capacity to register another's grief. In sum, Pohlenz views *eleos* as the primal affect of a creature who is fundamentally a social being, a *koinōnikon*

---

[2] W. B. Stanford, *Greek Tragedy and the Emotions: An Introductory Study* (London: Routledge, 1983), pp. 23–24.

[3] Wolfgang Schadewaldt, "Furcht und Mitleid?" *Hermes* 83 (1955): 129–71.

[4] See Max Pohlenz, "Furcht und Mitleid? Ein Nachwort," *Hermes* 84 (1956): 49–74. In his article, Pohlenz cites and follows Burkert, "Mitleidsbegriff," especially pp. 70, 80, and 114–16. See also Macleod, *"Iliad" XXIV,* pp. 5 n. 1, 13–14, and 27.

[5] On this point, see Scott, "Pity and Pathos," pp. 8–9.

zoon. To man's nature belongs not merely a physical but also a spiritual kinship with his fellows, and *eleos* cannot be understood apart from that kinship.

The apparent inconsistency between Schadewaldt's and Pohlenz' presentations of *eleos* may be resolved by considering more particularly the social environment in which *eleos* tends to be found. For a striking feature of *eleos* as it appears in the *Iliad* is the closeness of its association with the warrior's family. *Eleos,* to be sure, may be felt for comrades-in-arms, and even enemies,[6] but the appeal to pity is seen at its clearest in the context of intimate relations. We have already seen how the aged father begs his son to feel *eleos* (22.38–76). Other appeals to *eleos* include Andromache's plea in Book 6.407–39, or Cleopatra's moving account of the horrors befalling a town under attack (9.590–96), or Patroclus' emotional plea on behalf of the hard-pressed Achaeans (16.1–45). Because *eleos* is so closely associated with the family, it is at once an intense feeling such as Schadewaldt describes and transitive, in the sense Pohlenz identifies.

Below I consider *eleos* and its affinity with intimate relations in the *Iliad:* those between husband and wife and between parent and child. I also examine the wariness with which *eleos* is viewed by warrior society and the efforts made to discourage it and to warn against its peculiarly compelling force. Analyzing these two aspects of *eleos,* its affinity with the family and its suppression within warrior society, will enable us to get an idea of Homeric *eleos* that does justice to both its visceral and its transitive aspects. We will also be able to describe its place in the ethics of the warrior society.

III

Quite apart from the honor and fame that are so vital to his sense of himself, the warrior has intimate ties and passionate commitments to parents, spouse, children, brothers, and sisters: the members of his household or *oikos.* The relationship between the warrior and his intimates within the household, unlike that among the *philoi* in the warrior society, is not mediated by gifts, nor is it necessary that equity or parity be maintained. Indeed, family relationships are distinguished by the widest *disparity* of power among the members of the *oikos:* the wife and the infant are radically dependent on the husband/father. The goodness of such relationships is, nonetheless, an immediate given, and, unlike

[6] I consider *eleos* as it extends to enemies in the next chapter.

the values of renown and prestige, does not arise from the thought of the warrior's mortality or from the need to secure an "unperishing renown" against the day of death.

The members of the warrior's *oikos* are not simply "others" with whom he deals at arm's length: they are part of who he is. Because ties of blood or affection partly constitute the warrior's identity, the value of these ties persists, even when prestige and renown have lost their value (as they have, most signally, for the loser in battle). They continue to engage the person's deepest allegiance and his strongest emotions. They are, moreover, regularly associated with the warrior's feelings of *eleos* in the *Iliad*.

The close association between *eleos* and family connections in the *Iliad* is perhaps best illustrated in the encounter of Hector and Andromache in Book 6. Andromache expressly asks Hector to feel *eleos* for her (*all' age nun eleaire,* 6.431), and Hector does so, conjuring up the painful image of Andromache's slavery after his death (see 6.450–65, 484). Andromache's speech, which describes her dependence on Hector and her inevitable humiliation in the event of his death, was calculated to arouse just such pathetic scenes in Hector's mind.

> "Madman! Your strength will ruin you! No pity
> On your infant son or me, who have nothing: soon
> I will be your widow, for soon the Achaeans will kill you
> In massed attack. Better for me then
> To be buried without you. For no other
> Comfort is there, once you've met your fate—
> Only griefs. I have no father, no mother:
> Godlike Achilles killed my father
> And sacked the well-settled city of the Cilicians,
> High-gated Thebes. . . .
> I had seven brothers in my house—
> All in a single day went to Hades' realm.
> The swift, godlike Achilles slew them all
> As they tended their cattle and gleaming sheep. . . .
> Hector! You are my father and my lady mother
> And my brother! You are my fair husband!
> Take pity! Stay here by the tower—
> Do not make your child an orphan, your wife a widow!"
>
> (6.407–16, 421–24, 429–32)

Eleos, intense and rooted in particulars, expresses the ardor and force of the ties between Andromache and Hector. Unlike shame, which is a constant presence in the warrior's life, *eleos* is occasional and unpredictable; it overthrows the rational self-interest that shame promotes. Andromache asks Hector to act without regard to his prestige, and to be prompted by the purpose of saving her life—a purpose largely uncoded in the warrior society.

Eleos rests on the warrior's perception that his own good is deeply involved with another's well-being. Andromache reminds Hector of her complete dependence on him, and Hector's sense of his own good, too, is deeply tied to Andromache: rather than see her enslaved, he hopes to die:

> Let me die, and the earth pour and cover me
> Before I hear your cry as you are dragged away.
>
> (6.464–65)

Because it rests on the warrior's perception that another's well-being is deeply implicated in his own, *eleos* has a merging effect. Andromache and Hector imagine the same unbearable scenes, but under the sway of her deep attachment to Hector Andromache also takes up a male role by suggesting how her husband should arrange his men, and Hector unheroically hopes that death will spare him the sight of his wife's enslavement.[7] In the merging effect of *eleos,* the plight of the one pathetically begging the warrior becomes the warrior's own plight. Thus, *eleos* is partly a matter of "feeling concern for" (*kēdesthai*) another,[8] but because the one who begs is closely tied to the warrior and helps to constitute his sense of self, *eleos* is inevitably imbued with the warrior's feelings about himself, as well. The fear of death that he represses as a prestige-seeking warrior, he feels at the thought of death or harm befalling the person he loves. Thus, Hector's grief for Andromache is inseparable from his grief at the prospect of his own death. "Here is the wife of Hector," he imagines someone saying, "once the best warrior of the Trojans" (6.459–61). His grief for Andromache enables him in an indirect way to grieve for himself: *eleos* prompts him to wish for death but it also allows him to grieve at the prospect.

In its emotional coloring *eleos* bears a marked similarity to mourning, which is also an intense and primal feeling, yet a social one as well. Achilles' lament for Patroclus provides the most illuminating parallel.

---

[7] On the characterization of the hero, both in contrast to the feminine and by incorporation of traditionally feminine gestures or responses, see Hélène Monsacré, *Les larmes d'Achille* (Paris: Albin Michel, 1984), especially pp. 128–31, where she discusses Andromache as a double of Hector.

[8] On the connection between feeling pity (*eleairein*) and concern (*kēdesthai*), see, e.g., 6.51–55, 8.350–53, 11.665, and 24.174.

Achilles' emotions about his own life suffuse his feelings for Patroclus and lend those feelings some of their intensity: Achilles' outsized grief for his companion is at the same time sorrow for the dashing of his own hopes to be specially honored by the gods. Thus, Achilles' mourning for Patroclus inevitably becomes mourning for Peleus and ultimately for himself. In his lengthiest and most articulate lament for Patroclus, Achilles says:

> . . . I could suffer nothing worse,
> Not even should I hear that my father died
> (Who now, I think, sheds round tears in Phthia
> Missing me, his son: I, who amidst an alien people
> Wage war on the Trojans for dread Helen's sake), . . .
> For I think Peleus either is
> Dead or nearly dead from grief
> In hateful old age, and ever awaiting
> Sad news of me, to hear tell of my death.
>
> (19.321–25, 334–37)

Underlying his grief for Patroclus is Achilles' self-mourning, couched in memories of his father Peleus. Because Peleus is dead or dying of grief and because Achilles will never return to Phthia, Patroclus' survival was to have offered some relief from the consequences of Peleus' and Achilles' deaths by ensuring a continuity across the generations. Achilles had hoped that Patroclus would find Neoptolemus alive when the war ended and bring him back to Phthia (see 19.328–33). Patroclus' death thus brings home to Achilles the unrelieved and absolute nature of his own imminent demise, unmitigated now by his friend's survival.

The self-reference in Achilles' lament seems to be a general property of mourning. The old men (*gerontes*) who hear Achilles' laments also "groaned," but each one grieves at the thought of what he himself has lost (19.338–39). So too, the women who hear Briseis' lament for Patroclus "groaned for Patroclus as a pretext [*prophasin*], but each one for her own griefs" (19.301–2; cf. 19.338–39). The mourner's self-grieving, which emerges clearly from these passages, characterizes as well the experience of the one feeling *eleos,* and suggests the closeness of *eleos* and mourning.

Thus *eleos,* at least as it emerges in the scene with Hector and Andromache, seems to grow from the warrior's own fears of death. The other's distress vividly figures or calls to the warrior's mind thoughts of his own inescapable demise. It is significant that a sense of self-"mourning is possible for the warrior only indirectly, in his affections for his loved ones. Construed as a lone player on the battlefield, the warrior is obliged to view his own death dispassionately. The real passions lurking beneath that apparent indifference, however, are revealed in the warrior's ardent feelings for those closest to him, whose dearness makes of them the warrior's especial point of vulnerability.

In other words, the distinctive character of *eleos,* as presented in the *Iliad,* arises in part from its ability to express fears that must otherwise be discouraged and should not be acted on. In what follows, I will discuss the implications of this feature of *eleos* for an understanding of the warrior society and for the relationship between that society and the emotion of *eleos.* This relationship is worked out in four great scenes: the meeting of Hector and Andromache in Book 6, which we have already considered in part; Phoenix' speech during the Embassy in Book 9; Patroclus' plea to Achilles in Book 16; and Odysseus' advice to Achilles in Book 19. I discuss each of these scenes in turn.

The richness of the characterization of *eleos* in the scene between Hector and Andromache (6.390–502) arises in large measure from Hector's resistance to it. To act on the promptings of *eleos* and do as Andromache asks would flout the codes of behavior that Hector has been taught and of whose goodness he is deeply convinced.

> All these things weigh on me, wife. But awfully
> Am I ashamed before the Trojan men and long-robed women
> If I skulk away from war like a coward.
> Nor does my spirit bid me, since I have learned to be noble
> Always and to fight amongst the first ranks,
> Winning great fame for my father and for me.
>
> (6.441–46)

The claims of *eleos* are too intense and its effects too unruly for Hector to let himself be guided by them. Because it is uncoded, felt only occasionally, and unforeseeable as to its effects, *eleos* cannot provide a sure or steady basis for the warrior's conduct. It is worth noting that the conduct Andromache suggests would in fact be sound military strategy: Hector should set up his lines where the city is most vulnerable and where it could be defended in relative safety (see 6.433–39). Andromache does not, however, seek to persuade Hector as though she were a military strategist, nor does she base her appeal on the grounds of its soundness as tactics. She speaks, rather, as a beloved who dreads losing her husband. The sageness of her advice is almost beside the point: the appeal to *eleos* might serve to motivate any action.

As Hector's and Andromache's meeting makes clear, *eleos* is to a substantial degree inconsistent with the dictates of the warrior code, which accordingly requires that the undeniable power of this emotion be resisted and not be acted upon.

Nonetheless, the self-mourning that underlies both mourning and *eleos* shows that Iliadic characters cannot be treated wholly in terms of the warrior society and its values. While the warrior may truly welcome those values and look upon them as authentically his own, the desire for "unperishing renown" can only displace, not wholly eradicate, the mortal's dread of his own death. The ability of these deep-seated feelings to disturb the surface of the warrior society is suggested by Hector's obvious vulnerability to Andromache's appeal, and by his troubled resistance to it. It emerges just as strikingly in Phoenix's speech to Achilles in Book 9, when the embassy sent from Agamemnon seeks to persuade Achilles to return to battle. As I argue below, Phoenix is himself moved by the very feelings he warns Achilles against, and his whole speech evinces a notable ambivalence toward the family and its emotional life.

The speech of Phoenix (9.430–605) is central to the embassy that Agamemnon sends to Achilles, and Phoenix devotes the second half of his appeal to the story of Meleager and Cleopatra (9.524–605). Cleopatra approaches Meleager, her husband, in a time of danger, and describes for him (much as Andromache did for Hector) the evils that await. Meleager had been refusing to fight out of anger at his mother and had already rejected the earnest pleas of companions and parents. Not until Cleopatra tearfully pleads with him, describing "all the griefs (*kēdea*) that befall those whose cities are taken" (9.591–92), is Meleager's heart moved.[9]

---

[9] The ranking of those who unsuccessfully pleaded with Meleager—elders, father, sisters, mother, *hetairoi*, wife—resembles Hector's ranking of those for whom he laments—the Trojans, mother, father, brothers, wife (6.450–55). On the ascending scale of affections, see Nagy, *Best of the Achaeans*, pp. 104–6; see also Johannes Th. Kakridis, *Homeric Researches* (Lund: Gleerup, 1949), chapter 1. The graduated quality of the scale that Kakridis and Nagy posit should not obscure the tension existing between the mediated ties among comrades-in-arms and the immediate ties between the warrior and those dearest to him. Dieter Lohmann, *Die Komposition der Reden in der Ilias* (Berlin: de Gruyter, 1970), pp. 258–59, argues against Kakridis' theory of a traditional scale of affections in Phoenix's story, suggesting instead that the order of those supplicating Meleager reflects the sequence of suppliants in the embassy to Achilles. On this reading, the old priest (in the Meleager story) parallels Odysseus' role in the embassy, Meleager's father is analogous to Phoenix himself, and the *hetairoi* parallel Ajax, who expressly bases his appeal on the friendship between Achilles and the Achaeans.

The point that Phoenix wishes to make is that Meleager finally returned to battle and defended his city, but he did so without compensation or award. In the event, Phoenix relates, Meleager, "yielding to his heart" (9.598) returned to battle and saved the city: "No longer did they give him gifts many and pleasing, yet he repulsed the evil nonetheless" (9.598–99). Phoenix urges Achilles not to postpone defending his ships against Trojan attack until a time when, like Meleager, he must do so.

> . . . It would be a bad thing
> To defend the ships once they are ablaze. While they offer you gifts,
> Return to war. The Achaeans will compensate you like a god.
>
> (9.601–3)

A warning against *eleos* is implicit in Phoenix's cautionary tale. For it is clear that Meleager was prompted by pity for Cleopatra, whose dearness to Meleager emerges even in Phoenix's sketchy narrative (see 9.555–65). Meleager's "heart was stirred" (*ōrineto thumos*, 9.595), not simply because the enemy was at the gates, but because the wife he loved had described for him "all the evils that befall those whose city is taken." Similarly, Andromache had sought to stir Hector to action calculated to save her from danger, and her appeal was to Hector's capacity for pity. Because Meleager was moved to fight by *eleos*, he fought without regard to compensation. Phoenix's cautionary tale, then, contains the following sense: "You will ultimately fight out of *eleos* for those dearest to you, and if you wait until that happens, you will fight without compensation. Better to fight now and name your price."

Earlier in his speech to Achilles, Phoenix told a story about the dangerous ardor of relations within the *oikos*, placing them in implicit contrast to those that structure the warrior society. When he was a youth, his jealous mother asked Phoenix to seduce his father's mistress, and when the boy complied, he was cursed by his father with sterility or impotence (9.444–57). Phoenix's story of the quarrel with his father—a fascinating inversion of the Oedipus myth, since the father ultimately is able to destroy the son—is unmistakably significant for the disagreement between Achilles and Agamemnon.[10] Although both

---

[10] On the parallels between Phoenix's account of his youth and the story of the *Iliad*, see Judith A. Rosner, "The Speech of Phoenix: *Iliad* 9.434–605," *Phoenix* 30 (1976): 314–27; and Whitfield, "Restored Relation," p. 99. Ruth Scodel, "The Autobiography of Phoenix: *Iliad* 9.444–95," *American Journal of Philology* 103 (1982): 128–36, argues that Phoenix's story is intended to contrast Phoenix's situation (where departure from his father's household was justified) to Achilles' (where departure is not justified).

quarrels arise from rivalry over a woman, Phoenix seems more interested in how the situations differ. Agamemnon has merely taken away Achilles' woman, whereas Amyntor altogether deprived Phoenix of his virility. Phoenix seems tacitly to contrast the scope for destructiveness in familial relationships—and in particular between father and son—with the mediated and hence more easily reparable ties binding the warriors. In essence, Phoenix advises Achilles: "Do not treat Agamemnon's offense as though it were as deeply irreparable as a father's curse. Take advantage of the possibilities for reparation that society affords, and accept Agamemnon's gifts." Phoenix's account of his youth thus makes a point similar to his tale of Meleager—in both stories Phoenix urges Achilles to avail himself of the benefits of warrior society. He contrasts such benefits (compensation and reparability of harms) with the destructiveness of his own *oikos* in his youth, and with the irresistibly compelling emotion of *eleos* as it appears in the story of Meleager.

Yet there is a deep ambivalence at the heart of Phoenix's speech, for the old tutor seeks to obtain an attentive hearing by assuring Achilles of his benevolence toward him, basing his assurances on just those relationships against which he warns the younger warrior. Thus, Phoenix assures Achilles that he could never part from him, even if he could thereby regain his youth (see 9.434–48) and recounts how he nursed and tended Achilles as a child (see 9.485–95). Phoenix's recollections are surprisingly like those that an intimate uses in appealing to the warrior's *eleos:*

> I made you what you are, godlike Achilles,
> Loving you with all my heart: you would refuse
> To go to dinner or eat in the great hall,
> Unless I sat you on my lap,
> And offered you bits of food or wine.
> Often enough you wet the breast of my shirt,
> Spitting up wine as careless children will do.
> Thus, I suffered and toiled much for you—
> With the thought, the gods would never bless me
> With a son. I made you my child,
> Godlike Achilles, to ward off shameful destruction.
>
> (9.485–95)

Phoenix's recollections resemble those of Hecuba, who in begging Hector to "feel shame and pity" (22.82) reminds him of the breast that once comforted him and brought "forgetfulness of care" (*lathikadea mazon*, 83). The tenderness of his memories likens them, as well, to Andromache's meeting with Hector, in which the destiny awaiting their son Astyanax is a powerful part of the appeal to Hector's pity (see 6.407–8, 466–70). More particularly, Phoenix uses a phrase—"ward off baneful destruction" (*aeikea loigon amunēis,* 9.495)—which elsewhere expresses what dependents hope that the one in power will do.[11] As Phoenix uses it here, the phrase is intended to express the depth of his relation to Achilles, who has rescued him from the "shameful destruction" of a childless old age. But the phrase inevitably carries with it, as well, a sense of a dependent's appeal to be rescued by someone with superior strength.

A tension exists between Phoenix's intent and the meaning of his words, for he uses language that borders on that used by suppliants, but does so in a speech that seems intended, at bottom, to warn Achilles *against* feeling *eleos.* This tension also informs the image of the father, as this emerges from Phoenix's implicitly contrasting recollections of Peleus, who "loved [him] as a father loves a son" (9.481), and of his own father, who called down a curse on him. The father in Phoenix's speech is to be both cherished (like Peleus) and avoided (like Amyntor); he is benevolent and destructive. Indeed, the menacing ambiguity of the *oikos* is found within the Meleager story, where Meleager's mother prays for his death (9.566–71), and his spouse moves him to risk his life without compensation.

Relationships within the *oikos,* then, are capable of the greatest intimacy and the greatest destructiveness. In Phoenix's speech, the *oikos* compares unfavorably to society because the deep ambivalence of relations characteristic of the household renders them unsuitable and dangerous in the warrior society. Yet this ambivalence, far from being excluded from Phoenix's speech, in fact pervades it, for he is moved to advise Achilles by the very kind of feelings against which he implicitly warns him.

When Patroclus begs Achilles to reenter the battle or to send him in his stead (16.1–100), we are reminded of Phoenix's speech and of Cleopatra's supplication. The very names of the suppliants suggest the association, for *Patro-klos* and *Kleo-patrē* are inversions,[12] and the passages are closely linked by the significance of *eleos* in each. As we have

---

[11] See, e.g., in connection with the plague sent by Apollo, 1.67 and 1.456; in connection with the Achaeans' plight without Achilles, 1.341, 16.32, 75, 80, and 18.450; concerning the protection afforded by a god, 1.398, 5.603, 662, and 20.98. The linguistic evidence is assembled by Daniel R. Blickman, "The Role of the Plague in the *Iliad*," *Classical Antiquity* 6 (1987): 1–10, pp. 3–4.

[12] See Nagy, *Best of the Achaeans,* pp. 105, 110–11, following E. Howald, *Der Dichter der "Ilias"* (Zurich: Rentsch, 1946), p. 132.

seen, Phoenix was concerned with the spontaneous and irresistible nature of *eleos,* and warned Achilles against it. Those dangerous qualities also distinguish Patroclus' plea, and his exchange with Achilles develops into a mutual reading of the Meleager story, with each hero offering an interpretation. Their readings center on the problem of *eleos,* whose importance for understanding the relations between characters becomes ever more apparent as the *Iliad*'s narrative unfolds.

It is curious that Patroclus should base his appeal particularly on *eleos,* since Nestor, who had originally suggested the idea to Patroclus, clearly had a quite different appeal in mind. (See 11.790–803.) Contrasting Achilles' unequalled prowess with Patroclus' superior foresight and counsel, Nestor had encouraged Patroclus to encounter his friend precisely as a *philos,* essentially on the same level with Achilles. As Nestor presents it, Patroclus and Achilles have complementary skills and Patroclus should put his particular talent to use for his friend. Nestor's advice encourages conduct well within the bounds or considerations of the warrior society.

Although Patroclus takes Nestor's advice and asks to fight in Achilles' stead, he does not present himself as his friend's superior in counsel but instead weeps and rebukes Achilles. Approaching him in tears, Patroclus is likened by his friend, not unkindly, to a baby girl (*kourē nēpiē,* 16.7–8) crying to be picked up by her mother. Rather than address himself to his companion's sense of *aidōs,* Patroclus seeks to rouse *eleos* in Achilles, and in fact succeeds (cf. *oiktire,* 16.5). The intensity of *eleos* is shown here in its ability to invert reality, for even though Patroclus in fact is one of the preeminent warriors at Troy, "the equal of Ares" (11.604), he makes himself defenseless and girlish.[13] Patroclus' feminine quality bespeaks that "merging" effect of *eleos,* which tends to blur the polarization of the sexes and their different social roles under pressure of the emotional ties binding the warrior and his dependents.

Yet Achilles seems peculiarly unresponsive to a plea that is calculated

---

[13] Monsacré, *Larmes d'Achille,* pp. 91–92, notes that Patroclus presents in a positive light the qualities and offices normally associated with women: preparation of food, healing, and sweetness of disposition. Patroclus' concern for others is one of his distinguishing features: he shows exceptional kindness not only to Briseis (19.287–300) but also to Eurypylus (11.804–48 and 15.390–404). Menelaus mourns Patroclus as one who knew how to be "gentle to all" (17.671). Patroclus' feminine qualities, however, do not make him unique among the warriors: Homer comments elsewhere on the maternal quality of warriors insofar as they protect their comrades (see 9.323–27 and 17.4–6). Furthermore, Patroclus' feminine qualities do not at all prevent him from being one of the most daunting warriors among the Achaeans. The woman-like Patroclus is not to be likened to the "effeminate" Paris.

to arouse *eleos*. In sending Patroclus back to war, he seems to understand his story as one that concerns *timē* and the just punishment of Agamemnon's refusal to honor Achilles as he deserves. Achilles interprets the story up to this point as if it were parallel to Chryses' unfortunate encounter with Agamemnon. Just as Chryses, after being dishonored by Agamemnon, asked a god to bring a plague down on the Achaeans, so Achilles, through Thetis, had enlisted Zeus to bring death on the Achaeans on account of Agamemnon's arrogant misconduct. Further, the gods responded in both cases, and brought about the death of many Achaeans. When he sends Patroclus into battle, Achilles also echoes the prayer of Chryses, who interceded on the Achaeans' behalf when his daughter had been returned:

> Hear me, [Apollo] . . .
> . . . you heard my prayer once before
> And honoring me, you smote the Achaeans' army.
> Now, too, accomplish my prayer:
> Dispel the baneful plague from the Danaans.
>
> (1.451, 453–56)

Similarly, in sending Patroclus to relieve the Achaeans, Achilles prays:

> Zeus . . .
> . . . you heard my prayer once before
> And honoring me, you smote the Achaeans' army.
> Now, too, accomplish my prayer:
> I shall stay here by the assembly of ships,
> But I send my companion with the Myrmidons
> To fight: bring him glory, far-seeing Zeus . . .
> . . . May he return unscathed to the swift ships
> In full armor and with all his companions.
>
> (16.233, 236–41, 247–48)

Achilles, in other words, appears to understand his story this way: Agamemnon has offended Achilles (just as he had once offended Chryses) by failing to act as shame required, and Zeus has therefore punished Agamemnon and the Achaeans (just as Apollo had earlier punished them). Because Achilles, for whose sake Zeus has punished the Achaeans, now seeks to afford them some respite, Zeus will certainly hear his prayer (just as Apollo heard Chryses'). Far from responding in that urgent, self-forgetting way that an appeal to *eleos* envisions, Achilles calculates his best advantage. He agrees to Patroclus' proposal because in this way it will be even clearer to the Achaeans how much they need him.

Implicit in Achilles' and Patroclus' attitudes are two different "readings" of the Meleager story. Meleager had waited until the enemy was storming his city, and as a consequence had to fight as a matter of compulsion, without gifts (see 9.587–99). Achilles, far from relenting in response to Phoenix's story of Meleager, raised the stakes: not until the Trojans had actually set fire to the Achaeans' ships would he return to war. (See 9.650–55 and 16.60–63.) Once that happens, Achilles feels confident that, unlike the unfortunate Meleager, he will still be able to command the others' gifts. (See 16.83–86.)

In viewing the story as a challenge to his greatness and an opportunity to establish his preeminence among the warriors, Achilles interprets the Achaeans' sufferings in terms appropriate to the warrior society and its values, as the sign of his prestige and the honor in which Zeus holds him. A naive optimism is inherent in his response: the values of the warrior society seem truly "valuable," because, as the Achaeans' plight apparently demonstrates, they are upheld and enforced by the gods.

Patroclus' appeal to *eleos*, however, strongly suggests the inadequacy of Achilles' self-seeking response. The pathos of Patroclus' appeal does not at all arise from his own powerlessness (for he is in fact preeminent as a warrior); rather, it is based on the reality of human suffering, to which Achilles is relatively insensitive. When Patroclus, hurrying back to Achilles' tent, encounters the wounded Eurypylus, he feels sorrow for him (*oikteire*, 11.814), but his sorrow extends to the larger context of the Achaeans' misfortunes:

> Ah, wretches, leaders and guardians of the Danaans,
> So you were destined, far from friends and fatherland,
> To sate the dogs in Troy with your gleaming fat.
>
> (11.816–18)

Eurypylus' wounded thigh stirs a sense of pity in Patroclus because it calls to mind the deaths of many Achaeans. These deaths are conceived not as the result of some featureless lottery—distributing death indifferently to this man or to that—but in terms of their sadness. The grotesque image of the Achaeans' corpses feeding the Trojan dogs underscores the frustration of the soldiers' wish to be restored to friends and fatherland. Thus, while Achilles blithely takes the Achaeans' suffering as a confirmation that the gods truly honor him, Patroclus understands the Achaeans' misery as a sign, more generally, of human wretchedness.

Moreover, Patroclus bases his appeal more or less directly on his intimacy with Achilles, an unusual relationship among the warriors at

Troy.[14] Unlike most companions, Patroclus does not require arm's-length fair dealing, and his friendship with Achilles is not mediated by gifts or other exchanges of recognition for prowess. Patroclus' relationship to Achilles is characterized by a mixture of subservience and intimacy that makes it strangely like the relationship between a wife and husband.[15] Thus, Patroclus happily does Achilles' bidding: Achilles recalls how "quickly and nimbly" Patroclus prepared dinner (19.316–18; cf. 9.201–4) and Patroclus fears displeasing Achilles by delay in reporting the name of a wounded soldier Achilles has asked about (see 11.596–617, 648–54, 839–41). The rapport between Achilles and Patroclus is especially clear when Achilles sings a song of ancient heroes while Patroclus sits opposite and waits (9.186–91). Unlike other audiences, Patroclus does not "delight" in Achilles' rendition of the "fames of men," for his response is to Achilles rather than to Achilles' song. Achilles sings for solace (see 9.186), and Patroclus' silent attendance—"waiting until [Achilles] finished his song" (191)— conveys the depth of his concern for the singer.[16] These feminine qualities find their most intense expression in Patroclus' emotional appeal, and the pathos of his assumed feminine helplessness inevitably suggests a tragic finale, as in Andromache's doom-laden plea to Hector. Implicit in Patroclus' appeal, in other words, is the catastrophe about to befall both Patroclus and Achilles.

Achilles, who had trenchantly criticized the values of the warrior society in Book 9, now shows how closely he has in fact clung to them

[14] This close identification of Patroclus with Achilles is suggested by Dale Sinos, *Achilles, Patroklos, and the Meaning of "Philos"* (Innsbruck: Institut für Sprachwissenschaft der Universität Innsbruck, 1980), who elaborates the argument that Patroclus is Achilles' *therapōn* and functions as a "ritual substitute" for Achilles. See also Steven Lowenstam, *The Death of Patroclus: A Study in Typology* (Königstein/Ts.: Hain, 1981), pp. 126–31, 174–77, and Nagy, *Best of the Achaeans*, pp. 33 and 292–93. See also Nadia van Brock, "Substitution rituelle," *Revue hittite et asianique* 65 (1959): 117–46.

[15] The intensity of Achilles' feelings for Patroclus (see, e.g., 16.97–100 and 24.6) raises the question whether Achilles and Patroclus were lovers. Homer does not specifically allude to such a relationship, and E. Bethe, "Die Dorische Knabenliebe, ihre Ethik, ihre Idee," *Rheinisches Museum* 62 (1907): 438–75, p. 455, concluded that such a relation did not exist. See also Griffin, *Homer on Life and Death,* p. 104, n. 4; and K. J. Dover, *Greek Homosexuality* (Cambridge: Harvard University Press, 1978), pp. 197–98. W. M. Clarke, "Achilles and Patroclus in Love," *Hermes* 106 (1978): 381–95, argues that homoeroticism, if not homosexuality, is evident in the *Iliad;* see also Bernard Sergent, *Homosexuality in Greek Myth* (Boston: Beacon Press, 1984), pp. 250–58. As I argue below in Chapter 7, Achilles is a figure of impossible sublimity. It seems a part of his unreal loftiness that his relationship to Patroclus is charged with an erotic intensity but is without the carnal basis that such intensity implies in the everyday world.

[16] See Françoise Frontisi-Ducroux, *La cithare d'Achille: Essai sur la poétique de "l'Iliade"* (Rome: Ateneo, 1986), pp. 11–13 on Patroclus as an ideal image—in his combination of allegiance and subordination—of the poet's audience.

all along. His indifference to the others' plight and his calculations of his own best advantage are to be expected in a society that esteems *timē* above all else. Patroclus' deliberate appeal to *eleos,* however, shows the thinness of the society's values. Appearing initially as a suppressed emotion in heroic society, *eleos* becomes in Book 16 a force that exposes the insufficiency of the values governing that society.

Patroclus is a pivotal character in the *Iliad,* for with his death, it becomes tragically clear to Achilles that Zeus does not "honor" him, at least in the sense of respecting and deferring to his wishes. The fall of the companion dearest to Achilles is at the same time the death of Achilles' pretensions that he is preeminently honored by Zeus. When Thetis asks Achilles why he weeps—has not Zeus done everything Achilles asked for?—Achilles agrees:

> . . . the Olympian has indeed accomplished these things:
> But what pleasure in that, since my dear companion has died—
> Patroclus, whom I honored beyond all companions,
> As my own life?
>
> (18.79–82)

With the death of Patroclus, it becomes clear that the *Iliad* is not, ultimately, a story about the warrior code, or the search for "unperishing renown," but rather a story of griefs and the emotions—especially *eleos*—roused by human suffering. Achilles' mourning for Patroclus calls forth all those aspects of him that Phoenix had foreseen and warned against.

When Odysseus urges Achilles to give up his grieving for Patroclus (see 19.145–237), both his plea and the response he receives have much to show us about the nature of *eleos* in the poem. Their conversation is the *Iliad*'s most elaborate treatment of the tension between *aidōs* (which is especially associated with relations within the warrior society) and *eleos* (which has a particular affinity with relations between the warrior and his family). Moreover, as I shall argue, the speeches of Odysseus and Achilles in Book 19—and the debate about whether grief should or should not be kept in bounds—ultimately offer two competing conceptions of the poetics of the *Iliad.*

When Achilles refuses to eat, and evinces no interest in Agamemnon's gifts (see 19.199–214), Odysseus remonstrates:

> The Achaeans cannot grieve for the dead with their stomach:
> Far too many, in heaps, every day,
> Fall in war: when would there be a respite?
> No, we must bury the dead

> With unpitying heart, weeping for a day.
> Those who survive hateful war
> Must remember drink and food, the better
> To fight incessantly with our enemies,
> Our flesh clothed in stout bronze.
>
> (19.225–33)

Odysseus makes the suspect nature of *eleos* clear when he says that in disposing of its deceased, the warrior society must exhibit an "unpitying" (*nēlēs*) heart.[17] The use of *nēlēs* here is pointed, and seems to carry the full weight of its etymological meaning, "unpitying," for Achilles must relinquish the compelling and impulsive grief that arises from the loss of someone uniquely valuable and irreplaceable. To view the dead with "unpitying heart" is to view them with a certain equanimity as expendable, capable of being replaced by the survivors: a warrior must view the death of a companion in the same way that *aidōs* requires him to look upon his own death. Odysseus' speech has considerable power and persuasiveness, largely because he does not deny that death is an occasion for grief. Odysseus argues, rather, that precisely because of the overwhelming number of deaths—and, in consequence, the possibility of endless mourning—it is necessary to impose limits on the fervor and duration of grief; specifically, one weeps for a day, and then returns to the business of everyday life.

Odysseus' immediate objective is to get Achilles to eat, and so to solidify his reconciliation with Agamemnon and the Achaeans. In the course of his speech, however, "to remember drink and food" becomes an epitome of the warrior society's code and the warrior's attitude toward war.[18] To "remember" (*memnēsthai*, 19.231) drink and food is

---

[17] On *nēlēs* as "unpitying," see Burkert, "Mitleidsbegriff," pp. 22–27.

[18] Odysseus' speech has been the subject of a searching analysis by Pietro Pucci, *Odysseus Polutropos: Intertextual Readings in the "Odyssey" and the "Iliad"* (Ithaca: Cornell University Press, 1987), pp. 165–72. Pucci lays particular stress on Odysseus' use of the word *"gastēr"* ("It is impossible for the Achaeans to grieve for the dead with their stomach," 19.225), and understands the passage as an unflattering depiction of Odysseus—the man of *gastēr*—from a distinctly Iliadic and Achillean point of view. Thus, Pucci writes, "The *Iliad* enhances Achilles' sublime asceticism while implicitly debasing the mean concerns of Odysseus, as well as his—and the *Odyssey*'s—inability to understand the heroic poem of *kleos* and death" (p. 169). As I seek to show, the ethic Odysseus urges here is more cogent and compelling, even in Iliadic terms, than Pucci allows. For Odysseus articulates in a striking and powerful way the values of the warrior society and their basis in a tragic view of the human condition. Odysseus' reference to *gastēr* has a debunking effect on what may be the illusions of the warrior society but ultimately serves only to place the values of that society on a deeper and more secure basis. I agree with Pucci that Odysseus' use of *gastēr* is associated with a

to pay attention to the body's thirst and hunger—to consider the body's needs important and to act so as to satisfy them. Paying heed to hunger and thirst gives the work of war a distinctive rhythm—a pattern of fighting (when the stomach is satisfied) and rest (when the body is hungry). Survivors eat, Odysseus says, so that they may fight "incessantly always" (*nōlemes aiei,* 19.232). The "remembering of drink and food," however, shows in what way the soldier fights "incessantly"— that is, as a settled course of life rather than as a central obsession that makes everything else tangential and insignificant.

In refusing to sit down to a banquet with Agamemnon, on the grounds that this will delay his vengeance for Patroclus' death, Achilles had urged, "Let us remember war" (*mnēsōmetha kharmēs,* 19.148). The martial attitude embodied in this phrase is contested by Odysseus' advice to "remember drink and food." Remembering is a kind of single-mindedness for Achilles, and "to remember war" is precisely that adamant refusal to let go of war as one's sole and exclusive interest. Achilles' "remembering" of war is expressed in his indifference to reconciliation with Agamemnon and to the gifts intended to effect and symbolize the reconciliation:

> Glorious son of Atreus, Agamemnon, lord of men,
> Offer gifts if you like, as is appropriate,
> Or keep them by your side. Let us remember war
> Now. No time to stand here and make speeches
> Or waste time. A great deed remains undone.
> Just as Achilles will be seen in the front ranks
> Killing the Trojan troops with bronze spear,
> Let each of you remember and fight man-to-man.
>
> (19.146–53)

"To remember war," as Achilles means it, is to be indifferent to the body, so that one rushes into battle notwithstanding the body's hunger and fatigue. Indeed, "remembering war" in Achilles' sense—to remember the "great deed that remains undone" (*mega ergon arekton,* 19.150)—is to disdain the body's needs as beneath one's consideration in light of the important values at stake. (See 19.199–210.)

"To remember drink and food," then, as urged by Odysseus in response to Achilles' fervor for war and vengeance, expresses the need

---

poetic implicit in the poem, but I argue that the poetic in question, far from being antithetic to aristocratic "praise" poetry—as Pucci argues—articulates the periodicity, rhythm, and moderation inherent in the warrior code. I then argue that the *Iliad* ultimately suggests a different poetic, one based on griefs or *kēdea.*

to consider the dead (and, in particular, Patroclus) as less important than the on-going life of society and, in particular, the reconciliation of Achilles and Agamemnon. Odysseus urges this on Achilles partly because intimate attachments are less important than the mediated ties of the warrior society and the egotistic values of that society. The warrior society's ethic of seeking prestige and renown, as a response to a world where people die "in heaps" daily, possesses the virtues of moderation, prudence, and clear-sightedness. Thus, the warrior society is clear-sighted in its recognition of the reasons why one seeks prestige—because one is "neither immortal nor unageing" (see 12.322–28). It is prudent, in that, notwithstanding the common end of death, it ensures that the individual is not paralyzed. It finds a value in the individual's transient mortal existence; indeed, it makes mortality the very condition of this value—for, if one were not mortal and bound to grow old, there would be no value in risking one's life in order to achieve renown. Finally, the warrior code is moderate. The society's funeral rites provide a means for discharging one's natural grief at the sight of the fallen, and the conduct of these observances guides the individual in his experience of grief—the end of the rites should also be the end of mourning.[19] The friendly-mindedness (*philophrosunē*) that is a necessary part of the warrior society is neither outraged (the soldier is not expected to be indifferent to the dead) nor unduly encouraged (mourning should last but a day).

"Remembering drink and food" encapsulates the warrior society's qualities of prudence, moderation, and clear-sightedness, especially as these weigh against excessive desire for battle. The body's needs provide a kind of canon or rule for guiding the soldier's attitude toward fighting and for ensuring that his attitude is prudent and moderate. The soldier must fight valorously in the front ranks without regard to his life or safety; he is to be best "always" (*aien aristeuein,* see, e.g., 6.208). Yet modifying the rigor of this command is the consideration that one should be well-nourished before going to fight, and should desist when the body needs refreshment. The body and its appetites supply a discreet corrective to the absolute imperatives of the warrior code. Moreover, the need to eat captures the degree of comradeship or friendly-mindedness that should exist in the soldier's dealings with others in the society. For to heed one's need for nourishment and refreshment—allowing it finally to distract oneself from grief—ensures that the daily toll of death and bereavement does not stifle the on-going work of society. Finally, remembering drink and food shows a clear-

---

[19] See Redfield, *Nature and Culture,* pp. 179–82.

sightedness about fighting and its aims. Odysseus suggests a debunking and deliberately bathetic view of war. The warrior fights not out of any grand motives, but, in essence, simply as part of a natural process. This is how I understand one passage that has not drawn much comment.[20] Immediately after urging Achilles to remember drink and food so that he may fight, Odysseus adds:

> . . . Let no one
> Hold back [from fighting], awaiting another summons [*otruntus*]:
> For that summons will be an evil thing for the one left
> Behind by the Argives' ships. No, rising as one,
> Let us awaken fierce Ares against the horse-taming Trojans.
>
> (19.233–37)

The phrase "another summons" is uncharacteristically vague, but seems in this context to refer to a stimulus "other than" satisfaction of one's bodily needs. Odysseus' point becomes clear against the background of Achilles' intransigence throughout the poem. For Achilles has indeed insisted on some other, greater reason to fight. When Odysseus had offered Achilles gifts to compensate him for Agamemnon's offense, Achilles refused: no gifts could be sufficient to pay for risking his life. Phoenix's tale of Meleager, too, implicitly warned Achilles against waiting for something more than an apology and restitution. The "other summons" to do battle—which, in Achilles' case, is the death of Patroclus—has indeed proved to be an "evil thing" for him. To insist on lofty or compelling values to motivate one to fight, Odysseus suggests, is bound to end badly—to be an "evil thing" for the person who so insists.

Odysseus, then, could be understood as urging on Achilles much what the embassy had urged on him in Book 9—the necessity to be satisfied with such satisfaction as society has to offer. Yet Odysseus' argument in Book 19 seems the more penetrating, for he argues that the soldier fights, in the last analysis, simply because the world demands it. The natural rhythms of hunger and satisfaction should guide the warrior because war, like hunger, is essentially a matter of nature—

---

[20] Here I follow Allen's Oxford text. Edwards would punctuate differently, placing a period after ὀτρυντύς, to yield the sense: "Let no one of you hold back, awaiting some other summons; this is the summons; there will be trouble (κακόν) for anyone left by the ships." See Mark W. Edwards, *The Iliad: A Commentary*, Vol. *V, Books 17–20* (Cambridge: Cambridge University Press, 1991), *ad* 19.233–37. I prefer Allen's text, since it yields a more pointed sense than the one Edwards adopts: Odysseus is not generally reproving slackers but hinting that Achilles must not insist on having a compelling reason to fight.

a condition imposed on all—and not a matter of specific human purposes or desires.

To appreciate that war is essentially a matter of the kind of creatures we are reflects a practical, Odyssean lucidity, for it captures both what is terrible in mortal life and what assuages or soothes the terror. What is terrible is that war—which reflects and expresses the condition of all mortal life—does not grow from or answer to human purposes. Episodes that from a human point of view bring the most terrible losses and arouse the most painful feelings, are from Zeus's point of view merely means of accomplishing certain fated objectives (see 14.49–71). What is soothing, on the other hand, is the steady periodicity of life. The ebb and flow of the generations, dawn and dusk, hunger and satisfaction—all of these express the regularity of nature. War follows these rhythms. Men cannot stop war, or inaugurate an era of peace, but they can, by regarding the rhythms of day and night, enjoy some respite.

IV

The world, then, is fierce, yet the fierceness is contained within an alternating pattern. Much as Achilles' shield portrays a city at war, but balances this with a portrait of a city at peace, and contains both portraits within an overarching scheme (see 18.490–540), so the world of the *Iliad,* while essentially a world of strife, unfolds rhythmically and pulses and ebbs in a regular and intelligible way. The warrior should observe the periodicity of strife. "It is a good thing to obey the night," Idaeus says, by way of bringing the fighting to an end for a day (7.282). Conversely, Zeus despises Ares precisely because of his refusal ever to relent: "always (*aiei*) strife is dear to [him], and wars and battles" (5.890–91; cf. 1.176–77).

What Odysseus suggests is that the soldier should bring to the work of war something of the periodicity to be seen in bodily or other natural rhythms. This sense of the periodicity of strife—the cyclicality of victory and defeat—is implicit in the warrior's heroic indifference to death: it informs Sarpedon's words when he urges Glaucus into battle: "to see if we afford a boast to another, or another to us" (12.328). The same attitude can be seen in Paris' cheeky dismissal of his duel with Menelaus: "Don't rail at me, wife, with harsh words! If Menelaus, with Athena's help, has bested me now, later I'll do the same to him. For we have gods, too" (3.438–40).

"Remembering drink and food" epitomizes the alternating pattern that is characteristic of much in the *Iliad,* and captures both the terror underlying the warrior's life and the solace to be found in it. The warrior who thinks of the satisfied stomach as a sufficiently persuasive reason to fight is one who understands the basis of war in the structure of the world and the condition of mortal life. He understands that his fighting does not arise, in the first instance, from his own desire but from his own transiency. Likewise, the warrior who regards hunger as a good reason to stop fighting appreciates the periodicity of strife and its overarching order of pulses. Here, too, he appreciates that war does not respond to his desire, for he may—as Achilles does—deeply wish to fight on relentlessly. The warrior who "obeys the night" and seeks a respite from fighting acknowledges that war is not, ultimately, about his purposes. Yet he accepts, too, that which is benign in a world indifferent to his purposes, and makes its rhythms of strife and rest his own.

The power of Odysseus' argument is that it captures not only the spirit of the warrior society, but also many of our intuitions concerning the distinctive beauty of the *Iliad*. For the *Iliad* is a poem both of passion and repose, in which the most tragic human events are viewed from a quasi-Olympian perspective—broad and lofty, interested but distant.[21] Homer does not blink at the bloodiness of war or the fury of human passions. Again and again in the *Iliad*'s battle narratives he recounts tales of young soldiers cut down, beauty destroyed, the hopes of the old dashed, and the love of young wives frustrated. Yet in its narrative manner the *Iliad* seems to stand above the painful human events it recounts. These "griefs" have been refined into tales for later generations to hear (see *Od.* 8.579–80). The story, notwithstanding the emotional and physical violence of its subject, nonetheless evinces a beautiful and satisfying form. Thus, "remembering drink and food"— which engages the warrior in a rhythmic pattern of fighting and respite—seems connected, ultimately, to a poetic of the *Iliad* that sees its chief beauty in the balance between violence and aesthetic form.

V

Despite the power of Odysseus' arguments, Achilles remains un- moved. "Remembering drink and food" may epitomize what is noble and tragic in the warrior society but it ultimately excludes an emotion

---

[21] On the significance of the rhythm of natural process for the poetics of the *Iliad* and the *Odyssey*, see, e.g., Norman Austin, *Archery at the Dark of the Moon: Poetic Problems in Homer's "Odyssey"* (Berkeley: University of California Press, 1975), chapter 2; see also Jeffrey M. Hurwit, *The Art and Culture of Early Greece, 1100–480 B.C.* (Ithaca: Cornell University Press, 1985), pp. 71–73.

of central importance to Achilles: *eleos*. The survivors must bury the dead, Odysseus says, "with unpitying heart" (*nēlea thumon ekhontas*, 19.229). "Remembering drink and food"—paying attention to one's own body and its needs—is distinguished precisely by this relative indifference to others, a lack of deep emotional engagement with them.

There are at least two flaws in Odysseus' argument that prevent his words from finally persuading Achilles. First, Odysseus concludes from the great numbers of the fallen in war and the impossibility of grieving for all of them that it is advisable to grieve for none of them in particular. This argument, however, fails to address the real nature of Achilles' grief, which is not at all for the generality of the fallen Achaeans but for the specific and irreplaceable Patroclus. Second, from his assumption that the world is indifferent to human desire, Odysseus concludes that such desires should be avoided. "To remember drink and food," as Odysseus uses the phrase, is therefore to avoid strong wishes, such as arise from intimate attachments and issue in compelling sentiments like *eleos*. The warrior who insists on these stronger inducements to battle—stronger, that is, than the satisfaction of one's hunger—must inevitably suffer some evil (see 19.235).

Yet the indifference of the world to strong emotions like grief does not at all imply their worthlessness; indeed, the unresponsiveness of the world is itself the occasion and cause of such feelings. More important, Odysseus is wrong in his apparent assumption that strong attachments are not worthwhile simply because they must some day come to an end. Odysseus' advice fails to do justice to Achilles' sense of his desires and loves as being of compelling importance and of the deepest significance. Such a sense is not shaped by considerations of the structure of the world but is simply a given, which resists arguments urged against it.

Moreover, Odysseus' advice misses the importance that human griefs have for the gods. Although the gods do not suffer together with mortals, the spectacle of people's wretchedness, far from disposing the gods to comment on the folly of men's passionate feelings, moves the gods and stirs them to action.[22] Thus, Zeus is moved by pity for Achilles' grief at Patroclus' death (19.340) and bids Athena to place nectar and ambrosia on Achilles' lips so that he may not go hungry (see

---

[22] On the gods' pity for mortals, see Burkert, "Mitleidsbegriff," pp. 75–80, who points out the partisan quality of the gods' pity. He concludes that *eleos* is not a fixed disposition of the gods, but is occasional and represents, when it occurs, a moment of personal contact with and feeling for the threatened person.

19.347–48). Achilles' refusal to eat, which from Odysseus' point of view is imprudent, immoderate, and self-deluding, is from Zeus's standpoint worthy of pity.

That the warrior's pathos—the frustration of his ambitions and the dashing of his loves—is sufficient to rouse Zeus's pity demonstrates that in the world of the *Iliad* human emotions of grief or yearning are important and worthwhile in their own right, even if they cannot secure their object. So in feeling pity for Achilles' immortal horses as they grieve for Patroclus, Zeus comments on the wretchedness of those with whom the divine horses must share their lot:

> The son of Cronus saw and pitied the two, as they wept;
> Turning aside, he said in his heart:
> "Poor wretches! Why did I give you to lord Peleus—
> A mortal—when you are unageing and immortal?
> So you may share the griefs of miserable men?
> For there is nothing, I think, more woeful than man,
> Of all upon the earth that breathe and move.
>
> (17.441–47)

The plight of mortals does not put them beneath the gods' regard; to the contrary, it is largely their wretchedness that makes them of consuming interest to the gods. Achilles' immortal horses, like his immortal mother, are condemned to share all the sorrow of human life by virtue of being intimately associated with a mortal. Those aspects of life that are distinctively human—intimacy, passion, hope—cannot easily be assimilated to the serene and periodic rhythms of natural processes. Nonetheless, the anthropomorphic nature of the Homeric gods, themselves heir to the passions and capable of feeling pity for those who suffer, ensures the central importance of human suffering for Homer.

From this perspective, my previous description of the *Iliad*'s aesthetic qualities is clearly insufficient. That description focused on the rhythmic interplay of violence and rest, and found the aesthetic quality of the *Iliad* to inhere in the formal elegance of the interplay. Such a description omits, however, any treatment of *eleos* as it may be aroused in the audience by the epic poem; or, rather, it takes account of the piteous only insofar as it is contained within an overarching scheme or forms part of a pattern. Yet it is clear from the outset that the *Iliad* presents itself as a poem about the most turbulent and destructive emotions and their dire effect on others' lives. The first line of the poem announces that the song's theme is to be *mēnis* or "wrath", while the remainder of the prologue portrays the pathetic effects of Achilles' wrath, emphasizing not only the great number of the fallen but the excellence of those killed and the sordid fate of their corpses:

> Sing, o goddess, the wrath of Peleus' son Achilles—
> Destructive wrath that put countless woes upon the Achaeans,
> Sent to Hades the souls of many brave heroes
> But left themselves as food for the dogs
> And all the birds. So, Zeus's plan was accomplished.
>
> (I.1–5)

Achilles' wrath and its destructive consequences are, to be sure, contained within an ordering scheme: by means of this emotion and these deaths, as Homer says, "Zeus's plan was accomplished."[23] The intense subjectivity and self-involvement of feeling serve an objective purpose in the *Iliad,* unintended and unsuspected by the mortals in the throes of their emotions. The marshalling of even the most passionate states into an ordered "plan" is a considerable part of the *Iliad*'s beauty. Yet the pathetic images of the prologue have an importance above and beyond any place they may hold in Zeus's overall designs. Pathetic details like the "brave souls" lost to Hades or the mangled corpses strewing the ground—strictly speaking, irrelevant to Zeus's plan—are the very heart of the prologue. The details conjure up the piteousness of the deaths and show them to be final and irreparable—not containable within a rhythmic pattern of life and death. Against such a background, the "fulfillment of Zeus' plan" may seem to lend the further pathetic touch of a god who is indifferent to the sorrow that results from his "plan."

What is finally missing, therefore, from the aesthetic implicit in Odysseus' advice to Achilles is any role for *eleos* and the memory of griefs. That aesthetic, it will be recalled, was based on the "remembering of drink and food"—a remembering that precludes excessive attention to the death of others, and that is based on a sense of rhythms of bodily and other natural processes. The counter-aesthetic just sketched, however, is ultimately rooted in the remembering of grief: that is, a vivid experience through epic verse of the sorrows endured by

---

[23] It is not clear what "Zeus's plan" might have been, since no one in the *Iliad* ever suggests that Achilles' wrath was fulfilling some plan of Zeus. For a discussion of this question, see James Redfield, "The Proem of the *Iliad*: Homer's Art," *Classical Philology* 74 (1979): 95–110. What does emerge from the prologue, however, is the disparity between Zeus's plan and the human suffering that it costs. It may be that the reference to "Zeus's plan" is rhetorical "foil" to underscore the pathos of the human suffering that is to form the poem's true subject.

others. Epic poetry is exactly this memory of griefs—a making vivid, once again, of past experience. Understood as the sympathetic remembering by others of bygone griefs, epic is the distinctive fulfillment to which Helen and others look forward (see 6.357–58). Epic offers an "objective" experience of sorrow, in which the listener feels the characters' distress but in doing so learns about the kind of thing sorrow is, and its significance within human life.

Neither Odysseus nor Achilles in Book 19 gives expression to the distinctive kind of "memory of grief" conveyed by epic verse. Odysseus urges the importance of "remembering drink and food"; Achilles, in the throes of grief over the death of Patroclus, insists on "remembering war" (19.148) as a way of "remembering" Patroclus (cf. 19.314). Furthermore, we have found *eleos* to be an intense and wracking experience; the word does not seem to suit an audience's response to epic poetry. Rather, the kind of memory appropriate to epic verse, and the kind of *eleos* appropriate to the audience of epic verse, bear a distinct likeness to the memory of griefs and to *eleos* as roused by the suppliant in the victor: the experience of griefs as objects of reflection. I shall consider in the next chapter the kind of memory roused by the suppliant, and the kind of *eleos* that rests upon such a memory.

CHAPTER 4

Memory and Supplication

I

No act of supplication in the *Iliad* is so elaborately prepared as Priam's supplication of Achilles in the final book. The ceremony is the means decreed by Zeus himself to effect the return of Hector's corpse to the Trojans for burial. That the supplication of Achilles by Priam is decreed and overseen by the gods raises its dignity and lends it a monumental quality that befits the conclusion of an epic poem. The lively interest of the gods in human affairs—the pity that the gods feel for Hector and their anger at Achilles (see 24.22–54)—makes these events larger than life: more exhilarating and more exciting, because of the gods' attentive participation, than anything else in the world.

There is an unmistakable, *Odyssey*-like element of fantasy in the gods' oversight of these final moments in the poem. The counsel of gods that opens the last book of the *Iliad,* the subsequent flight of Iris to Troy, the companionship of Hermes leading Priam to Achilles' tent—all these recall the opening scenes of the *Odyssey* almost point-for-point: specifically, the council of the gods, Hermes' resultant visit to Calypso, and the disguised Athena's escort of Telemachus. Indeed, the purpose of the gods' plans in the *Iliad*—to restore the son's dead body to the father—seems like a tragic mirror of the gods' plan in the *Odyssey* to restore the living father to the son.[1] Zeus provides for the

[1] I do not make any claim concerning the relative date of the poems, or suggest that *Iliad* 24 contains allusions to our *Odyssey* or that it was composed after the *Odyssey*. It seems likelier that the similarities between the two poems spring from a shared tradition. The "mirroring" of the two scenes may be a function of the complementarity of the two poems: the *Iliad,* as the story of the hero who does not return home, and the

supplication of Achilles by Priam as a way of honoring Achilles (see 24.65–76), as elsewhere suppliants honor warriors by acknowledging the victor's preeminence and offering him wealth. Yet Zeus affords Achilles a hitherto unheard-of honor: the king of the Trojans himself will come and kiss his hands to plead for the return of his son's body. There could scarcely be a more extravagant proof of the greatness of Achilles' victory.

This honoring, however, is far different from the recognition that Achilles had sought and in which he once had such confidence. It has the peculiar property of reflecting both good and evil fortunes and it expressively conveys the glory and the vulnerability of human existence. Achilles had originally sought to obtain a proof that Zeus honored him, to be demonstrated by the deaths of his fellow Achaeans at the Trojans' hands. (See 1.352–56, 407–12, and 503–10; cf. 9.607–10). The death of his dearest companion Patroclus, however, demonstrated in a grimly ironic way that Zeus does not honor Achilles, at least not in the sense that he dependably carries out Achilles' wishes for unrivalled prestige. Priam's supplication truly honors Achilles for his excellence but at the same time reflects Achilles' inability to keep those he most cherishes alive and happy. The goodness of victory is both recognized and circumscribed.

Even before Priam arrives, it is clear that Achilles will agree to return Hector's body. When Thetis tells him of the gods' plan, Achilles accedes immediately:

> So be it. Let him bring ransom and take the body,
> If Zeus himself wishes it so strongly.
>
> (24.139–40)

The very terseness of Achilles' response suggests that he is already predisposed to do what the gods command. Nonetheless, Priam's appeal and its effect on Achilles are the crucial part of the supplication—the means by which the frustration of Achilles' stubborn grief for Patroclus becomes insight into his grief and that of others. Although the gods elaborately prepare Priam's secret visit to Achilles, what actually happens between the two men after Priam arrives in the enemy

---

Odyssey, as the story of the hero who does. On the parallels between *Iliad* 24 and the *Odyssey,* see Nicholas Richardson, *The "Iliad": A Commentary, Vol. VI: Books 21–24* (Cambridge: Cambridge University Press, 1993), pp. 21–24. On the *Iliad* and *Odyssey* as "parallel products of parallel evolution," see Nagy, *Best of the Achaeans,* pp. 26–41. See also the "Conclusion" below.

camp flows from each one's own experience and memories. Hence, notwithstanding the gods' broad role in breaking the impasse, the action in Book 24 is not imposed artificially on the preceding action but emerges from it.

In this chapter, I argue that Achilles ultimately resolves the searing memory of Patroclus' death—not by "forgetting" it, as Odysseus had urged, but by coming to understand it. In other words, the action of the *Iliad* reaches its climax when its hero achieves insight into experience and confers significance upon it. Achilles' understanding of his loss is a forming or trans-forming of blind emotions to a cognitive end. The poem's climax grows from the preceding action in a way that is surprising yet coherent: Achilles never forgets but he discovers a new way of remembering. This mode of remembering is finally impossible within the warrior society and requires a different kind of community, a *philotēs* that is established by Priam's act of supplication.

II

Priam's first words upon entering Achilles' tent are an invocation of memory: *mnēsai patros soio,* "remember your father" (24.486). Priam's appeal is immediately distinguished from Odysseus' more practical advice, for the old king expressly urges Achilles to fill his mind with all the thoughts that have most deeply distressed him. The *Iliad* is in large part the story of Achilles' memory. Thus, he cannot be reconciled to the Achaeans even after Agamemnon has offered gifts because, as he tells Ajax, "my heart swells in anger whenever I remember (*mnēsomai*) how Agamemnon insulted me as though I were some migrant of no account" (9.646–48). Later, Achilles clings to the memory of Patroclus, and vows that he will never forget him: "Even if they forget the dead in Hades, yet even there shall I always remember my dear companion" (22.389–90).

As Richard Martin has pointed out, characters in the *Iliad* do not, by and large, remember simply for the pleasure of it; remembering typically has an exterior goal.[2] The warrior's memory on the battlefield has an almost physical nature: to "remember strength" is to gather one's powers and to renew one's effort. (Cf. such phrases as "they

[2] Richard P. Martin, *The Language of Heroes: Speech and Performance in the "Iliad"* (Ithaca: Cornell University Press, 1989), p. 80. On memory as "mindfulness," see Jean-Pierre Vernant, "Aspects mythique de la mémoire," in *Mythe et pensée chez les Grecs* (Paris: Maspéro, 1965); and Ford, *Homer: The Poetry of the Past,* pp. 53–54. See also below, Chapter 5.

remembered battle" and "remember strength," *mnēsanto de kharmēs,* and *mnēsasthe de thouridos alkēs.*)[3] Through his memory, the warrior feels with a new intensity the importance of what he does and the value it has for him. Thus, in defending the body of Patroclus, Menelaus calls upon his comrades "to remember the wretched Patroclus, for he knew, while alive, how to be gentle to all; and now death and fate have overwhelmed him" (17.669–71). Menelaus invokes memory as a means of leading the warriors to fight with fiercer determination and greater success.

Memory is also closely associated with mourning and grief at the loss of those dear to one. So, for example, Achilles vows: "I will never forget (*epilēsomai*) [Patroclus], as long as I dwell among the living and my legs can move me" (22.387–88). It is precisely in order to nurse his memory that the mourner starves himself of bodily necessities. Thus, Achilles goes sleepless in order to "remember" (*memnēmenos,* 24.4) Patroclus:

> . . . Nor did sleep
> That quells all take him, but aimlessly he strayed
> Yearning for Patroclus' manhood and noble might
> And all the things he accomplished at his side, and all the troubles
> endured—
> Traversing the wars of men and the troubled waves:
> Remembering these things, he wept a hot tear;
> Now lying on his side, now again
> On his back, now on his belly.
>
> (24.4–11)

Andromache, too, in grieving for Hector, regrets the absence of any detail about his final moments that would enable her to keep her memory of him fresh and continually painful:

> To me especially dire griefs are left;
> In death you did not lift your hands from your bed
> To tell me some wise word, which always
> I might remember (*memnēimēn*), as I wept day and night.
>
> (24.742–45)

As described in the *Iliad,* the mourner's memory, like the warrior's on the battlefield, has an almost physical force. Rather than being

---

[3] See, e.g., 4.222, 8.252, 14.441, and 15.380; 6.112, 8.174, 11.287, 16.270, and 17.185; cf. 13.721–2. See Martin, *Language of Heroes,* pp. 77–88.

simply a tribute to the deceased, it is a means to keep him present and so to deny the death. Indeed, the power and vehemence of the mourner's grief suggests that mourning serves to repress the thought of his own impotence—that is, his inability to revive the one he loves. Thus, the mourner's grief-stricken recollection is passionate, insistent, and adamant. It excludes other influences and rejects others' counsel.

So, when Achilles first learns of Patroclus' death, "a black cloud of grief cover[s] him" (18.22), he pours dust on his hair, and "disfigure[s] his lovely countenance." Achilles tears his hair and wails in a way terrible to hear; he appears to bystanders to be on the verge of suicide (18.23–35). He refuses to bathe, goes sleepless, and abstains from sex (see, e.g., 23.38–48 and 24.4–5, 128–32). Similarly, after Hector has been killed, Hecuba shrieks and tears her hair (22.405–07) and Priam filthies himself by rolling in a pile of dung (22.414; see also 24.159–65).[4]

Finally, memory is a vital component of *eleos;* indeed, the significance of memory in *eleos* is one of the features that most likens it to mourning. As we have seen, Andromache and Cleopatra seek to inspire *eleos* in their husbands by awakening a passionate memory of the grief that threatens. So Hecuba, pleading with Hector not to face Achilles in battle, appeals expressly to his memory: "Remember (*mnēsai*) these things, and ward off the enemy from within the walls" (22.84–85). The memory that Hecuba seeks to provoke in her son bears the same features as the mourner's memory. She asks Hector to "remember," essentially, how he will be mourned should he die: her exposed breast suggests the vehemence of the bereaved mother's grief. Hector will be stirred to feel *eleos* if he bears in mind not only the way Hecuba nursed him as a baby, but how she will be unable to bury him properly if he dies at Achilles' hands (see 22.82–89). This memory is less a recollection of the past than a lively sense of the intimate and inextricable ties between them. In bidding Hector to remember "the breast that brought forgetfulness of care" (*lathikēdea mazon,* 22.83) Hecuba invites her son to identify with her as closely as possible. The

[4] Compare the remarks of John Peradotto, *Man in the Middle Voice: Name and Narration in the "Odyssey"* (Princeton: Princeton University Press, 1990), p. 134, who stresses the experience of emotion as enveloping the subject: "Our way of understanding or at least of expressing emotion—as something emanating from a subject toward an object, like a missile thrown by someone at someone else, or as something exchanged between two parties—is essentially itself highly metaphoric, and may blind us to a way of experiencing and expressing the emotion that concentrates on the activity as a kind of envelope embracing those involved with little apparent interest in distinguishing what we would call 'agent' and 'patient.'" Peradotto's metaphor of emotion as "enveloping" the person captures the way the Iliadic mourners seem to experience their grief.

memory that Hecuba invites does not offer intellectual perspective on the past, but an intimate rapport. This emotional identification of the son with his mother is to issue in *eleos*.

III

So far, we have seen memory as a faculty that reignites emotions in all their consuming power. The memory characteristic of the person who feels *eleos* for a suppliant differs, however, from the mourner's memory. The suppliant cannot hope to inspire the passionate intensity that a wife or a mother or father can. Rather, the suppliant asks the other to call that passionate intensity to mind and to reflect on it. The *eleos* elicited by the suppliant is a "memory of grief," but not one in which the person feeling it is immersed in the immediate experience of loss. In supplication, the one feeling *eleos* necessarily remembers his griefs from a distance. The suppliant implicitly asks the victorious warrior to generalize from his own experience to another's similar experience of loss. As invoked by the suppliant, then, memory represents a disengagement from the immediate experience of sorrow. The very intensity of grief, which had blinded the mourner to anything else, becomes a powerful means of insight into another's life when it is recalled. Achilles' grief over Patroclus, and the lengths to which it had driven him, enable him to sense vividly the pain that has driven Priam to kiss the hands of his son's killer.

Engagement in the experience of grief is essential to the memory evoked by the suppliant, but so is a disengagement from that experience. It is only by being engaged in his loss and feeling it intensely that the person can know what the experience is like, but to be aware of the feeling—to compare it to other things and to be able to say what it is like—the person must stand back from the immediate throes of the experience. To understand a grief one must be close enough to feel the pain in the experience of sorrow, yet sufficiently distanced that one is not overwhelmed by it (as the mourner, for example, is). This distinctive disengagement enables the pitier to reflect on the experience and to extrapolate from his own to another's.

Achilles has, indeed, often "remembered" his father, especially in the latter half of the poem, in connection with Patroclus' death and his own misery, and such memories partly fueled his savagery in killing Hector and refusing him burial. The memory that Priam encourages, however, is different from Achilles' unaided or self-initiated memories of Peleus. Priam invites Achilles to remember Peleus while looking upon another old man—Priam himself. The memory that Priam envisions is one that sees Peleus less in the special terms of his relationship with Achilles, and more in terms of his similarities to other old men:

> Remember your father, godlike Achilles,
> Old as I, on the baneful threshold of old age;
> Perhaps the neighbors surrounding him
> Besiege him, and he has no one to ward off battle and destruction.
>
> (24.486–89)

To remember the father, in the sense intended by Priam, requires a step back from and out of whatever limits the son's perspective on his relationship with him. Achilles, that is, is asked not simply to feel his father's grief but to use such feelings as a means of understanding the emotions that characterize the relationship between other fathers and sons as well. The objective memory to which Priam invites Achilles consists in transferring the feelings he has for Peleus to the feelings that exist between other fathers and sons. The memory Priam evokes in Achilles is deeply emotional but is described in such a way as to bring out its similarities to Priam's own grief. For after Priam has finished speaking, the two men are said to remember (*mnēsamenō*), each one his own sorrows:

> The two of them remembering: Priam, fallen before Achilles' feet,
> Keenly wept for man-slaying Hector;
> Achilles wept for his father, and sometimes then
> Patroclus.
>
> (24.509–12)

The use of the dual number in *mnēsamenō* binds together the different and contrary subjects of Priam's and Achilles' griefs under a single head. Patroclus and Hector were mortal enemies and no less so are the men who weep for them, but the common act of memory (*mnēsamenō*) brings out the deep similarity of the experience, notwithstanding the antagonism of the persons whose deaths brought it about. Indeed, the very hostility between the objects of Priam's and Achilles' grief sharpens the likeness between the mental and emotional experience of those who remember.

Remembering emerges as a reconciling force, something that exists apart from historical circumstances and the hostilities that arise in such conditions. To the extent that memory is merely a mode of access to painful events of the past, it serves to perpetuate hostilities: because of his passionate remembering of Patroclus, for example, Achilles' enmity toward the Trojans took on a deeper dye and became an implacable hatred for them. As it emerges in this scene, however, the act of memory is important in its own right, apart from the particular objects recalled. It does not serve either Achilles or Priam merely as a tool for recalling past events, but rather reflects each man's sense of the importance of those events—the toll they took on him and the sorrow they cost him. Insofar as it flows from Achilles' sense of the significance of the very experiencing of events, memory lets him feel sympathy even for those furthest removed from his affection, since the experience of death, separation, and loss is everywhere much the same. *Eleos,* then, as felt by Achilles for Priam, partly rests upon an appreciation of the importance of memory apart from the past emotions and experiences to which it allows access.

The memory evoked by the suppliant—based as it is on the similarity of one's own to another's experience—has a cognitive element, for by likening one's own griefs to others' experience of them, one recognizes that griefs are a necessary constituent of a mortal's life. So Achilles, in feeling pity for Priam, tells him of the jars of good and evil gifts beside Zeus's throne, which determine the shape of the person's life.

> Two jars sit by Zeus's door
> Of evil gifts he gives, and one of good.
> The man to whom Zeus, who delights in thunder, gives a mixture,
> Now happens on evil, and now on good. . . .
> So, the god gave Peleus shining gifts
> From his birth: for he surpassed all men
> In happiness and wealth; he ruled the Myrmidons;
> They gave to him—a mortal—a goddess for his wife.
> But god gave him, too, an evil: for him,
> No issue of hearty children in his halls,
> But one son he sired, destined for an early death. For I do not
> Tend him in his old age, but far from home
> I sit in Troy, bringing griefs to you and to your sons.
>
> (24.527–30; 534–42)

Achilles' parable of the jars serves in several ways to make the experience of grief into something intelligible. First, the subjective experience of sorrow is explained by deriving it from something wholly different—a divine process of selection and mingling. The grief felt at the loss of a son or beloved, because it is bewildering in its intensity, can be understood only by being referred to something outside itself, that is, to something unemotional. Elsewhere in the *Iliad,* too, the gods plan out the largest outlines of human affairs without regard to the human misery that will result. The point is not the malice or even the cruel indifference of the gods. Rather, it is a comfort to the distressed to refer the painfulness of emotions to a source having little to do with the emotion.[5] The intelligibility of the explanation is a means of quelling the pain of the experience. Second, the parable of the jars places the experience of grief within a rhythmic pattern of mingled good and evil gifts. The very intelligibility of grief, conceived as part of a rhythm, counsels against an excess of emotions, for it is part of the understanding of grief (at least in the case of Peleus and Priam, and others who have received a mingling of gifts) that any sorrow is but part of a cycle of good and evil things sent by Zeus. More somberly, the understanding of grief counsels moderation because the rhythm is not to be stopped: an evil gift gives on to yet another evil. The continuousness of the rhythm must prevent the mourner from trying to stop time at the point of some unbearable grief. "Bear up," Achilles concludes his address to Priam, "and do not grieve adamantly in your heart. Your grief will accomplish nothing, nor will you raise up your son before suffering another evil" (24.549–51).

More fundamentally, however, griefs become intelligible by being acknowledged as a necessary part—a constitutive element—of the person's life. In the earlier parts of the poem, Achilles had been far from such a view of his sufferings. Although aware from the very beginning of the shortness of his allotted life, Achilles had not looked upon his early death as in any deep way a frustration of his desires, which reposed, rather, in his prestige among his fellows and in his expectation that Patroclus would care for Achilles' son and father (see 19.321–37). When these desires are frustrated, Achilles' response is blind fury at those who were the causes of his pain. To speak of evils as gifts from Zeus's jars, however, is to view the ills of one's life as a part of its fabric. On this view, evils are not simply, or even primarily, pains inflicted from without by particular enemies; considered more deeply, they are woven into mortal life itself. The parable of the jars, then, clearly reflects Achilles' sense of himself as a *kind of being*—one who is exposed to harms by his very nature.

In generalizing or extrapolating from his experience to conjure up another's, Achilles re-forms or restructures his sense of himself. It requires only the most rudimentary sense of self to respond angrily to

---

[5] On the "gifts of the gods" as a motif in archaic Greek poetry, see W. G. Thalmann, *Conventions of Form and Thought in Early Greek Epic Poetry* (Baltimore: Johns Hopkins University Press, 1984), chap. 3, especially pp. 84–85.

attacks: the warrior needs only a sense of self-love or the desire to preserve himself, and a sense of something outside and hostile to that self. Such is Achilles' sense of self in the earlier parts of the poem. Achilles possesses a confident sense of his own preeminence and when this sense is offended he responds immediately and recklessly in order to vindicate his claims to superiority.[6] Achilles' ultimate ability to appreciate the similarity of another's experience to his own, however, reflects a more complex self. In appreciating his resemblance to another, Achilles no longer confines his reactions to the immediate stimulus but can see in another's distress the kind of danger to which he is *in general,* or *as a kind of being,* exposed. In this new awareness, Achilles attains a more complex appreciation of the other person, as well, for he understands Priam in his own right, apart from the pain Priam's son has inflicted on him. Achilles finds in the old man a compelling image of the mortal lot, which he now understands to be *his* lot.

Eleos, as Achilles feels it for the suppliant Priam, is complex. It is deeply connected with elemental emotions and, in particular, is inseparable from the pitier's feelings about his own death. Yet Achilles' *eleos* gives such feelings a memory and an expectancy. It reflects an awareness of himself as a kind of being with much to fear and an appreciation that his own experiences of fear, grief, and hope resemble the experiences of others. As an emotion thoroughly imbued with elemental feelings, *eleos* is scarcely altruistic but it does represent a sublimation of the immediate throes of grief. When he feels it for a stranger, Achilles is able to re-experience his own sorrows in a more distanced way through another's experience.

Because memory can be objectified, *eleos* can be something other than the primal feeling Schadewaldt described. The *eleos* Achilles feels for Priam, which grows from the very passions he had previously felt in an unreflecting and emotional way, comes to constitute an insight into his grief and an understanding of it. The *Iliad* tells the story, in other words, of a hero's attainment of perspective on himself and appreciation of himself as a kind of being—the very ground, according to Pohlenz, from which *eleos* grows and which it presupposes. *Eleos* finally takes on an ethical significance in the *Iliad,* in the sense that it contributes to and reflects Achilles' vision of himself as a being like others. The *eleos* that Achilles feels toward Priam comes close to our notion of pity. The *Iliad* dramatizes the emergence of pity (a reflective sense of sorrow and its role in human life) from fear, understood

---

[6] It is this quality of immediate response to external stimuli that Fränkel sees as generally characteristic of Homeric man. See Fränkel, *Early Greek Poetry,* pp. 77–79.

broadly as an unreflecting and passionate response to one's own vulnerability.

Thus, Achilles' advice to Priam "to let the griefs in [his] heart rest" is fundamentally different in tone and spirit from Odysseus' advice to Achilles in Book 19, notwithstanding the surface similarity of the two passages. Odysseus had urged on Achilles the impossibility of perpetual mourning and begged him to eat. Achilles does the same with Priam, but where Odysseus had urged Achilles to eschew pity and so give up grief (cf. *nēlea thumon ekhontas,* 19.229) Achilles urges Priam to do so precisely from a sense of pity. Odysseus had wanted Achilles to participate in a meal as a sign that he joined once again whole-heartedly with the Achaeans—sharing their values, their enemies, and their friends. The meal and, by extension, the friendship to which Achilles invites Priam is of a markedly different kind, for it is clear that Achilles and Priam remain enemies and their mutual hostility lurks just below the surface. Achilles even threatens to kill Priam when the old man tries to refuse Achilles' invitation to eat (see 24.552–70). Later on, in hoisting Hector's body onto Priam's cart, Achilles' attendants take care to keep the body out of the old king's sight, for fear he cry out and stir Achilles to violence (24.582–86). The bitter hatred between the two men thus underlies their whole encounter.

It would be a mistake, therefore, to see Achilles' hatred for Priam as a vestige of his savagery that persists once he has returned to a more "humane" self. The *eleos* he feels for Priam does not spring from kindliness, nor does it evince the friendly-mindedness that Odysseus had urged on him. Rather, his *eleos* reflects Achilles' tragic sense of himself as the kind of a being that is exposed to evils and it does not at all entail forgiveness of the person who has inflicted the evils. The pity Achilles feels is instilled with the sense of bereavement that made him savage: his *eleos* is not a forswearing of the feelings roused by bereavement so much as an understanding of them.

IV

In the parable of the jars, Achilles obviously sees himself as like Priam—a being whose life comprises goods and evils. Yet, perhaps more remarkably, he also sees himself as resembling his father Peleus, and Achilles' orientation toward Peleus in the parable of the jars is subtly but significantly different from what it has been. For in earlier parts of the poem, Peleus was little more than a function of Achilles' grief for himself—as such, tenderly remembered, but not finally distinguishable from Achilles. So Achilles had conjured up his father most vividly as mourning for none other than Achilles himself. Even in yearning for Peleus, Achilles bolstered his sense of being uniquely and preeminently important.

As remembered by Achilles at Priam's behest, however, Peleus is a being separate from Achilles, with his own life history of joys and sorrows (see 24.534–42). While Achilles still understands his absence as one of Peleus' great sorrows, this sorrow is now seen primarily as an evil gift sent from Zeus. Peleus is no longer merely a reflex of Achilles' immediate emotional state. As now remembered or imagined, he is comparable to Achilles, to be sure, but ultimately a distinct person with a distinct history. The father is now clearly demarcated from the son, and the two are understood as subject alike to the same laws and experiencing the same pattern of Zeus-sent joys and sorrows.[7]

From this new perspective, Achilles is finally able to act in regard to Peleus. Up until now, however much Achilles might mourn his father's lonely old age, there was nothing he could, or would, do to comfort it. Action was impossible, since the father's commands that the son obey the dictates of shame conflicted with his implicit appeals to the son's pity: the father at once commanded the son to stay on the battlefield and pleaded with him to return home. Priam's supplication at last affords Achilles the opportunity to act in accord with shame and pity alike: indeed, this is precisely what Priam asks Achilles to do (see 24.503).

In returning Hector's body to Priam, Achilles at last finds a means of expressing his relationship to his own father. As the spectacle of Priam begging for the return of his son makes clear, the son, in the world of the *Iliad,* is restored to the father only in death. The sight of the shattered relation between Priam and Hector sets Achilles' relationship to his own father in a broader context of generations severed and the peaceful continuity of life from father to son violently interrupted. The final scene of the *Iliad* implicitly corrects Glaucus' assertion that the generations rise and fall with a leaflike regularity (see 6.145–49). The rhythmic pulse of the generations' growth and decay, as described by

---

[7] Achilles himself takes on a Peleus-like role in the latter part of the poem. Thus, his grief for Patroclus is expressly compared to the grief a father feels for his son's death (23.222–25). Furthermore, when Priam appears suddenly in Achilles' tent, the amazement (*thambos*) felt by the onlookers is compared to that felt when a homicide arrives seeking the protection of the wealthy host (24.480–83). The simile implicitly likens Achilles to Peleus, who received Patroclus as a suppliant and extended protection to him. (See 23.84–90; *cf.* 9.444–84; 16.570–76.) See Robin R. Schlunk, "The Theme of the Suppliant-Exile in the *Iliad,*" *American Journal of Philology* 97 (1976): 199–209.

Glaucus, conveyed the inevitability of the mortal's death but missed the impassioned grief that the warrior's fall inflicts on those who love him.

The spectacle of the old father gathering the son's remains captures precisely this sense of the ardor of intimate relations and the grief aroused by the passage from generation to generation. It expresses the inherent and irresolvable conflict in the son's relationship to the father—a relationship in which the son's pity prompts him to return to his father, while his shame demands that he not. The restoration of Hector's corpse to Priam, then, conveys Achilles' feelings about the unbridgeable distance between himself and his own father. Achilles' understanding of his experience does not, however, make of him an essentially private character, whose existence in a traditional poem such as the *Iliad* would be implausible. Achilles' attainment of understanding finds expression, above all, in an emotion felt for another— pity—and action undertaken on the prompting of the emotion. Achilles' self-understanding is, at bottom, really his sense of his resemblance to others.

Indeed, Achilles' progress in the *Iliad* could be described as a movement from the private to the public. Only in the last book does Achilles whole-heartedly accept the gifts that are offered to him, no longer considering them inadequate (as he did in Book 9) or of no importance (as in Book 19). Not until the poem's conclusion, therefore, does Achilles become a willing participant in the system of gifts and exchange that are the public currency of his society. Furthermore, Achilles' self-understanding reflects his emergence from a state of intensely passionate feelings. Such feelings are necessarily private, because they cannot be shared by others, nor can they be adequately expressed in all their intensity, as Achilles learns from his frustrated attempts to abuse Hector's body.[8] It is only in responding to Priam's supplication and so achieving a new understanding of his own experience, that Achilles attains to that balanced sense of the perennial sadness of life that captures both his own and Priam's experience. His meal with the old king and his restoring of Hector's body grow from his sense of himself as a creature largely constituted by sorrows.

---

[8] In a well-known study, Adam Parry argued that Achilles' great speech to the embassy in Book 9 reveals a language inadequate to the expression of his passionate anger. See Adam Parry, "The Language of Achilles," *Transactions of the American Philological Association* 87 (1956): 1–7. I do not agree with Parry that Achilles' language in Book 9 is incoherent, or that the *Dichtersprache* cannot express sentiments at odds with the code of the warrior society. See David B. Claus, "*Aidōs* in the Language of Achilles," *Transactions of the American Philological Association* 105 (1975): 13–28. None-

In short, having exiled himself from a society and public life whose compromises were finally too constraining, Achilles ultimately emerges into a new public sense of himself and discovers words and gestures—essentially, those of supplication[9]—adequate to this sense. He cannot, however, return to a contented life as a soldier under Agamemnon's command. Achilles remains inescapably alienated from the warrior society and its demands that offenses be overlooked or that sorrow for the loss of one's dearest should be pragmatically placed aside. Rather, his attainment of self-understanding seeks expression in forming a friendship or *philotēs* with Priam—again, the first time in the poem that Achilles actively seeks out such a relationship. The friendship Achilles inaugurates with Priam suggests that mortals are not simply confined to recognizing passively the indifference of the world. They can come to understand it and can find ways of responding and of expressing their response. The friendship to which Achilles invites Priam is just such an expressive vehicle.

This *philotēs* or fellowship is of a distinctive kind, for it is based on a Achilles' sense of himself as a kind of being. In offering him food, Achilles tells Priam the story of Niobe, who lost all her children and, in her distress, mourned and fasted for nine days. Then she ate and afterward was transformed from a woman immersed in passionate mourning for her slain children to a rocky cliff—a part of the landscape—that "ruminates upon the griefs sent by the gods" (*theōn ek kēdea pessei,* 24.617). Niobe's mourning for the loss of her children passes from the hectic grief that rejects everything into something more perennial and less passionate. The sadness of the transformed Niobe, like the sadness of the one who has achieved an understanding of his griefs, is a kind of settled awareness.[10] Niobe's metamorphosis provides a useful image of what happens in Book 24. For Achilles does not "give up" his grief, as Odysseus had urged; rather, by seeing the similarity between his own and another's experience, he transforms it into something less spectacular than his passionate laments, but deeper and wiser. His pity is a metamorphosis of his savagery.

The meal affords Achilles a means of expressing this transformed sense of grief. Throughout the society Homer describes, the meal is a token of fellowship,[11] but Achilles invents or discovers in it a more

theless, Parry's argument is suggestive for Achilles' inability to discharge or fully express his grief for Patroclus, either by word or deed, before Priam's supplication.

[9] On the significance of supplication in this final scene, see Chapter 5.

[10] On the expressiveness and "legibility" of landscapes, see Ford, *Homer: The Poetry of the Past,* pp. 141–42. Ford's observations seem especially relevant to Niobe.

[11] On the *dais* and its significance for communal life, see M. I. Finley, *The World of*

profound meaning, expressing the resemblance of the person who feels *eleos* to the one who elicits it. The meal, which elsewhere serves to honor the banqueters and to single out those most worthy of reward, here conveys their similarity as the kind of beings whose lives are distinguished by suffering. Unlike the Achaean warrior society, the *philotēs* of Achilles and Priam is not founded on a common project or on cooperative effort, nor does it involve the partners' having common friends and common enemies. It is based on pity, not on shame, and enables its participants only the better to understand what each has experienced.

The friendship that issues from Priam's supplication of Achilles in the final book of the *Iliad* climaxes a series of supplications by Priam's sons, in which the suppliant uses the rhetoric of *philotēs* in hopes of winning over the other.[12] Thus Priam's son Lycaon pleads with Achilles to remember the *philotēs* they shared as joint participants in a common banquet (21.64–135). While Achilles rejects Lycaon's supplication, it is significant that he does not turn a deaf ear to it. He in fact accepts Lycaon's claim and calls him "friend" (21.106). Achilles, however, draws a conclusion from the tie of "friendship" different from what Lycaon had sought. Lycaon had hoped to avoid death, but the only basis on which Achilles is willing to recognize a friendship with this man is that the two of them—the preeminent warrior Achilles and the hapless and cowardly Lycaon—must alike die:

> Now, friend, you shall die too. Why weep so?
> Patroclus died, who was far better than you.
> Do you see the kind of man I am—how beautiful and large?
> I come from a good father; my mother is a goddess:
> Yet, even so, death and mighty fate hang over me.
>
> (21.106–10)

Lycaon looks for friendship in hopes of escaping the destiny common to all. To grant what he asks would be, for Achilles, to belie the only basis on which any conceivable friendship with him could exist. The *philotēs* Achilles articulates in response to Lycaon's plea looks for-

---

Odysseus (New York: Viking Press, 1977), pp. 123–26; Nagy, *Best of the Achaeans,* pp. 127–28; Suzanne Saïd, "Les crimes des pretendants, la maison d'Ulysse, et les festins de *l'Odyssée,*" in *Etudes de littérature ancienne* (Paris: Presses de l'Ecole Normale Supérieure, 1979), pp. 14–21; Griffin, *Homer on Life and Death,* pp. 14–16; and A. L. Motto and J. R. Clark, "Isē Dais: The Honor of Achilles," *Arethusa* 2 (1969):109–25.

[12] See 20.463–72 (supplication by Trōs); 21.64–135 (supplication by Lycaon); and 22.111–28 (Hector's imaginary supplication of Achilles).

ward to the kind of friendship he shares later with Priam. Both are based on what Walter Burkert has called the "community of death," in which each one expresses for the other the constitutive role of evils and mortality in his life.[13]

Hector, too, had briefly imagined commencing a friendship with Achilles by supplicating him. Having rejected his parents' frantic pleas that he return to safety inside the city walls, Hector momentarily entertains the desperate thought of throwing himself on Achilles' mercy (see 22.111–30). By rendering himself completely helpless and hence womanlike, Hector seems to hope for the kind of intimacy shared by "a maiden and a youth."

> But what if I should throw down my knobbed shield,
> And mighty helmet, lay my spear against the wall,
> And go up to blameless Achilles, face to face,
> And promise him Helen and wealth besides—
> All that Paris brought in hollow ships
> To Troy—since she was the cause of the war:
> Give all these back to the Atreids, and among the Achaeans
> To distribute all that the city holds inside . . .
> But why does my spirit say such things!
> I mustn't approach him; he would not pity me
> Nor feel shame, but kill me, in my defenseless state,
> As though I were a woman, once I took my armor off.
> He was born from oak or rock: there is no way
> To speak fondly with him, as a maiden and youth,
> A maiden and youth speak fondly—the two of them together.
>
> (22.111–18, 122–28)

Hector entertains the possibility of deliberately making himself helpless by giving up progressively more lavish ransom: his armor, Helen, his own property, the wealth of Troy. This munificence suggests, at least, that Hector wants Achilles to give him an end to war, but Hector's supplication is notable for its lack of a clear purpose. It is significant that he never articulates precisely what he hopes to accomplish by all his renunciation. Rather, Hector seems to have a vague wish to make Achilles all-powerful by becoming powerless himself: if Achilles were entirely in command of goods and evils, perhaps he would give Hector everything he most deeply wishes.

Hector paradoxically imagines using his power as the most important warrior among the Trojans in order to make himself like a woman

[13] See Burkert, "Mitleidsbegriff," p. 97.

to Achilles. So, for example, he rejects the idea of supplication, since Achilles would remain unmoved and kill Hector as though he were a defenseless woman (22.124–25). More strikingly, what Hector hopes is to have the same kind of intimate conversation with Achilles as "a maiden and youth" share (22.127–28). Hector lingers on the picture of their conversation, repeating, almost as if in a ballad, "the maiden and youth, the maiden and youth." His use of the dual number to describe their conversation (*oarizeton,* 128) underscores the intimacy of their talk as a couple.

Hector's inner soliloquy catches the ambiguity of feminine helplessness in the *Iliad.* Women are powerless before the onslaughts of war, but their very powerlessness seems to open the possibility of an intimacy with the warrior that other males, themselves engaged in securing prestige and renown among their fellows, cannot enjoy. The woman does not offer the warrior competition. More fundamentally, however, she becomes a part of the warrior's tragic conception of himself, his point of vulnerability. So, as we have seen, Hector agonizes at the thought of losing Andromache, and Meleager is stirred to reenter the wars by Cleopatra's anguished description of the horrors threatening them. Hector's talk with Andromache in Book 6 and Meleager's with Cleopatra in Book 9 represent just the kind of intimate conversation that Hector here seems to imagine between himself and Achilles.

The intimacy Hector hopes for is impossible, but it resembles the intimacy that Priam and Achilles ultimately share. As we have seen, a suppliant seeks to arouse in the victor's mind vivid memories of those dearest to him, and to direct the emotional charge of such memories back to the supplication. As the contrast between Hector's imagined supplication and that of Priam makes clear, however, the relationship between the victor and the suppliant is not itself an intimate relationship, but arises from the joint memory of other such ties and from the common experience of their painful severance. The *philotēs* between Achilles and Priam does not possess the immediacy that characterizes the relationship between a warrior and those he most loves. It is not itself an intimate relationship but, rather, is based on the *memory* of such relations. Indeed, it is precisely through their *philotēs* that Achilles and Priam each transforms the passionate memory of his deepest ties into a more seasoned or objective awareness of their importance and their tragic destiny.

Hector's imagined supplication suggests the powerful emotions attaching to the warrior's intimate loves that provide, so to speak, the raw material for Priam's and Achilles' *philotēs.* Yet in seeking the kind

of fond conversation enjoyed by maidens and youths—the immediacy
and continuity of the warrior's deepest emotional ties—Hector madly
hopes for more than supplication can possibly give. Unlike the intimacy Hector briefly imagines, the *philotēs* between victor and suppliant, resting as it does on pity and the understanding of grief, has
little or no practical use. There is no benefit (*prēxis,* 24.524) to be had
from "chilly laments," says Achilles, nor can there be much use or
benefit, he might have added, from the friendship that replaces passionate grief. Because of pity, it is true, Priam obtains the body of his
son; yet this climactic supplication seems to suggest, by the very modesty of what is asked for and obtained, the essential uselessness of pity
and of the understanding on which pity rests. In his imagined supplication, Hector had hoped to achieve impossible goods through impossible means—to use exchange magically, so to speak, to obtain everything he most deeply wished simply by disgorging extravagant wealth.
In the final book, however, Priam's request for the dead body of his
son contrasts with all the things one might want—an end to war, the
chance to live in peace with one's family and loved ones—but which
pity cannot give.

The essential uselessness of this friendship for anything other than
the joint contemplation of human destiny likens it to the friendship
between the Achaeans and Chryses that concludes the story of
Chryses' fateful supplication in the first book of the *Iliad.* After Apollo
has sent the plague on the Achaean army and Agamemnon has re-
lented, an embassy of Achaeans travels to Chryses to return his daughter. There Chryses and the Achaeans sacrifice a hecatomb to Apollo,
and after Chryses asks that Apollo "ward off destruction from the
Achaeans" (1.456), the priest and the Achaeans join in a common
banquet (1.457–68). The meal concludes with paeans sung by the
Achaean youths in honor of Apollo, which the god delights to hear
(1.472–74).

The friendship between Chryses and the Achaeans that finds expression in the meal they share is different from that existing among the
Achaeans within the warrior society. For this reconciliatory friendship
and the meal inaugurating it take place under the sign of the gods'
power over men. Agamemnon had thought to exercise his prerogatives
as king and as victor in refusing the old priest's request for the return of
his daughter. The sequel, however, has shown only too powerfully the
limits confining the victor's prerogatives and the relative nature of any
mortal's victory. In place of a hierarchy distinguishing victor and loser,
we find in the meal shared by Chryses and the Achaeans a hierarchy
distinguishing mortals, on the one hand, from the gods who easily

undo the pretensions of the victorious, on the other. The fellowship of the table that Chryses and the Achaeans share is a fellowship based on the common mortal subjection to the gods.

Such too is the friendship between Achilles and Priam. The meal they share, following the example of Niobe, is a recognition of the place of evils in men's lives. It expresses their understanding that sorrows are "gifts" allotted by Zeus from the jars beside his throne, and that they are part of the very fabric of mortal existence. The climactic *philotēs* between Achilles and Priam that resolves the action of the entire poem, therefore, is implicit and inchoate in the *Iliad*'s opening sequence, which describes Agamemnon's refusal of Chryses' supplication and the ultimate reconciliation between the Achaeans and the priest of Apollo. The opening sequence contains the motifs of the father's supplication for the return of his child, as well as the distinctive friendship that ultimately arises between the suppliant and the victor— a friendship arising from each one's recognition of the circumscribed nature of the distinctions dividing them. The climactic scene, which alludes to and resolves the action in the rest of the poem, returns to the opening motifs of the father's supplication and the *philotēs* between suppliant and supplicated, but now with incomparably greater emotional effect.

The coincidence of the beginning and the conclusion of the *Iliad* points not to a formal symmetry governing the design of the poem but, rather, to a powerful concentration of subject matter. The *Iliad* could be read as a meditation on the ceremony of supplication: in it, the connections between supplication and the values governing the society and the lives of its characters—their shame, their capacity for *eleos,* their penchant for memory—are explored and the significance of supplication concomitantly deepened. Supplication emerges as at once a ceremony expressing the predominant values of the warrior society and as a critique of those values. Ultimately, it makes possible what in the Iliadic world is the only possible resolution of the wrath (*mēnis*) which is the announced subject of the poem. The poem's opening and the close—not to mention the supplication scenes that recur at the major junctures in the *Iliad*'s story—suggest that the notable concentration of the narrative, notwithstanding the monumental size of the poem, derives from its being an evocation, from start to finish, of a single ceremony. In the next chapter, I consider more closely the significance of supplication in this final scene and throughout the poem.

CHAPTER 5

Supplication and the
Poetics of the *Iliad*

I

Supplication is the ceremonial occasion for Achilles' climactic experience of pity for Priam and the *philotēs* he inaugurates with him. In asking that Achilles remember his father, Priam does not want him simply to conjure up thoughts of Peleus, but specifically to do so while looking on his suppliant. The structure of supplication is such that Achilles transfers onto Priam the vivid experience of his feelings for his father. The comparability of the victor's and the loser's experience inheres in this structure, which in turn underlies and informs Achilles' climactic insight into his grief and wrath.

The ceremony of supplication has sometimes been described formally as a traditional public action that consists of a more or less set and predictable group of words and gestures. So, for example, in the most thorough study of this ceremony among the ancient Greeks, John Gould describes supplication as a "game" with certain rules. Supplication, for Gould, represents an "inversion" of the normal rules of social intercourse, which is characterized by competition and by challenge and counter-challenge. "The ritual of supplication. . . puts a new arrival 'out of play' in terms of the normal 'game' of competition, precisely because the suppliant's behavior is an inversion of normal expected behavior."[1]

Notwithstanding the excellence of Gould's article, there are several difficulties with his formalist description of supplication. First, supplication does not constitute a simple time-out from the normal game

---

[1] Gould, "Hiketeia," p. 95.

of competition; since suppliants in the *Iliad* regularly promise wealth in return for what they ask, the ceremony is a means by which a victorious warrior gains prestige among his fellows, and to that extent, it participates in the values of *timē* and *kleos* that animate warrior society. Because the suppliant must acknowledge the other's victory over him, supplication is a form of praise—indeed, it is one of the most spectacular forms of praise available to the warrior. Further, the description of supplication in terms of "games" and "rules" misses the compelling importance of those needs or desires that impel someone to supplicate. It is a peculiar description of a person begging for his life that he is "out of play." Rather, it seems an essential part of the suppliant's power to move the victor that he shows in a particularly clear way the crucial value of what he seeks in supplication. For the suppliant, the goods that power has to offer—prestige, fame, renown—have ceased to have value: supplication, therefore, shows what motivates the person in extremis, and what values continue to animate people even after their worldly ambitions have been lost.

Finally, Gould cannot give a coherent account of supplication within the formalist terms he uses. Supplication emerges from his treatment as an "ambivalent ritual,"[2] for the suppliant does not merely abase himself before the other but also appropriates him physically. Supplication is at once a plea and a threat: a "mime of aggressive symbolical significance. . . but a mime whose aggressive implications are contradicted by the inversion of normal competitive behavior-patterns which is also a definite feature of the ritual."[3] While there is a tension in supplication, a formalist description leaves this tension at the level of a simple contradiction. Supplication, I have said, is a form of praise, but it is praise from the distinctive and troubling perspective of the loser—the one for whom the attainment of such values is no longer possible. The suppliant's gestures of self-abasement serve in significant part to make clearer the crucial importance of other goods—his own life or the life of his child—for whose sake he makes bold to confront the victor. The loser thus brings into high relief for the victorious warrior the significance of his own love for those dearest to him and of his love for his own life as something uniquely precious-sentiments that he, as a rule, is constrained to deny. To the extent he is moved by the suppliant, the warrior is shown to be more complex than one who seeks only renown or prestige—that is, one whose values are given by the warrior society

---

[2] Ibid., p. 100.
[3] Ibid.

and who can be wholly understood within the official terms of that society.

Supplication is not a prescribed set of stereotyped words and actions but is better approached, in the words of Clifford Geertz, as a "commentary upon the whole matter of assorting human beings into fixed hierarchical ranks and then organizing the major part of collective existence around that assortment."[4] On this view, which presents supplication within a broader cultural context, supplication is a story people tell themselves about themselves, and does what a poem or a play does: it takes up emotionally charged realities—power, subjection, prestige, grief, memory—and orders them into structured action, so as to throw into relief their essential nature.[5] Supplication shows the equivocal nature of victory, which has the godlike power to assure the warrior of "undying renown" but necessarily comes at the cost of another's misery. Because the suppliant shows in a dramatic way the transiency of power, he can awaken the hero's sense of vulnerability, much as the warrior's dependants—father, wife and children—do. Supplication illuminates victory as a sign at once of the hero's power and of his immersion in mortal things.

Because supplication underscores the deeply ambiguous character of victory, which it both celebrates and circumscribes, it can scarcely be said to inculcate a society's sacrosanct or unquestionable beliefs. Here I part company with Agathe Thornton, who presents supplication in the *Iliad* as a ceremony that puts a moral constraint on the one supplicated to do as asked, and brings punishment on the one who refuses.[6] For Thornton, the parable of Atē and the Litai (9.502–12) is paradigmatic for supplication throughout the *Iliad*. After Atē (or "Reckless Folly," a divine force visited on the person) has caused some injury or offense, the Litai (or "Suppliant Prayers") come hobbling after, seeking to make amends. The man who feels shame before (*aidesetai*) them, Phoenix says, wins their benevolence; should one reject their pleas, however, they beg Zeus to send Atē on him as well. The "Suppliant Prayers" are lame and wrinkled and unable to look the aggrieved person in the eye (9.103)—physically, the very opposite of Atē, who is strong and surefooted (505). Although the wretchedness of their appearance might

[4] Geertz, "Balinese Cockfight," p. 448.

[5] Ibid. See also Goldhill, *Poet's Voice,* pp. 73–75, who writes, (p. 74), "The interplay between the claims of the institution [of supplication] and the acceptance of the institution by the figure of power constitutes supplication as an uneasy instantiation of the control and contestation of power."

[6] Thornton, *Homer's "Iliad,"* pp. 113–42.

appeal to one's sense of pity, the point of the story is that these apparently infirm and helpless creatures must nonetheless be respected, for they have a powerful protector. The punishment for the person's refusal to feel shame is exposure to the very kind of madness that initially caused the offense.

Phoenix's parable shows the connection between shame as it structures the relations among the warriors in the warrior society and supplication. In pleading with the victor to feel shame, the suppliant asks him not to press to the hilt the privileges and powers that he enjoys. Such restraint is an attitude vital to social cohesion, and refusal to feel shame in regard to the suppliant, therefore, has wider repercussions in the society at large—as shown most clearly in Agamemnon's refusal to feel shame before Chryses and the consequences that ensue.

Phoenix's story, which strictly speaking concerns a plea for reconciliation rather than supplication as such, is motivated by his attempt to persuade Achilles to accept Agamemnon's gifts. To see it as the key to all occurrences of the ceremony, I think, underestimates Phoenix's rhetorical purpose and puts more weight on the parable than it can comfortably bear. Phoenix's story, properly understood, confirms the complexity of supplication's significance. Taken together with other occurrences of the ceremony in the *Iliad,* it shows how supplication both confirms and questions the values of the warrior society. The suppliant's plea to feel shame links supplication to the values of the warrior society; the appeal to *eleos,* however, and the deep pathos expressed by the suppliant's gestures, call forth values that such a society regards warily and at times actively discourages.

Partly because supplication is open to ambiguity and ambivalence, it can be genuinely illuminating. It does not press a particular belief or principle on the participants but allows a host of meanings to crystallize around it. The formal properties of supplication make the act of pleading self-referential; suppliants do not simply beg for something, they draw attention to the fact that they are begging.[7] The stereotyped gestures link the present occasion to a tradition of human misery. This linking serves a rhetorical function, for the suppliant implicitly claims a larger significance for his need. The suppliant tries to show that what has happened to him, to quote Aristotle, is "the kind of thing that happens."[8] He sets his own catastrophe within the contours of what he implicitly claims is the shape of mortal existence. Indeed, a succinct

[7] See Goody, "'Greeting,' 'Begging,' and the Presentation of Respect."
[8] Aristotle, *Poetics* 1451b5 (*hoia an genoito*). Aristotle is contrasting history, which recounts "what happened," with poetry, which tells "the sort of thing that happens." I discuss below the implications of supplication for the poetics of Homer's epics.

way to describe the action in Book 24 would be to say that in it Achilles comes to appreciate supplication as the kind of thing that happens—as an especially luminous image of the human condition. Supplication, then, which uses "emotion for cognitive ends," is a positive agent in Achilles' attainment of insight into who and what he is.[9]

The final scenes of the *Iliad* present a poetic vision of what supplication is capable of meaning, rather than a reliable ethnographic account of supplication among the ancient Greeks.[10] Yet it would be misleading to treat supplication in the *Iliad* as simply a poetic artifact. Iliadic supplication is not wholly distinct from the ceremony's appearances in Greek tragedy or from the accounts of it in the Greek historians.[11] Indeed, the most striking gesture of supplication as it is portrayed in the *Iliad*—the suppliant's embrace of the other's knees—is not peculiar to ancient Greece. Agathe Thornton has described *theteke,* a parallel to Greek supplication among the Limba (a people in northern Sierra Leone), in which someone pleads by uttering one of the standard phrases used to beg for forgiveness, and then sometimes claps, puts a hand on the other's ankle as a sign of humility, or in extreme cases lies prone on the ground.[12] Prisoners in the Bangladesh war pleaded for their lives by kneeling before their captors and holding them by the knees,[13] and some of the most arresting images from the Persian Gulf War of 1990 were television shots of Iraqi prisoners embracing the knees of American soldiers.

Notwithstanding the formality of supplication, its gestures of genuflection and embrace have an almost instinctual force, which may account for its troubling mixture of humiliation and aggression, and for its ability, too, to touch a responsive chord in those supplicated. How-

---

[9] The phrase is from Geertz, "Balinese Cockfight," p. 449.

[10] It is clear that supplication as it appears in the *Iliad* has been subjected to considerable poetic elaboration. The repetitiousness of the Iliadic suppliants' appeals to *aidōs, eleos,* and memory appears to owe as much to the properties of the Homeric *Dichtersprache* as to the actual language used by suppliants. So, too, the theme of the father that seems central to so many of the supplications depicted in the *Iliad* links supplication to the larger thematic concerns of the poem. Finally, the importance of ransom in Iliadic supplications cannot be understood apart from the values of wealth and prestige that underlie the warrior society. Pedrick, "Supplication in the *Iliad* and the *Odyssey*," discusses the artful variation of supplication scenes and warns that the poet's elaboration of his traditional material poses a serious methodological problem for anyone using Homer to write a history of supplication.

[11] See the account in part (i) of Gould, "Hiketeia."

[12] See Thornton, *Homer's "Iliad,"* app. 4, pp. 170–71.

[13] A photograph of Bangladesh war prisoners is reproduced in Walter Burkert, *Structure and History in Greek Mythology and Ritual* (Berkeley: University of California Press, 1979), fig. 4. See also the instances cited by Gould, "Hiketeia," p. 101.

ever that may be, supplication is not only a social tradition but a dramatic event in the suppliant's life, and necessarily draws its meaning in part from the individual's purposes in having recourse to it. To understand supplication fully, then, requires an acquaintance with its specific occasions and its situation within the particular lives of its participants. This is precisely what the *Iliad* enables us to do: Priam's ceremonial plea emerges so forcefully because it bundles together the values that underlie the warrior society depicted in the poem. We can appreciate the ability of supplication to clarify grief from its power to resolve the story of Achilles' wrath.

On this view, the *Iliad* is a reading of supplication; it not only shows the link between this ceremony and the values enforced and repressed by society, but depicts the various roles supplication plays in the lives of those who participate in it. To be sure, the *Iliad* does not offer a reliable objective account of supplication, but it presents a valuable subjective picture of the ceremony from the perspective of a society that practiced it. Supplication is thus an important factor in grasping the narrative coherence of the *Iliad* and suggests more generally the fruitfulness of ceremony for an understanding of the oral narrative poem.

The plot of the *Iliad* traces a development between two successful supplications: Thetis' supplication of Zeus in Book 1, in which she bids Zeus to "honor her son" (*timēson moi huion*), and Priam's supplication of Achilles, by means of which Zeus conclusively honors Achilles and guarantees that he will have glory, or *kudos*.[14] These two supplications bring out different aspects of prayer, and the contrast between them will enable us to sharpen the focus on Priam's ceremonial prayer to Achilles.

Thetis' supplication is one of the grandest and most ornate descriptions of supplication in the *Iliad*:

> And then she sat beside him, and took his knees
> With her left hand; with her right, she held his chin,
> And pleaded with Zeus, the son of Cronus and lord:
> Father Zeus, if ever I helped you among the immortals
> By word or deed, accomplish this hope for me:
> Honor [*timēson*] my son, who of all men is the most short-lived.
> For now Agamemnon, the lord of men,
> Has dishonored [*ētimēsen*] him. He took and holds Achilles' gift of
>   honor [*geras*].

(1.500–507)

---

[14] Zeus assures Hera that he will arrange for the release of Hector's corpse in such a way that Achilles will be honored more than Hector: *ou men gar timē ge mi' essetai* ("for

Thetis' prayer, in which she discreetly lays claim to Zeus's benevolence,[15] is characteristic more generally of the stance adopted in the Greek prayer, as this is evidenced in Homer and elsewhere in Greek literature.[16] The typical prayer begins with an elaborate naming of the deity addressed; the god is invoked through a cluster of epithets, often referring to the god's favorite places. After asking the god to "hear," the person who is praying reminds the deity of past services performed or of earlier displays by the god of benevolence to the one seeking his favor now. A future service may be promised, usually a sacrifice. The prayer concludes with the actual request, expressed concisely and directly.[17] A characteristic example is Chryses' prayer to Apollo:

> Hear me, god of the silver arrow, who dwell on Chryses
> And godly Killa, and rule Tenedos in power,
> Smintheus. If ever I built a temple that pleased you,
> Or burned the fat thighs
> Of bulls or sheep, accomplish my wish:
> Let your arrows take vengeance on the Danaans for my tears.
>
> (1.37–42)

What is striking in Greek prayer is that the one supplicating the gods does not, typically, appeal to the gods' pity, but seeks to offer a kind of exchange: a favor now in light of past works pleasing to the gods or a promise of such a work in the future. The typical prayer, in other words, is similar to the kind of supplication used by warriors on the battlefield, in which the suppliant lays stress rather on his ability to repay his captor than on appeals to the other's shame or pity. The form of Greek prayer does not bespeak the suppliant's weakness; rather, it casts the one praying in a position of strength, as one with the wherewithal to negotiate with the gods. It reflects a stance in which the suppliant has some claim to the god's benevolence because of past or future favors.

---

they will not be honored alike"), 24.66. He later tells Thetis that he is ordering Achilles to release Hector's body so that he may give glory to Achilles: *autar egō tode kudos Akhillēi protiaptō* ("I grant this glory to Achilles"), 24.110.

[15] Thetis tactfully alludes to an episode that Achilles had urged her to mention (1.396–406): she once had rescued Zeus before he established his dominion over the other gods. See Slatkin, "Wrath of Thetis."

[16] On Greek prayers, see Burkert, *Greek Religion,* pp. 73–75; Kurt von Fritz, "Greek Prayer," *Review of Religions* 10 (1945-46): 5–39; F. Schwenn, *Gebet und Opfer* (Heidelberg: C. Winter, 1927); K. Ziegler, "De precationum apud Graecos formis questiones selectae," (Diss., Breslau, 1905); and C. Ausfeld, "De Graecorum precationibus questiones," *Neue Jahrbücher Supp.* 28 (1903): 502–47.

[17] Occurrences of prayer in the *Iliad* are collected in Dietrich Mülder, "Götteranrufungen in *Ilias* and *Odyssee,*" *Rheinisches Museum* 78 (1929): 35–53.

What Thetis' prayer ultimately begets in the *Iliad* is yet another prayer. For Zeus grants Thetis' request and finally honors Achilles by sending the king of the Trojans to pray for the return of his son's corpse—the concluding example of a successful supplication in the *Iliad*. As it emerges in this final example, however, prayer is a sign of mortal vulnerability rather than of the mortal's claim of entitlement to the benevolence of those in power. For although Priam has wealth to offer Achilles and does in fact offer it, it is clear that Achilles does not have that benign disposition toward Hector's father that would induce him to accept an offer of exchange. Hence, Priam is constrained to appeal to the other's pity and does so precisely because of Achilles' indifference to his desire. The *Iliad* moves between these two poles: Thetis' prayer, which expresses confidence in her power to bring about her wishes (by offering an exchange of goods), and Priam's, which expresses the indifference of the world to the suppliant's wishes.

Priam's supplication could be seen as an unmasking of the stance reflected in the form of Greek prayer. Certain things—one's own physical life, for example, or one's child—initially appear wholly within one's control, and power over them is essential to one's deepest sense of self. The suppliant, however, has had these apparently inalienable goods suddenly alienated—and not simply removed from his control but put into the hands of an adversary. The one praying to the gods assumes a posture in which he can negotiate with the gods, whereas the suppliant, at least insofar as he is exemplified by Priam, has no such confidence. He finds his life and his self wholly in the power of someone essentially uninterested in him and predisposed to disregard his pleas. Far from being able to deal with Achilles from a position of strength, Priam ultimately has only the other's memory of mortal wretchedness with which to persuade him. The expressive force of supplication lies in large part in its confrontation of suppliant's desire and victor's power.

Indeed, there is a latent instability even within Thetis' initial supplication of Zeus. Although Thetis does not appeal especially to Zeus's pity, she uses gestures that express a suppliant's wretchedness, in which such an appeal is powerfully implicit. These gestures are redolent of emotions and values essentially outside those recognized and upheld by the warrior society. Yet, Thetis uses these emotionally charged gestures in order to achieve her son's honor (*timē*)—one of the central values of the warrior society. The object of her earnest plea is to a degree inconsistent with the very earnestness with which she urges it. More than that, the urgency that informs the suppliant's—and, in particular, Thetis'—gestures bespeak values and affections that ultimately overwhelm Achilles' search for prestige. In short, Thetis' supplication, which uses inherently powerful images of despair and abasement, points to the resolution of the *Iliad,* in which the very ability of supplication to provide a compelling image of Achilles' new sense of mortality and loss brings the poem to its climax.

Priam's supplication is ultimately Zeus's answer to Thetis' prayer in Book 1 that he honor her son. Yet the kind of honor that Zeus offers Achilles in the last book of the *Iliad* implies that Zeus does *not* honor mortals—in the sense of accommodating their wishes and doing just what they ask. Rather, as Achilles tells Priam, Zeus metes out evil fortunes as well as good from the jars beside his throne. Zeus's honoring of Achilles is paradoxical: the god's honor (Priam's supplication) gives Achilles the opportunity for obtaining insight into the world, but part of Achilles' insight is that the gods are ultimately aloof from mortal concerns. The gods, for all their participation in the events at Troy, are absent when they might attend to the warriors' vital concerns. For example, Zeus truly wants to save his son Sarpedon from death, but is made to admit the impossibility of this by Hera (see 16.426–61). Rather than interfere in the outcome of the battle between Sarpedon and Patroclus, Zeus—"the father of gods and men" (16.458)—pours drops of blood upon the battlefield to "honor his own son" (*paida philon timōn*) (460). Zeus's honoring of Sarpedon, like his later honoring of Achilles, contains the idea that the gods are distant or absent: honoring is what the gods do instead of granting the warrior his deepest wishes. Zeus's impotence in regard to Sarpedon is essentially like that of other fathers in the *Iliad,* who can do nothing for their sons except bury them and give them the honors befitting the dead (see 16.456–57). The shower of blood in Sarpedon's honor, like Priam's gathering of the son's remains, expresses the father's larger inability to save his son, and shows that the world is finally indifferent to the individual's desires.

Supplication can be described as the ceremony of the father's absence. The suppliant and the one who is supplicated both encounter an absence: no benign power watches over and protects the individual. The suppliant adopts the small stature and the importunate gestures of a child, but it is just the point of supplication that the one supplicated is *not* a kindly father and that, indeed, there is no powerful and beneficent parent. This is signalled by the elderly Priam's taking on the childlike position of the suppliant, while the young Achilles is cast in the role of the father. This inversion of son and father implicitly reflects the unattainability for Achilles of his own father and the absence of a power that reliably honors and protects him.

Supplication stands out among the human ceremonies described in the *Iliad* because, in at least this final instance, it succeeds. Other ceremonies are described in the poem, with careful attention devoted to the elaborate procedures the characters undertake to assure a successful outcome. So, for example, in Books 3 and 4, the Achaeans and Trojans seek to end the hostilities by means of a duel between Menelaus and Paris. The narrative not only stresses the goodwill of each side but describes in detail the impressive ceremony with which the two armies solemnize their pact. The solemn preparations amount to a ritual, in the sense I identified in Chapter 1, for they adhere to established formulas that convey a particular and unmistakable message to the participants. Two rams are to be sacrificed—one white, one black—in honor of the Earth (Gē) and the Sun (Hēlios), who are to witness the parties' oaths (3.103–4, 276–80). The sacrifice thus invests the duel with a cosmic significance and impresses on both sides the unique importance of this event. Trojans and Achaeans call down curses on the head of any who would violate the treaty (see 3.276–301) and both sides look forward to the end of war and the beginning of friendship (111–12, 250–54).[18] The humans' best-laid plans, in the event, are overthrown by the gods, when Hera promises to give up any one of her favorite cities in return for a promise that Troy will be destroyed (see 4.30–72). The gods' pact-making ironically signals the failure of the mortals' efforts, through treaties, to avoid further deaths and destruction. The episode suggests the ultimate inefficacy of ritual in the *Iliad*. People seek to solemnize their agreements by the invocation of the gods, but the narrative shows that the gods are not recruited by mortals' say-so.[19] Indeed, supplication succeeds partly because it is a ceremony, ultimately, of the gods' absence: it is the memory of the gods' final indifference to human desires that awakens *eleos*.

II

By the poem's conclusion, Achilles has moved past that certain healthy insensitivity to suffering—others' and one's own—which is necessary for committed fighting on the battlefield. In doing so, he approaches the perspective of the *Iliad's* poet. The sense of pity Achilles attains at the close of the *Iliad* has imbued the poem from its very

[18] On oath sacrifices, see Burkert, *Greek Religion,* pp. 250–54; and G. S. Kirk, *The Iliad: A Commentary,* vol. 1 (Cambridge: Cambridge Universitiy Press, 1985), pp. 302–11.

[19] Agamemnon's efforts to solemnize his reconciliation with Achilles in Book 19.257–65 hardly succeed in reassimilating Achilles into Achaean warrior society.

beginning, for the *Iliad* is characterized throughout by its embracing sympathy, which encompasses Achaean and Trojan alike. By the poem's end, Achilles' sympathy is neither partisan (it is not confined to any one side in the war) nor special (it is not confined to a particular group of intimates). While derived from a passionate experience of grief for those dearest to him, Achilles' sympathy is broad-ranging, extending even to the father of his bitterest enemy. By inviting Priam to give up his adamant grieving for Hector and to reflect on the inherent sadness of human life, Achilles expresses a sympathy like that of the poet, who describes the deaths even of unimportant soldiers in a way that underscores their pathos—the grief inflicted by the death on father or wife, or the sadness of youth cut down in all its beauty.[20]

The *Iliad* could be understood, then, as a poem in which the hero attains finally an understanding of the poetics implicit in it,[21] for these poetics have to do with the memory of grief. Because it preserves the memory of evils once inflicted and griefs once endured, the poem is a fulfillment to which the characters within the poem look forward. The experience of grief is fulfilled in becoming an object of song, a theme for others to ask about and to take an interest in. Song partly complements the values of the war society by providing the unperishing renown that the warriors anticipated. Yet at the same time, epic poetry— at least as exemplified in the *Iliad*—is hardly confined to providing the compensation in renown that the warrior society promises. The *Iliad's* hero, almost from the outset of the poem, calls into question the reliability and value of such compensation. Thus, *aoidē* also shows the limits of the warrior society. It tells the story of the painfulness of loss and asserts the importance of the experience of grief.

Supplication provides a model for construing epic poetry and its complex relation to the warrior society. Like Homeric epic, supplication is a form of compensation that honors the victorious.[22] Yet supplication also marks out the limits of the warrior society by showing

---

[20] See Griffin, *Homer on Life and Death,* pp. 103–43 for examples.

[21] I find myself in disagreement with one of the central points of Martin, *Language of Heroes.* Martin argues that a poetic of the *Iliad* can usefully be based on the formal speech-acts of the poem's heroes. I agree with Martin that a poetic of the *Iliad* is implicit in the story it tells and in the speeches of its characters; but I believe that it distorts our understanding of the *Iliad* to locate the poetic primarily in the speeches of the heroes speaking as confident and undefeated warriors. The *Iliad* ultimately stands outside the heroic society, and does not view the warriors in the shame-based way they have been trained to think of themselves. Martin's approach cannot do justice to Priam's suppliant speech and Achilles' emotional reply, which, in my reading, truly climax and resolve the action of the poem.

[22] See Lynn-George, *Epos,* pp. 200–209, who suggestively compares epic (conceived as compensation for the warrior's life) and supplication as a form of exchange.

those values that remain compelling even after the goods of renown and prestige have ceased to be valuable. Song and supplication alike seem to be situated liminally, as a part of society and yet apart from it.

This similar "situation" of poetry and supplication in regard to society leads on to yet other points of resemblance. The relation between the suppliant and the victor is suggestively close to that between the poem and its audience. The suppliant seeks to create in the victor as vivid a picture of suffering as he can: he wants the victor to summon up in a lively way the experience of grief and to enter imaginatively into the suppliant's own distress. Similarly, the Homeric poem affords the opportunity to the listener to imagine scenes from far away and long ago, and yet to feel the emotions of the characters as though they were his or her own.[23]

The poet does for his audience much what Cleopatra did for Meleager. When the enemy were already storming the city, Cleopatra told her husband:

> . . . all
> The griefs [kēde'], as many as befall those whose city is taken:
> They kill the men; fire destroys the city;
> Strangers lead off the children and the deep-girdled wives.

> (9.591–94)

Cleopatra conjures up for her husband a scene calculated to rouse his emotions: she tells him a tale of griefs. In seeking to awaken in Meleager a vivid imagining of the scene described, she does not describe an event that actually happened, but to paraphrase Aristotle, of the kind that typically happens.[24] The poet, like Cleopatra, tries to evoke in the listener a powerful image of the scenes described. His narrative is imbued with memory, a concept deeply characteristic of the internal poetics of epic poetry.[25] In the invocation to the Catalogue

---

[23] On vividness as the distinct pleasure that the Homeric poems seek to provide, see now Ford, *Homer: The Poetry of the Past,* pp. 54–55, 125–29.

[24] See Aristotle, *Poetics,* 1451b5–b12.

[25] On memory and its importance for the poetics of archaic Greek poetry, see Pucci, *Odysseus Polutropos,* pp. 19–22; Thalmann, *Conventions of Form and Thought,* pp. 147–49; Penelope Murray, "Poetic Inspiration in Early Greece," *Journal of Hellenic Studies* 101 (1981): 87–100; William Stephen Moran, "*Mimnēskomai* and 'Remembering' Epic Stories in Homer and the Hymns," *Quaderni Urbinati di Cultura Classica* 20 (1975): 195–215; and Vernant, "Aspects mythiques de la mémoire," in *Mythe et pensée*; and J. A. Notopoulos, "Mnemosune in Oral Literature," *Transactions of the American Philological Association* 69 (1938): 465–93. See also the discussion of memory in Martin, *Language of Heroes,* pp. 77–88.

of the Ships in Book 2, the poet asks the Muses to "call to mind" (*mnēsaiath'*) all who went to Troy (2.492). To sing is just "to remember": when, in the *Hymn to Apollo,* the Delian maidens sing their song (*humnon aeidousin*) they are "remembering" (*mnēsamenai*) the men and women of old (*h.Ap.* 160–61; cf. 150). The importance of memory to the production of song is inscribed in the Muses' very genealogy, for they are—as Hesiod tells us—the daughters of Memory (Mnēmosunē, *Theogony* 53–55). Indeed, the very purpose of epic song is to perpetuate the memory of the warriors by narrating the "fames of men."[26] As Albert Lord in particular has stressed, the poet's memory is not memorization or a meticulous recording of past events,[27] but rather a kind of mindfulness,[28] which consists in his making a scene powerful and vivid in his mind, so that he can speak it *"kata kosmon"*—just as it was, even though he has not actually witnessed the events themselves, nor heard of them from some one who had (see *Od.* 8.489–91).[29] The poet's excellence is that he conveys to his listeners a similarly vivid experience of the scene.

The listener's aesthetic response to the grief suffered by the characters in the poem, like that of the one supplicated, could be described as an emotional experience of the place of griefs in human life. The aesthetic response is emotional, yet cognitive as well, for the listener does not simply suffer griefs but appreciates their significance as the hallmarks of mortal life. The paradoxical delight that the listener derives, notwithstanding the grief conveyed by the song, is precisely the greater understanding of sorrow afforded by song.

The delight or pleasure that Achilles feels in looking upon Priam is a model for the listener's experience of the poem. It is a part of Achilles' peculiar nature as a character that he not only endures evil, but survives it and comes to understand it. Achilles is not exactly a "tragic" hero, since he is not ruined by his misfortune but achieves a climactic insight into it. He at once undergoes evil and observes it. Even in their distress, therefore, he and Priam are nonetheless able to delight, as they

---

[26] On the poetics of epic poetry as a perpetuation of the fames of men, see Nagy, *Best of the Achaeans,* p. 95; and his earlier *Comparative Studies in Greek and Indic Meter* (Cambridge: Harvard University Press, 1974), pp. 244–55. See also Walter Marg, *Homer über die Dichtung* (Munster: Aschendorffsche Verlagsbuchhandlung, 1957), p. 17.

[27] See Lord, *Singer of Tales,* chap. 4; and Ford, *Homer: The Poetry of the Past,* pp. 49–50.

[28] On memory as "mindfulness," see Vernant, "Aspects mythiques de la memoire," in *Mythe et pensée;* and Murray, "Poetic Inspiration."

[29] See Bruno Gentili, *Poetry and Its Public in Ancient Greece* (Baltimore: Johns Hopkins University Press, 1988), pp. 7–8.

expressly do in one another's looks and voice, after they have concluded their meal.

> But when they put off the desire for drink and food,
> Dardan Priam wondered at Achilles—
> His size and look were like the gods'.
> Achilles, too, wondered at Dardan Priam,
> Looking upon his good face and hearing him speak.
>
> (24.628–32)

Achilles' delight is partly, no doubt, in the august eminence of Priam's features, but it consists, perhaps more fundamentally, in his appreciation of Priam's resemblance to his own father: the moment is as close as Achilles will get to looking upon Peleus. Achilles' delight, in other words, arises from his new ability to see his father's likeness in another. It is a delight in his new understanding of his suffering and of its resemblance to others' experience.

Achilles' delight is like the listener's aesthetic pleasure in the vicarious experience of grief. For this pleasure, too, consists in the deepened understanding of sorrow that epic *aoidē* affords. The listener, like Achilles, conceives of himself, in response to the song, as a being in whose life evils are a necessary element. The most genuine pleasure of such a creature is not to escape grief (for, ultimately, griefs are inescapable), but arises from understanding them as constitutive of the person.

This pleasure finds expression in the emotion of pity, understood as the blend of engagement and disengagement—of passion and reflection—that I have sought to describe above. From the vantage point of the final scene of the *Iliad,* we may now return to a problem posed at the beginning of this study—the relation between pity and pleasure. The argument developed over the course of these chapters suggests that pity and the pleasure it paradoxically affords are not to be avoided, as Plato claims. For the pity that Achilles feels at last is hardly a spectacular display of grief such as Plato criticizes: rather, it represents the decisive consignment of such passionate displays to the past.

Achilles can feel and act on *eleos* in regard to Priam only because he has moved beyond the unreflecting and unrestrained torments he first felt at Patroclus' death. Pity, as felt for the stranger, is a distinctly reflective emotion. It responds emotionally to another's grief but also involves a thoughtful awareness of grief and its place in human life. The pleasure of pity consists, then, in the learning it imparts concerning the pitier's own misery and his likeness to others.

For Aristotle, *eleos* required "purification" (*katharsis*) through the medium of tragedy. In the *Iliad,* on the other hand, pity—as Achilles ultimately feels it for Priam—does not stand in need of such purification, for as presented in Book 24, pity *is* the purification of the mourner's passions. Pity represents, so to speak, a "second order" emotion: it is an emotion arising from the understanding of one's emotions. More specifically, *eleos,* as felt for the suppliant, is the mourner's emotional registering of the necessary place of griefs in his life, and his assimilation of them into his sense of the kind of being he is. Thanks to his pity, the mourner can generalize past his own experience and use his sorrows as a powerful means of insight into another's life. Pity emerges from grief, but because it represents an understanding of grief, it issues in delight.

III

Like the singer, the suppliant is in his society but not quite of it: suppliant and singer alike are necessarily outside the dominant values of their society and hence able to consider them critically. This outsider's stance in regard to the warrior society celebrated in the *Iliad* is one reason why epic poetry and supplication resemble each other, and why supplication is a fruitful source for the poetics of epic poetry. Even more fundamentally, however, it is a matter of life-and-death importance for the suppliant to make clear to others the similarity of all human suffering and the ineluctable quality of grief. The urgency and clarity of the suppliant's need renders his speech an especially articulate expression of the mortal condition; he is, so to speak, a poet *avant la lettre.*

To say that supplication provides a basis for elaborating a poetics of the Homeric poems is to claim that epic song is essentially human speech, spoken from within the stress and urgencies of mortal circumstances. As we have seen, prayer to the gods grows from the hope that human speech can reach past the mortal world to a power capable of rescuing the mortal and securing for him what he most deeply wants. Supplication—prayer transferred from the realm between gods and men to the purely human realm between mortal and mortal—suggests that there is no such benign power. It implies the absence of the gods as benign parents who care for their children's lives: a successful supplication, such as Priam's, is one in which the suppliant brings home to the other a sense of that absence.

Because it is so similar to prayer—speech that aspires to move the gods to act as one wishes—supplication ultimately suggests the impossibility of transcending human speech. The suppliant's speech and gestures are not a powerful tool ensuring the fulfilment of his desires. He does not unleash a ritualistic power, nor does he exercise an unambiguous moral authority over the other.[30] The suppliant's speech and gestures are merely a means of persuasion: his words do not reach past the human realm, and within that realm find only an indifferent other who must somehow be led to do what the suppliant wants.

To the extent that supplication provides a model for the poetics of epic *aoidē,* then, it suggests that song, too, does not attain to a final authority or escape the contingencies and uncertainties of mortal existence. Like supplication, a song's tale of griefs concerns the absence of powers or authorities that rescue the mortal from the conditions of mortality. The *Odyssey* is a poem about the return of the parent and husband, but as I shall argue in subsequent chapters, it is more deeply about the truth that the father never returns, for Odysseus never brings about the regime of security and order that Telemachus and others expect. The *Odyssey,* as the story of Odysseus' non-return, is a poem about the kind of thing poetry is: it suggests that, as a tale of grief, epic poetry is but human speech, and as such, necessarily concerns absence.

---

[30] I refer here, respectively, to Gould, "Hiketeia," who stresses the ritual efficacy of the suppliant's physical contact, and Thornton, *Homer's "Iliad,"* e.g., p. 142, on supplication as moral compulsion.

SUPPLICATION AND POETICS IN THE *ODYSSEY*

CHAPTER 6

Telemachus' Supplication

I

    Supplication provides a model for the poetics implicit in the *Iliad*, and in Part II I will extend that model and apply it to the quite different world of the *Odyssey*. First we must consider the poetics that emerge from *Iliad* 24 against the background of statements within the poems themselves concerning their origins and purpose. The *Iliad* seems to understand itself essentially as divine speech intended to convey knowledge, and to be based not on the suppliant's ability to conjure up vivid scenes of human suffering but on the gods' ability to convey reliably what happened in the past. Thus, the *Iliad* begins with a prayer to the Muse to sing the story of Achilles' wrath, and, as Homer later makes clear in introducing the Catalogue of Ships, the poet's authoritative account of the forces amassed in the Trojan War is possible only because the Muse, who was present then and knows everything, brings what she knows to the poet's mind.

> Tell me now, Muses who dwell on Olympus,
> For you are goddesses, you are present and know all,
> While we only hear report and know nothing—
> Who were the leaders and rulers of the Danaans.
> I could not speak or name that host,
> Not if I had ten tongues and ten mouths,
> An invincible voice and a heart of bronze
> Unless the Olympian Muses, Zeus's
> Daughters, bring to my mind all who went to Troy.
>
>   (*Il.* 2. 484–92)

The poetics expressly announced in the *Iliad* is one of presence: because the Muses are goddesses and immortal, they were actually present at the events whose story they relate to the poet, and therefore know those events (*pareste te, iste te panta,* 485). As so construed, poetry represents a singular exception to the conditions of mortal life; because of it, mortals are not wholly confined to hearing reports (cf. *kleos oion akouomen,* 486). Poetry flows from a source that is decisively outside human affairs, and therefore not subject to the ambiguities and uncertainties of human speech.[1]

Moreover, understood as it is at the opening of the Catalogue of Ships, *aoidē* complements the warrior ethic by assuring the warriors of that "unperishing renown" (*kleos aphthiton,* cf. *Il.* 9.413) for which they give up their lives. Without the gods, *kleos* is a sign of human ignorance: it is that fallible "report" of past events that does not offer sure knowledge (see 2.486). Thanks to the gods' reliable knowledge of the past, however, *kleos* becomes "renown"—a trustworthy dissemination of distant events.[2] The claims of epic poetry to derive from the gods, then, serve to support the values of the warrior society by ensuring that death can in some measure be escaped. *Aoidē* furnishes a sole instance of immortality in human affairs. By suppressing his fear of death and courageously facing it on the battlefield, the warrior can hope to attain through *aoidē* a kind of immortality.

The "divinity" of epic poetry is in substantial part a mythic reflex of its traditional character. Because *aoidē* was handed down from generation to generation, it lacked a single, identifiable source but rather evinced the seemingly godlike properties of being perennial and ubiquitous. Moreover, because traditional song constituted in effect a shared knowledge of the past, it served as a means of social cohesion. As Havelock and others have argued, epic song amounted to a kind of cultural "encyclopedia" or storing place for the collected lore of the society.[3] Because everyone knew it, song counted as "knowledge"; it

---

[1] On the invocation of the Muses in *Iliad* 2, see the discussions by Ford, *Homer: The Poetry of the Past,* pp. 60–61, 72–73; and Pietro Pucci, "The Language of the Muses," in *Classical Mythology in Twentieth-Century Thought and Literature,* 11, ed. W. M. Aycock and T. M. Klein (Lubbock: Texas Tech Press, 1980), pp. 163–86. On eyewitness knowledge as the surest knowledge, see the references in Jenny Strauss Clay, *The Wrath of Athena: Gods and Men in the "Odyssey"* (Princeton: Princeton University Press, 1983), p. 13 n. 8.

[2] See Ford, *Homer: The Poetry of the Past,* p. 77.

[3] See Eric A. Havelock, *Preface to Plato* (Cambridge: Harvard University Press, 1963), pp. 61–96. See also Gentili, *Poetry and Its Public,* pp. 1–8, who links the notion of the poet as a repository of cultural information with the concept of divine inspiration.

was the object of social consensus. Conceived of as something heard from the Muses, song was the common ground—the common language—that enabled members of the society to argue their disagreements, but the common ground could not itself be criticized or disputed.[4]

I will refer to the concept of *aoidē* described above by speaking of "song-as-knowledge." Implicit in the Homeric epics, however, is a different poetic, which can be described under the rubric "song-as-understanding." This alternate conception of epic poetry can, in the first instance, be characterized negatively: it does not claim to attain to a point outside mortality and its conditions, and consequently it does not afford knowledge, for it cannot achieve complete presence to the past. *Aoidē* is not, however, simply a sign of human ignorance. Put positively, song-as-understanding is a memory of griefs, or *kēdea;* as such, it is an account of mortal existence from within the contours and limitations of that existence. Although it cannot afford a sure and dependable knowledge about the past, it nonetheless affords an "understanding" of what grief is like. It seeks to stir an emotional response in its listeners, which is at the same time an insight into the experience of griefs. Rather than complementing the values of the warrior society, this poetic construes song as arising from and addressing the fears suppressed by the warrior society. As I suggested at the conclusion of the first part, song (more precisely, song-as-understanding) has to do with absence—specifically, the absence of the gods as kindly guardians who bring about the individual's deepest wishes. The *Odyssey*—in which, as I shall argue, Odysseus never truly becomes present as an authoritative restorer of justice—is a poem about absence, and, more generally, therefore, about the kind of thing poetry is.

Supplication is essential to this poetic of song-as-understanding. Not only is this poetic implicit in Priam's supplication of Achilles in *Iliad* 24, but it is a vital part of discussions of poets and poetry in the *Odyssey*. As we shall see, such discussions in the *Odyssey* are regularly presented in the context of supplication or in contexts that strongly suggest supplication. That context materially affects our understanding of what the characters have to say about poetry or poets, and points toward song-as-understanding as affording a more adequate poetic than "song-as-knowledge" for both the *Iliad* and the *Odyssey*.

---

[4] On the poetics of song as something beyond criticism, see the discussion by George B. Walsh, *The Varieties of Enchantment* (Chapel Hill: University of North Carolina Press, 1984), pp. 12–14.

II

In the second book of the *Odyssey*, Telemachus calls an assembly in order to denounce publicly the self-proclaimed suitors who have infested the household of Odysseus. After Telemachus' impassioned denunciation has degenerated—thanks to the ringleader Antinous' sophistic rebuttal—into a kind of impasse between him and the suitors, two eagles appear overhead, tearing at each other with their talons, to the amazement of the onlookers (see 2.150–55).[5] One of those present at the assembly, Halitherses, "unsurpassed in the knowledge of birds and at speaking what is destined" (2.158–59), interprets the eagles' flight:

> Hear now, Ithacans, what I say.
> To the suitors especially I reveal these things:
> For a great woe is in store for them. Odysseus
> Will not be far from his loved ones, and now already
> Is at hand, planning death and fate for them. . . .
> . . . I am not inexperienced at prophecy, but expert:
> For I say that all has been accomplished for him
> As once I said, when the Argives set sail for
> Troy, and wily Odysseus among them.
> I said that after suffering many evils, and losing all his companions,
> Unknown to all, in the twentieth year,
> He will return. All this will now come to pass.
>
> (2.161–65, 170–76)

As we have seen, Halitherses' skill in prophecy is vouched for by Homer, and what he says is in fact true: Odysseus is indeed about to return in the twentieth year, after suffering many evils and losing all his companions. Halitherses' interpretation is a shaky one, however, for it is imposed on an event that hardly appears to support it. The two eagles seem evenly matched: they tear at each other's cheeks and necks (2.153) without any clear superiority being established. The omen seems an unlikely indication of the swift and sure destruction that Halitherses claims is imminent.

Moreover, the proofs Halitherses adduces in support of his interpretation are of the weakest. For he seeks to buttress his current predic-

---

[5] On omens in the *Odyssey*, see Rebecca W. Bushnell, "Reading 'Winged Words': Homeric Bird Signs, Similes, and Epiphanies," *Helios*, n.s., 9 (1982): 1–13; and Agathe Thornton, *People and Themes in Homer's "Odyssey"* (London: Methuen, 1970), pp. 52–57. See also Steven H. Lonsdale, *Creatures of Speech: Lion, Herding, and Hunting Similes in the "Iliad"* (Stuttgart: Teubner, 1990), pp. 112–15.

tion of Odysseus' imminent return by recalling his old prophecy that Odysseus would return in the twentieth year. Far from supporting his interpretation of the eagles, Halitherses seems to undermine it by suggesting that he has a motive for twisting the omen into a prediction that Odysseus is at hand.[6] Thus Eurymachus, the second unofficial leader of the suitors, has little trouble in undercutting Halitherses' interpretation. Eurymachus need only assert that Halitherses has offered his interpretation in order to obtain gifts from Telemachus, and that the eagles' flight is merely a chance event, not a divine manifestation (see 2.178–86). Halitherses' interpretation is internally so weak that it loses its effect at the simplest (and most self-serving) suggestion that it is prompted solely by greed.

The contrast with Calchas in the first book of the *Iliad* is striking. There, too, Homer expressly vouches for the seer's skill: "by far the best of augurs, who knew the past, the future and the present" (*Il.* 1.69–70). When Calchas announces that Apollo has been angered by Agamemnon's treatment of his priest Chryses, there is never the slightest doubt that Calchas has genuine access to the mind of the gods and that he accurately recites what is objectively true. Agamemnon—rather like Eurymachus—is angered by the seer's prophecy, but the difference between their responses is instructive. For Agamemnon nowhere calls Chryses' veracity into question nor does he suggest that the seer is seeking to curry favor with others.

Eurymachus switches attention from that which is spoken to the speaker—from the sign to the sign's interpreter. The effect is to undermine seriously the force of Halitherses' pronouncement: the message of Odysseus' imminent return is shown to be baseless and possibly to have its source in Halitherses' view of his best advantage. More deeply, Eurymachus' ad hominem attack on Halitherses calls into question the objective "significance" of any event. According to the suitor, the flight of eagles has no objective meaning; people merely foist a meaning onto external events for their own self-interested reasons.

The objective "meaningfulness" of eagles—as harbingers, for example, of Odysseus' imminent return—rests upon a world that is morally ordered and in which villains like Eurymachus will certainly get their just deserts. It is not only what the eagles signify but the very fact of their significance that attests to a moral order. Eurymachus' assertion that the eagles mean nothing, therefore, implicitly denies both that the

[6] On Halitherses' interpretation, see Alfred Heubeck, Stephanie West, and J. B. Hainsworth, *A Commentary on Homer's "Odyssey,"* vol. 1 (Oxford: Clarendon Press, 1988), note on 2.161ff.

suitors will be punished and that a cosmic moral order exists. Eury-machus boldly substitutes his own cynical "prophecy" (*tauta d'egō seo pollon ameinōn manteuesthai*, 2.180): Odysseus is dead, and Halitherses should be (2.182–84).

Eurymachus' defiance marks him at once as a scoundrel, but it is striking that—although he is a villain in what appears to be a poem celebrating a moral order—he is not refuted by Halitherses or exposed for what he is. Rather, the suitor's personal attack on the seer's motives successfully blunts the force of Halitherses' solemn pronouncement, so that the assembled Ithacans fail to rally decisively behind Telemachus. More troublingly, it is difficult to say why Halitherses' reading of the eagle omen—which seems willfully imposed on the evidence and is only tenuously supported by a similar prophecy Halitherses made twenty years previously—is entitled to deference. Eurymachus' "anti-interpretation" of the eagles' flight creates an unresolved and troubling uncertainty, for although his words are appropriate to his evil nature, they are more persuasive than they have any right to be. It is difficult to counter Eurymachus' argument that the seer's prophecy is based on nothing so much as his own wishes, and that such wishes are inevitably self-seeking.

In Eurymachus' attack on Halitherses' prophecy and indeed throughout these early scenes on Ithaca, the *Odyssey* conveys the char-acters' inability to attain to certainty about their situation and their confinement to individual constructions or interpretations of possible meanings of the events. The Telemachy is in large part about the Ithacans' failed efforts to escape mere interpretation and to impose meaning on an ambiguous situation. Odysseus' absence is the chief source of the Ithacans' quandary, largely because he fits into no easily identified category: he is neither a warrior who died young and cele-brated nor a man who lived a long and prosperous life. Thus, Tele-machus says, if his father had died at Troy, the "Panachaeans would have raised a memorial in his honor," and he would have bequeathed a "great renown" (*mega kleos*) to Telemachus (see 1.237–41). Alter-natively, Telemachus says, Odysseus could have lived at home to a ripe old age and handed his possessions over to his son (see 1.217–18).

These different paths—death at Troy, long life at home—were the two options available to Achilles in the *Iliad:* either to die young with an "unperishing renown," or to live without fame into a ripe old age (see *Il.* 9.412–16). The similarity between the alternative lives available to Achilles and Telemachus's alternative wishes for his father suggests that these represented readily and widely understood courses that a life could take. Telemachus is, in a way, indifferent to which of these two lives—early heroic death or long prosperous life—should be his father's lot, for either one would afford those back home an idea of where they stood. Odysseus' disappearance falls into neither category, and hence leaves Telemachus simply baffled. "I would not have grieved so much," he says candidly, "even if my father had died" (1.236), since such a death at Troy, duly honored by the Achaeans, would have at least given Telemachus his father's renown as his birthright.

Even the gods seem unable to make sense of Odysseus' absence from home and the sufferings he endures as a result. In the opening scene of the poem, Athena at first contrasts Odysseus (who has done nothing to offend the gods) with Aegisthus (who admittedly deserved his violent death) (see 1.45–62). As he emerges from this contrast, Odysseus looks like one who is to be pitied for his sufferings; indeed, all the gods, save for Poseidon, do pity him (*eleairon*, 1.19).

Later, however, when Athena contrasts Odysseus with Aegisthus' victim, Agamemnon, Odysseus' lot appears considerably happier:

> As for me, I would sooner wish, after enduring many sorrows,
> To reach home and look upon my day of return,
> Than to arrive and be slaughtered by the hearth, as Agamemnon
> Died by Aegisthus' guile and his own wife's.
>
> (3.232–35)

Odysseus' lot looks alternately piteous and fortunate, depending on the one with whom Odysseus is contrasted.[7] Again, contrast with the *Iliad* is instructive. For there, too, the absence of Achilles' father Peleus from the action at Troy rendered him "plastic"—capable of meaning different things. As we have seen, characters invoked Peleus' authority

[7] Uvo Hölscher argues that the House of Atreus story sets forth three types of heroic fate—represented by Aegisthus, Orestes, and Agamemnon—which together make up a unity of possible outcomes for the hero. See Uvo Hölscher, "Die Atridensage in der *Odyssee*," in *Festschrift für Richard Alewyn*, ed. H. Singer and B. von Wiese (Cologne: Böhlau, 1967), pp. 1–16. We may compare the inconsistent accounts in the *Iliad* of Peleus' departing advice to Achilles, which construct a synoptic view of heroic society. In the *Odyssey*, however, the House of Atreus story often conveys the elusiveness of Odysseus, as Hölscher also suggests. See S. Douglas Olson, "The Stories of Agamemnon in Homer's *Odyssey*," *Transactions of the American Philological Association* 120 (1990): 57–71, p. 63, who stresses that no single authoritative interpretation of the significance of Agamemnon's story ever emerges either for Homer's audience or for the characters within the poem. The most elaborate recent study of the House of Atreus story in the *Odyssey* is Marylin A. Katz, *Penelope's Renown: Meaning and Indeterminacy in the "Odyssey"* (Princeton: Princeton University Press, 1991). I address Katz's study below in Chapter 9. Also on the House of Atreus story in the *Odyssey*, see Edward F. D'Arms and Karl K. Hulley, "The Oresteia Story in the *Odyssey*," *Transactions of the American Philological Association* 77 (1946): 207–13.

for different and even inconsistent propositions, but Peleus' varying significance was never stressed and the audience's attention was never drawn to this variability.

Far different is the *Odyssey,* where Odysseus' absence is manifestly susceptible to different and obviously inconsistent interpretations. Odysseus, in the first two books of the *Odyssey,* is relegated to being a figment of others' constructions of him. The clear incompatibility of the different versions of him makes each account unreliable—merely an "interpretation." The different interpretations of Odysseus in the first several books of the *Odyssey* underscore and deepen the implications of Odysseus' absence: Odysseus is not merely distant in a geographical sense, he is beyond the ability of those on Ithaca—and even the ability of the gods—to encompass and explain him. The signal feature of the ill-starred assembly called by Telemachus is that even apparently unassailable claims—for example, denunciations of the parasitic suitors—fail to have their effect because, thanks to the obscurities brought about by Odysseus' absence, they can be impeached and undermined. Instead of Odysseus' authoritative presence—as husband, father, lord of the household, and king of Ithaca—we have only shifting interpretations of signs and inconclusive arguments about the meaning of Odysseus' continued absence.

III

Against a background of blurred distinctions and interpretations that do more to obscure than to clarify, Telemachus leaves Ithaca and seeks to get word of Odysseus. He sets out for the Peloponnese in order to meet Nestor and, later, Menelaus, and to question them concerning his father. Telemachus plans to base his course of action on what he hears from these men: he will learn whether his father lives or has died, and will act accordingly (see 1.287–92).

When he meets Nestor, Telemachus supplicates him, or, at least, couches his appeal in the language of the suppliant. Yet, Telemachus' supplication is deliberately paradoxical: unlike other suppliants, he expressly begs Nestor to feel neither shame (*aidōs*) nor pity (*eleos*), even though these are the emotions that normally prompt a person to do what the suppliant asks. Only by rooting out such emotions, Telemachus feels, can he obtain the candid and reliable report he so badly desires. This "supplication-in-reverse" sets the *Odyssey* in self-conscious relation to supplication scenes such as occur throughout the *Iliad.* Tele-

machus' plea both continues and inverts such pleas, and forms a basis
for elaborating a "poetics of supplication" for the Homeric poems.

> So now I come before your knees, if you be willing
> To tell that man's dire destruction, if perhaps you saw it
> With your own eyes, or got word from another
> Wanderer. His mother bore a man of woes:
> Yet do not be softened, feeling shame or pity,
> But tell me how you came upon the sight.
> I beg of you, if ever my father, noble Odysseus,
> Carried out a promise by word or deed
> Among the Trojans when you Achaeans suffered woes,
> Remember it now, and tell me truly.
>
> (3.92–101)

Telemachus' plea is far removed from any actual supplication; yet
the allusion to supplication is certainly not inappropriate to the situation. Telemachus is moved to supplicate in the first place because his
father's disappearance has left him in an intolerable situation:

> All the others—all that fought at Troy
> We have heard about; where each suffered a baneful death.
> But the son of Cronus has made my father's death unheard.
> For no one can tell me clearly when he died,
> Whether he was subdued by enemies on land,
> Or at sea amongst the waves of Amphitrite.
>
> (3.86–91)

Odysseus' prolonged absence has not only left Telemachus without
news of his father but has deprived him of a robust sense of his own
sonship as well. "My mother tells me I am [Odysseus'] son," Telemachus confides to the disguised Athena, "but, as for myself, I do not
know: for no one knows his own parentage (*gonon*)" (1.215–16). News
of his father is vital to the young Telemachus in commencing his adult
life, as the return of a slain child was necessary to the old man bringing
his life to its conclusion. Telemachus' recourse to the vocabulary of the
suppliant is appropriate to his situation.

What Telemachus earnestly desires, above all, is hard knowledge. It
is precisely because he does not "know" who his father is (*ouk oid'*,
1.216) that he has come to Nestor. Zeus has made his father's "dire
destruction" (*lugron olethron*, 3.87) "unheard" (*apeuthea*, 3.88). Telemachus wants to be in the essentially passive situation of one who hears

a report uttered authoritatively: Nestor is to tell what he knows either because he has seen it himself or heard it from another (see 3.93–95). Nestor's candor is essential to Telemachus' purpose of obtaining a reliable report about his father. Any emotions that might lead Nestor to temper or "sweeten" (cf. *meilisseo*, 3.96) his account—to withhold from Telemachus, for example, information establishing Odysseus' death—would wholly defeat the purpose of Telemachus' visit. Thus, Telemachus begs Nestor to feel neither pity nor shame: such emotions can only distort or cloud the straightforward report by Nestor of what he knows.

Telemachus is in the anomalous position of a suppliant whose plea can only be frustrated if the other feels pity or shame. What Telemachus wishes to avoid, above all, is the need to interpret what Nestor says: for example, to glean from hints and evasions in Nestor's account what has happened to his father. Telemachus does not wish to grapple with Nestor's account—to try actively to understand it. The need to interpret would only enmesh him more in the web of interpretation that has made life on Ithaca so uncertain.

Telemachus' paradoxical supplication has unmistakable implications for the poetics of the *Odyssey*, for he speaks in a language appropriate to epic song. Telemachus states the purpose of his visit succinctly: "I came to hear of the broad fame (*kleos euru*) of my father" (3.83). Although *kleos euru* is taken by some to mean simply "news,"[8] it should not be shorn of its literal sense ("broad fame") and its usual associations with the renown disseminated by poetry. Furthermore, Telemachus is sure that his father is dead and that any account of him will necessarily be one of "dire destruction" (*lugron olethron*, 3.87)—the typical theme of many songs performed with the *Odyssey*.[9] For song, as it is presented in the *Odyssey*, is typically about "ruin" or "destruction"—the recurring words are *oitos* and *olethron*. So, for example, the singer Phemius, who performs for the suitors, sings of the "dire homecoming" (*noston . . . lugron*) that the angered Athena sent on the Achaeans returning from Troy (see 1.325–27); in Telemachus' words, Phemius' song describes the "evil destruction" (*kakon oiton*) of the Danaans (1.350). Demodocus, the court singer of Alcinous, sings of the "quarrel (*neikos*) between Odysseus and Achilles" (8.75) which signalled the

---

[8] See W. B. Stanford, *The "Odyssey" of Homer*, vol. 1 (Houndmills: Macmillan, 1959), note on 3.83. See also Heubeck, West, and Hainsworth, *Commentary*, note on 3.83; and Edwards, *Achilles in the "Odyssey*," p. 71 n. 2.

[9] As Sheila Murnaghan, *Disguise and Recognition in the "Odyssey"* (Princeton: Princeton University Press, 1987), p. 157, writes, "[Telemachus] does not search for his father but for the ending to his father's story, the conclusion to the narrative that will at once testify to his father's life and confirm that it is over."

"beginning of woe (*pēmatos arkhē*) for the Trojans and Danaans through the counsels of great Zeus" (8.81–82). It was a song, as Odysseus later describes it, about the destruction (*oitos*) of the Achaeans (8.489). Later, Demodocus sings about the "destruction (*oitos*) of the Argives, Danaans, and Troy" (8.578).

The "dire destruction" of a people or city is preeminently the theme for *aoidē*, with its powers to celebrate and to perpetuate in memory. Odysseus' peculiar fate, however, is that the gods have buried his "destruction" in obscurity: they have made it the very opposite of "that which is heard" (*kleos*) by rendering it "unheard" (*apeuthea*, 3.88).[10] Odysseus is a paradoxical hero: his fame (*kleos*) reaches the heavens (9.19–20) but because the Furies have "snatched him away without renown" (*akleiōs*, 1.241), no one is so obscure as he. Telemachus' supplication aims at routing the obscurity, so that his father's "broad fame" may shine through. Such fame will be his legacy as Odysseus' son and will make him less resolutely agnostic about his parentage. He will have not only his mother's say-so, but the common agreement of all—the broadly spread fame—that he is indeed Odysseus' son. The dissemination of fame is preeminently the work of song conceived as transmitting knowledge. In the absence of a song about Odysseus' "destruction," Telemachus begs Nestor to make up for the song that is lacking, with a report that can claim to be authoritative. Nestor is to "speak [that man's] dire destruction" (*lugron olethron enispein*, 3.93); in other words, Nestor is to provide an account that will function like song to "speak the destruction" of a man.

Supplication has been elaborated in this scene into a vehicle of Homer's poetics, for while Telemachus is seeking news of his father, he uses language that is closely associated with the description of epic *aoidē*. Clearly, it is song-as-knowledge that provides the model for the account Telemachus wants. Just as the singer (of song-as-knowledge) merely relays what the Muses speak, so Nestor should tell in as straightforward a manner as he can what he knows. Again, what the Muse reports is reliable because, as a goddess, she was present at the events and therefore knows them (see *Il.* 2.485); similarly, Nestor's account will be reliable, Telemachus hopes, because it is based on what Nestor has seen himself or heard on good authority.[11]

In Telemachus' view, pity is an emotion that can only obscure the

[10] On the distanced and self-conscious use of *kleos* in the *Odyssey* generally, see Charles Segal, "*Kleos* and Its Ironies in the *Odyssey*," *L'Antiquité classique* 52 (1983): 22–47; and more recently Katz, *Penelope's Renown*, pp. 20–29.

[11] On the passive response appropriate to song-as-knowledge, see Walsh, *Varieties of Enchantment*, p. 14.

transmittal of information, by leading the speaker to temper or modify the bitter truth of his account; Telemachus therefore begs Nestor not to feel it. Yet pity, as I suggested at the close of the first half of this study, is an inherent part of song-as-understanding. A speech by Nestor imbued with pity could not transmit knowledge. It *could* afford understanding, but understanding, to the extent that it requires active judging and interpreting by the listeners, cannot release Telemachus from that "web of interpretation" he wishes to escape. What results from Telemachus' peculiar situation—being in dire need of candid speech— is a supplication at odds with itself: a solemn plea that the other feel none of the emotions appropriate to supplication. This internal contradiction suggests the impossibility of what Telemachus seeks: he asks Nestor to speak of events he has witnessed, yet to feel none of the emotions appropriate to such events. More generally, Telemachus' quest for information that is absolutely reliable and does not call for judgment or interpretation cannot succeed, for there is no such information to be had. Telemachus does indeed learn the truth about his father (4.555–60) from Menelaus, whose source was the omniscient god Proteus, but the news of Odysseus and Calypso—"the one who hides"—is of no use to Telemachus. It neither confirms Odysseus' death nor gives assurance of his imminent return, but merely perpetuates the inherent obscurity of the situation.

In one sense, Telemachus' mission to the Peloponnese is a failure, since he does not dispel the obscurity imposed on Odysseus by the gods. In another way, however, the mission is a resounding success, for Telemachus does grow to be his father's son in the benign light of Nestor's and Menelaus' admiring regard. Athena had breathed courage (*tharsos*) into the nervous Telemachus partly so that "he might have noble fame among men" (3.77–78). Telemachus' novel supplication, which stands the ceremony on its head, is calculated to win him fame. It shows him to be his father's son not only in its cleverness but in its appropriateness to the situation.

Thus, Nestor is seized by wonder (*sebas*, 3.123) when he looks on Telemachus. Having hailed Odysseus as unsurpassed in cunning intelligence (*mētis*) and tricks (*doloi*), he praises Telemachus' words (*muthoi*) as being similar (*eoikotes*) to his father's. "Nor," he adds, "would you expect a young man to speak so appropriately (*eoikota*) (3.123–25). *Eoikos* catches both the similarity of Telemachus' clever speech to Odysseus' tricks and the appropriateness of his anomalous supplication to the circumstances.[12] Telemachus' speech is praiseworthy both for its

---

[12] See Heubeck, West, and Hainsworth, *Commentary*, note on 3.124–25. On Tele-

cleverness and appropriateness. It marks him at once as being like his father and yet commendable in his own right, a young man whose speech belies his youth. Telemachus' own burgeoning powers ought to be sufficient for him in dealing with the menace confronting him. Telemachus does not succeed in obtaining secure and useful information about Odysseus, but he is afforded the opportunity to understand his sonship, by judging the excellence of his own speech and the effect he is able to produce in his listeners. His own powers are as much of his father's presence as he needs.

It is noteworthy that Nestor, Menelaus, and Helen in fact all respond emotionally to Telemachus—despite his urgent request that they not do so—and such emotions are potentially what is most illuminating to Telemachus about his relationship to his father. Thus, Menelaus notices his young visitor weeping at Menelaus' warm reminiscences of Odysseus, and debates whether he should leave the young man to his memories or ask him straight out if he is Odysseus' son (4.116–19). Helen, too, debates whether to say what is on her mind in regard to the young stranger: "Shall I lie or speak the truth?" (4.140). Menelaus and Helen both feel the pity and shame, or the embarrassment, that Telemachus later asks Menelaus not to feel (4.326). Nestor and Menelaus both praise Telemachus for the eminence of his heritage and offer their assurances that he is worthy of his father (see 3.123–25, 199–200, 375–79 and 4.148–54, 611). Their words do not offer Telemachus sure knowledge, but rather a sense of his own mettle. If Telemachus is seeking his father—Nestor, Menelaus, and Helen seem to say—he need look no further than himself.

We are left with a paradox. As Eurymachus' attack on Halitherses' solemn pronouncement indicated, no human speech—no matter how august or apparently authoritative—is beyond criticism. Moreover, as the unending debate about Odysseus' whereabouts and the significance of his absence indicates, no human speech can lay undisputed claim to objective truth: the reliability of any statement can be undermined by pointing to the self-interested motives of the person who speaks. That said, the emotional speeches of Nestor and Menelaus do have power to teach Telemachus about himself. They cannot answer his questions and so determine his course of action in regard to the suitors, but they can assure him of his mettle and his status as a son, through the pity and respect they feel and express.

Because Nestor and Menelaus answer Telemachus' request in sur-

---

machus' "likeness" to Odysseus, see Peter V. Jones, "The *Kleos* of Telemachus: *Odyssey* 1.95," *American Journal of Philology* 109 (1988): 496–506, pp. 501–6; and Edwards, *Achilles in the "Odyssey,"* pp. 28–30.

prising and unexpected ways, we are led to question his odd supplication and the poetics that underlie it. Indeed, the *Odyssey* is structured here to suggest that Telemachus has misconstrued the nature of song and its application to his search. The very terms of his supplication imply the impossible nature of his mission—a supplication that begs a person to avoid the very emotions that elsewhere conduce to a suppliant's success. Indeed, we have seen how the emotions his hosts have for Telemachus—emotions Telemachus has asked them *not* to feel—are what is most truly revealing concerning Telemachus' parentage. The *Odyssey* seems implicitly to assert, against Telemachus, the nature of song as something necessarily and properly imbued with pity and shame. Song is just the opposite of that unemotional (and, therefore—Telemachus thinks—reliable) account for which Telemachus supplicates. Song is enlightening, but it enlightens in the manner of supplication—that is, by arousing emotions in the listener and inviting him to reflect on them.

Telemachus' inverted supplication and the response it excites in Nestor illuminate the poet's invocation of the Muses in the second book of the *Iliad;* indeed, they sound like a variation on that invocation. As we have seen, the poet prays to the Muses because he is powerless without them to tell of the troops that fought at Troy (see *Il.* 2.484–93). What stands out in that invocation is the poet's radical dependency. His invocation is different from other prayers addressed to the gods, in that the poet has no *quid pro quo,* that is, nothing to offer the Muses in return for their help.[13] The very absence of a proposed exchange itself implies the depths of human ignorance ("for we hear only reports, and know nothing" *Il.* 2.486), and hence the crucial importance of the Muses' help. Yet by stressing the profundity of his ignorance, the poet's invocation unavoidably casts doubt on the claim of *aoidē* to afford an escape from it. For if ignorance is truly and necessarily part of moral existence, can it be so magically cured by a kindly goddess's intervention? In short, the poet's suppliant mode suggests the impossibility of what he asks.

Telemachus' self-contradictory supplication expands on the tensions to be found in *Iliad* 2, where it is the poet who begs the Muses for help. Both suppliants seek reliable news about the past, and in both cases the very modality of supplication suggests the impossibility of what is so urgently sought. Telemachus' urgent plea that the other feel none of the emotions that usually attend urgent pleas brings into sharper focus

---

[13] On the form of Greek prayer and the emphasis it places on exchange, see above, Chapter 5.

the inherent contradictions in the poet's request that the Muses relieve him of the ignorance that is the mortal's lot.

In response to Telemachus' paradoxical supplication, Nestor speaks with unabashed emotion about Troy, and in doing so implicitly revises the invocation of the Muses in the second book of the *Iliad*. Nestor responds to Telemachus' request (which had, in fact, been for an un-emotional account) as though Telemachus had asked him to "remem-ber his grief" (cf. *emnēsas oïzuos*, 3.103). His account is more rhetorical than factual, and is designed to convey the sadness of the passage of great men:

> There war-like Ajax lies, there Achilles,
> There Patroclus, like the gods in counsel,
> There my own son—strong and blameless—
> Antilochus, unsurpassed in races and battles.
>
> (3.109–12)

Nestor's account conveys the pathos of the memories Telemachus has provoked, by stressing, too, the sheer enormity of the losses:

> Who
> Of mortal men could speak all these things?
> Not if you stayed five years, or six years
> Could you tell all the evils the godlike Achaeans suffered.
>
> (3.113–16)

Nestor's pathetic portrayal of the losses suffered by the Achaeans bears a suggestive resemblance to the invocation of the Muses. There, as here, the speaker emphasizes the inability of any mortal being to en-compass the theme (3.113–14 and *Il*. 2.486, 488–92). Nestor's piling up of time ("Not if you stayed five years, or six years") recalls the Iliadic poet's piling up of foil ("Not if I had ten tongues, ten mouths, an unbreakable voice, and a bronze heart," *Il*. 2.489–90). Yet, although Nestor uses language like that found in the invocation, he uses it to substantially different effect. For Nestor is not praising the knowledge of the Muse, but conveying the immensity of griefs. He is introducing an all-too-human reminiscence, rather than a transcendently guaran-teed account of distant events.

IV

One of the distinctive features of the *Odyssey* is that poets are actu-ally characters in it and performances of epic poetry form part of the narrative. Thus, the very story of the *Odyssey* provides the occasion for statements about the kind of thing that *aoidē* is. Below, I deal with two of these in particular: Odysseus' praise of Demodocus in Book 8, and Phemius' description of the poet's calling in Book 22. While poetry is described in both passages in a way that arguably suits "song-as-knowledge," it is significant that each takes place in a situation at least highly redolent of supplication and, in the case of Phemius, in the context of an actual ceremonial supplication. As I argue, that context must considerably modify what is said about poetry's claims to afford knowledge, and suggests instead a poetic of what I have called "song-as-understanding."

At an evening banquet among the Phaeacians, Odysseus praises the song Demodocus had sung earlier that day about the quarrel of Achilles and Odysseus.

> Demodocus, I praise you above all mortals!
> Surely, the Muse, Zeus's daughter, or Apollo was your teacher.
> For you sing the destruction of the Achaeans only too well—
> All that the Achaeans did and suffered and toiled,
> As though you yourself were present or heard from another!
>
> (8.487–91)

Odysseus' praise suggests that Demodocus has some unearthly access to matters that would normally be outside his ken. His ability to give accounts that have an eyewitness authenticity indicates his special affinity with the gods—the Muse or Apollo. While Odysseus' words could be construed as describing a conception of song like that reflected in the poets' invocation at the beginning of the Catalogue of the Ships in the second book of the *Iliad,* the differences are subtle yet significant.

Demodocus' song does not flow directly from the Muse; rather, it apparently springs from Demodocus' own talent, which has merely been trained or perfected by the gods. In Odysseus' graceful compliment, the Muse or Apollo is not *dictating* Demodocus' words (as the poet in *Iliad* 2 apparently envisioned that the Muses would); rather, these gods are imagined to be Demodocus' *teachers (Mous' edidaxe. . .ē Apollōn, 8.488).* As Odysseus says, "Among all men on earth, singers have their portion of honor *(timē)* and respect *(aidōs)*, because the Muse has taught them the paths of song and she loves the tribe of singers" (8.479–81). It is not merely song, as such, but the talent of the individual singer that affects the audience. Eumaeus' later description of the *aoidos* is to the same effect: the singer who has learned from the Muses how to sing produces "lovely" or "charming" *(himeroenta, 17.519)* words. His audience "yearns eagerly" (*amoton memaasin,* 17.520) to hear him and he "enchants" his listeners (*ethelge,* 17.521).

In the *Odyssey* song is a human activity, a form of human speaking, and a good song naturally elicits an audience's praise. So Odysseus hails Demodocus' first song of events at Troy and promises to spread his fame "among all men" if he produces a song on the subject Odysseus next suggests (8.487–98). Odysseus does not credit Demodocus with actually having knowledge of the events he recounts (or speaking the words of a god with knowledge). Rather, he praises him because he speaks as if he were an eyewitness with knowledge.

The Muse, to be sure, inspires the singer, but he is something more than her mouthpiece.[14] The singer vaunts of his uniqueness: Phemius claims to be *autodidaktos,* or "self-taught" (22.347). Rather than simply continuing the knowledge of events of old, he takes pride in producing something new. As Telemachus says, men especially celebrate the newest song (1.352).

Odysseus' praise for Demodocus thus reflects a view of the *aoidos* different from that found in *Iliad* 2, although Demodocus' power to speak so accurately about events he has not witnessed remains something divine and uncanny. Odysseus' response to the song he requests, however, shows *aoide* in a decidedly untranscendental way that clearly relates it to supplication. After praising Demodocus' skill, Odysseus suggests a specific topic for the poet's next song:

> . . .Sing the prodigy of the wooden
> Horse, that Epeius made with Athena,
> That Odysseus brought to the acropolis as a deceit,
> Having filled it with men who ravaged Troy.
>
> (8.492–95)

The song Demodocus sings in response arouses Odysseus to the most copious weeping:

> Odysseus
> Melted; a tear moistened the cheeks at his eyelashes.
> As a woman falls around her beloved husband and weeps,
> After he has fallen before the city and its people,
> While warding off the day of cruelty from city and children—
> She looks upon him dying and breathing his last,
> And prostrate beside him shrilly howls, while behind her,

---

[14] See Pucci, *Odysseus Polutropos,* pp. 230–32, on the constant effort in the *Odyssey* to circumscribe the responsibility of the Muses, and so to claim a certain autonomy for the poet.

The enemy prod her back and shoulders with spears
To take her off into bondage, to a life of toil and sorrow;
Her cheeks are worn with the most piteous woe:
And so Odysseus dropped a piteous tear.

(8.521–31)

Odysseus' response to Demodocus' song—weeping like a woman whose city has just been conquered—recalls the appeals made by women in the *Iliad* to arouse *eleos* in their husbands. Cleopatra described for Meleager "all the kinds of things that befall those whose cities are taken" (*Il.* 9.592) and Hector, in responding to Andromache's appeal for pity, imagines her desolation as she is led off into slavery after Hector's own death (*Il.* 6.447–65). What appeared in the *Iliad* as emotionally charged scenes are self-consciously recast here in the context of a poetic performance. The painful scenes of death and loss that Andromache, Cleopatra, and Patroclus conjure up in their pathetic appeals are used here to depict aesthetic response.[15]

The parallel between *aoidē* and supplication can be extended. The song that stirs Odysseus to weep like a woman being led off into captivity is different from the song that he apparently had envisioned. Odysseus had wanted, it seems clear, a song about one of his greatest victories—the stratagem that brought Troy down.[16] Demodocus' song, however, as described by Alcinous, is less a song of praise in Odysseus' honor than it is a tragic song about the "destruction (*oiton*) of the Argives, Danaans, and Troy," (8.578). Demodocus, to be sure, praises Odysseus, for he sings how "renowned Odysseus" (*agakluton Odussēa*, 8.502) headed a company of men who "sat in the Trojan agora, while hidden within the horse" (503). He sings, too, of Odysseus' excursion with Menelaus to the house of Deiphobus, and the fierce battle that ensued (8.517–20). Yet, Demodocus' song is less about Odysseus' intelligence and courage than about the fate (*aisa*, 8.511) that doomed Troy.

---

[15] A similar use of highly pathetic scenes from the *Iliad* in expressly aesthetic contexts in the *Odyssey* can be seen in Telemachus' snappish response to Penelope's demand that Phemius change the topic of his song. "Speech will be the men's concern—and especially mine, since power over this house belongs to me" (*muthos d'andressi melēsei / pasi, malista d'emoi: tou gar kratos est' eni oikōi*, 1.358–59). Telemachus' words inevitably recall Hector's farewell to Andromache: "War will be the men's concern—and especially mine—all who were born in Troy" (*polemos d'andressi melēsei / pasi, malista d'emoi, toi Iliōi eggegaasin*, Il. 6.492–93). The two passages differ markedly in their emotional coloring; yet it remains significant that what had appeared in the *Iliad* as a pathetic scene imbued with *eleos* is used in the *Odyssey* as part of a debate about aesthetic response.

[16] On the implications of the story of the wooden horse for the later portions of the poem dealing with Odysseus' return to Ithaca, see Ø. Anderson, "Odysseus and the Wooden Horse," *Symbolae Osloenses* 52 (1977): 5–18.

Demodocus sings about the Trojans' debate concerning what to do with the horse—to test it, destroy it, or preserve it (8.507–09). Their debate, however, seems predestined to lead to the most disastrous decision possible, since Troy's destruction was fated, "once the city contained the great wooden horse, where sat all the best of the Argives, bringing death and destruction to the Trojans" (8.511–13). Demodocus' song redounds to Odysseus' praise, but from the distinctive viewpoint of *aoidē:* Demodocus, that is, treats the story of the wooden horse as a song about destruction (*oitos*)—of Greeks as well as of Trojans (cf. 8.578)—and specifically about the destruction of Troy as an instance of fate, or *aisa* (cf. 8.511).

In its relationship to Odysseus (who is both its hero and its audience), Demodocus' song bears a distinct and suggestive similarity to the kind of speech characteristic of the suppliant. For like the suppliant's speech, Demodocus' song necessarily redounds to Odysseus' praise, but at the same time—and, again, like the suppliant's plea—shows the human toll that victory takes. The song reveals to Odysseus the kind of thing victory is. Thus, Odysseus' emotional response to the song mirrors Demodocus' poem: Odysseus' tears resemble those of the Trojan woman who has lost her husband in the fighting during the sack of Troy, and who is about to be led off into captivity by the Achaeans. Odysseus is brought, by Demodocus' song, to see his victory from the point of view of those who were destroyed by it.[17]

Odysseus' tears are not, to be sure, tears of regret: Demodocus' song is no more intended to make Odysseus "repent" his clever stratagem, than the suppliant's speech is meant to make the warrior repent his victory. The point, rather, of both Demodocus' song and the suppliant's speech, is to broaden the victor's understanding of victory from the limited perspectives of his current success to a more encompassing vision of the sorrows caused by victory and the griefs inherent even in the victor's life. Odysseus' tears, then, spring from something like *eleos*. The war widow's sorrow (*akhos*) is called "most pitiable" (*eleeinotaton*, 8.530); the piteousness of her sorrow, moreover, is the point of comparison with Odysseus, whose tear is also called "piteous" (*eleeinon*, 8.531).

Odysseus' response to Demodocus' song and its similarity to the pathetic scenes of loss described by Cleopatra and Andromache in the *Iliad* together throw a different light on the kind of thing that song is.

---

[17] That the simile describes a scene that would be appropriate in Demodocus' song is noted by Goldhill, *Poet's Voice*, pp. 53–54; and R. B. Rutherford, "The Philosophy of the *Odyssey*," *Journal of Hellenic Studies* 106 (1986): 145–62, pp. 155–56. Such scenes appear at *Od.* 9.41 and *Il.* 6.44–65, 9.591–94, 16.830–33, 19.291–300 and 22.59–76. See Heubeck, West, and Hainsworth, *Commentary*, note on 8.523–30.

Demodocus is able to sing of events he has never witnessed *kata kosmon*—"just as they were." Yet Odysseus weeps at Demodocus' account not because of its accuracy but because of the vividness with which the singer conjures up the events recounted in his song. Odysseus' tears strongly suggest an affinity between *aoidē* and supplication and indicate that the singer, like a suppliant, seeks to rouse a vivid memory of grief in the person listening. Odysseus' strongly emotional response shows that what is most significant about Demodocus' performance is not the poet's divine power to speak accurately about events to which he has had no personal access, so much as his power to convey the emotions inherent in an event.

Song, as it emerges from this scene, does not principally convey reliable knowledge about bygone events, but rather, at its best, produces skillful accounts that vividly convey what the events were like. "Like a singer, you skillfully (*epistamenōs*) spoke the dire griefs of all the Argives and of yourself," Alcinous praises Odysseus (11.368–69).[18] In the unusual instance where a member of the audience happens to have participated in the narrated events, there is an independent check on the accuracy of the poet's song. Even without such an independent check, however, a listener can say whether or not a song is well-formed and skillfully done. For the skillful quality of the narrative does not rest on its literal accuracy but on its ability to convey a sense of what the events were like. It is the generalizing power of a skillful song that inspires the appropriate emotions in the audience and encourages the listeners to reflect on what they feel.

The several parallels between Demodocus' song and supplication prompt me to suggest one more parallel: that Odysseus' "piteous tear" (8.531) in response to the widow's "most pitiable grief" (8.530) reflects his better understanding of his victory. Through the song of the wooden horse—a tale, as Demodocus presents it, of the "destruction of the Argives, Danaans, and Troy" (8.578)—Odysseus is not confined to the victor's perspective. His tears evidently reflect a sense of the painfulness that is inextricable from victory, and the simile comparing his tears to the widow's implies that, in responding to Demodocus' poem,

[18] The word *epistamenōs* (11.368) refers to technical expertise elsewhere in the *Odyssey:* for example, the way a skilled carpenter hews timber and planes it straight (see 5.245, 17.341, and 21.44), or the way experienced hunters bind the wound of an injured companion (19.457). *Epistamenōs,* therefore, refers to the "well-formedness" of Odysseus' tale—the shapeliness of the narrative that makes it similar to the products of singers (*aoidoi*), who are the technicians of narrative. On *aoidoi* as technicians of narrative, see 17.381–85, where Eumaeus speaks of the singer (*aoidos*) as a "public worker" (*dēmiourgos*) to be classed with prophets, healers, and carpenters. See also Gentili, *Poetry and Its Public,* p. 14. On *epistamenōs,* see Ford, *Homer: The Poetry of the Past,* p. 37.

he can see his victory from the victim's point of view as well. One of Odysseus' signal traits is that he knows the "mind of many men" (*Od.* 1.3), and, more particularly, as I will show in Chapter 7, that he anticipates how others (e.g., the relatives of the slain suitors) respond, in anger or sorrow, to his violence. On this reading, Odysseus' response to Demodocus' song is of a piece with his character elsewhere in the poem.

If this suggestion is accepted, then, Odysseus' ability in this scene to appreciate his victory in terms of its great human cost links him to Achilles in the final book of the *Iliad*. Both men are brought to a coign of vantage from which they can appreciate both the magnitude of victory and the inescapability of grief. Significantly, however, the hero's understanding—which is brought about in the *Iliad* by the old king's supplication that the hero "remember" (that is, vividly imagine the pathetic scenes Priam describes)—is created in the *Odyssey* by *aoidē* and its vivid narrative of pathetically colored scenes of loss. *Aoidē* resembles supplication not least in its ability to afford its listeners an intensified experience of others' grief and an insight into one's own experience of it.

Perhaps the most striking instance of the affinity between *aoidē* and supplication in the *Odyssey* occurs in the aftermath of Odysseus' slaughter of the suitors, when Phemius, the singer of epic verse, supplicates Odysseus to spare his life:

> I kneel before you, Odysseus; feel reverence and pity me.
> Sorrow will visit you hereafter if you slay
> The singer who sings for gods and men.
> I am self-taught; a god has implanted in me
> Lays of every kind. I am fit to sing before you
> As before a god. Do not cut my throat!
> Telemachus, your own son, will tell you
> It was not my will or desire to come to your home
> To entertain the suitors at their banquets.
> Outnumbered and overpowered, I was brought by force.
>
> (22.344–53)

Phemius claims a powerful authority for song, which he presents as having close affinities with the gods: the singer's audience comprises not only mortals but gods as well, and song has its ultimate source in the gods. Phemius' claims have a pathetic ring to them, however, since he makes them while pleading for his life. His dire situation to a considerable extent belies his pretensions to a godlike authority. Phemius' plight flows inexorably from introducing *aoidoi* into the *Odyssey's* cast of characters and inserting them into the society described in the poem. As something produced by mortal singers, *aoidē* is immersed in the "real" world and is subject to the political struggles for domination in that world. Phemius is in the grip of the power struggle on Ithaca, first compelled by the suitors to entertain them and now threatened with death for having done what he was forced to do.

As Pietro Pucci has pointed out, Phemius is now in the same predicament as he claims to have been when the suitors held sway: he is under the threat of violence.[19] The poet's vulnerability to power, as Pucci suggests, inevitably casts doubt on the veracity of what he sings. Previously, Phemius sang songs that pleased the suitors. His song of the Achaeans' "dire" (*lugron*) return home was acutely distressing to Penelope because of its unhappy implications for Odysseus' fate (1.325–27); these same implications could only comfort the suitors and assure them of a continued idyll at the expense of Odysseus' household.

With a change in power, however, Phemius changes his allegiance and promises to "sing before [Odysseus] as before a god" (22.348–49). Phemius himself emphasizes his flexibility, announcing that he can sing "lays of every kind" (*oimas pantoias*, 22.347–48). It appears, then, that the singer is at the mercy of his audience: he must sing whatever he thinks will please the particular group for whom he performs on any given occasion. This same point was made more mildly by Telemachus, when he observed that poets are not to blame for their songs since their song is dictated by the audience's preference for whatever is newest (see 1.346–59).

Phemius' subjection to political forces considerably undercuts his claims to divine authority. While Odysseus in fact spares Phemius' life, he does so because Telemachus intercedes on his behalf, rather than from any reverence for the singer's prestige. Yet, if the poet cannot claim to an authority that transcends the struggles of the mortal world, is he therefore lacking in any authority? I would argue that *aoidē*, even construed as human speech, is something more than a reflection of the wishes or whims of its audience. Phemius' song of the Achaeans' *nostoi* was genuinely able to convey the painfulness of the "dire" events befalling the warriors during their return home. His song may have reassured the suitors, but that does not detract from its power to represent vivid pictures of sorrowful experiences. Penelope's tears tell partly of the partisan quality of Phemius' song but, perhaps more

---

[19] See Pucci, *Odysseus Polutropos*, pp. 229–35.

importantly, also reflect the real power of his song to move those who hear it.

As presented in the *Odyssey*, therefore, *aoidē* is authoritative but its authority is not of that transcendent kind that belongs to the Muses (privileged knowers of the distant past). It is like the paradoxical authority exerted by the suppliant, who articulates compellingly for his listener what the experience of grief or loss is like. In the next chapter, I consider in more detail the distinctive authority of *aoidē*.

CHAPTER 7

Morality and the Belly

I

Aoidē seems wedded to a particular view of the relation between gods and men. When characters in the *Odyssey* speak about *aoidē,* they typically refer to it as dealing with evils imposed on mortals by the gods. So, for example, Alcinous says, in asking his guest why he weeps at the poet Demodocus' songs: "[The gods] have apportioned destruction (*olethron*) to men so that there may be song (*aoidē*) thereafter" (8.579–80). Similarly, Telemachus defends Phemius, whose song about the Achaeans' disastrous return home from Troy has proved so distressing for Penelope, by saying that singers are not "to blame" (*aitioi*) for the evils they sing about; rather, Zeus is "to blame" (*aitios*) since he gives whatever lot he pleases to everyone (see 1.347–49). Phemius' song in the first book of the *Odyssey,* too, concerns the "dire return of the Achaeans, which Pallas Athena sent on them" (1.327).

As narratives about the evils sent on mortals by the gods, the *aoidai* performed in the *Odyssey* resemble the *Iliad,* which concludes with Achilles' insight that griefs have their ultimate source in the lots meted out by Zeus. More deeply, the poetic implicit in that final scene is inextricably linked to a view of griefs as inherent in the very fabric of mortal life; such a view underlies that broad sympathy with the griefs of Achaeans and Trojans alike that animates the *Iliad* throughout and that finally finds expression in the *philotēs* between Achilles and Priam. If we bear in mind the typical theme of *aoidai* in the *Odyssey*—griefs sent to mortals by the gods—and the similarity of this theme to Achilles' insight in *Iliad* 24, the opening speech of Zeus in the first book of the *Odyssey* seems to address a question of poetics.

Ah! how mortals always hold the gods responsible!
For they say evils come from us: but they themselves
By their own folly have evils beyond their fated portion—
As, even now, Aegisthus has transgressed his portion,
By marrying Agamemnon's wedded wife, and killing him on his day
    of return,
Although he knew it meant utter destruction, since we had warned
    him
Through Hermes the watchful, the slayer of Argos,
Not to kill him or to court his wife.

                                        (1.32–39)

Zeus's comments at the very beginning of the *Odyssey* seem to take up
and criticize Achilles' insight at the end of the *Iliad*.[1] Achilles' insight
was precisely that the gods *are* responsible for the evils in men's lives.
Zeus, however, points to a class of evils that, he claims, are "beyond
what is fated" (*hyper moron,* 1.34). Because these are the evils that men
bring about themselves by their own conduct, moral judgments are
highly relevant to such conduct. To comprehend the evils Aegisthus
endured, not only must one understand human fate, one must also be
able to judge human conduct. Zeus's complaint implicitly questions
the ability of *aoidē,* construed as a remembering of evils inherent in
mortal life, to convey a true understanding of such evils. For *aoidē*
seems to confine itself to—or at least to emphasize—the evils imposed
on mortals. If so, song ignores one of the most important things about
evil, that it is in substantial measure brought about by mortals' own
folly. In this chapter I shall try to show that the *Odyssey* implicitly
defends *aoidē* against Zeus's critique.

    Zeus's observations about men's responsibility for their own foolish
deeds have often been taken as a programmatic statement, setting forth
a more advanced conception of the gods and a more enlightened view
of divine justice and human responsibility than is to be found in the
Iliad.[2] Lloyd-Jones rightly cautions against seeing a moral progression
from the *Iliad* to the *Odyssey,* but even he finds that "moral issues are
infinitely simpler" than in the *Iliad*.[3] There is much in the *Odyssey* that
seems to confirm the view of the poem as embodying a straightfor-

---

[1] See Clay, *Wrath of Athena,* pp. 215–16, on the relation between *Iliad* 24 and Zeus's
speech in *Odyssey* 1.

[2] See, e.g., Dodds, *Greeks and the Irrational,* p. 32.

[3] Hugh Lloyd-Jones, *The Justice of Zeus* (Berkeley: University of California Press,
1971), p. 31. For more on the supposed "new morality" reflected in the *Odyssey,* see
Clay, *Wrath of Athena,* pp. 213–39; and Bernard Fenik, *Studies in the "Odyssey"* (Wiesbaden: Steiner, 1974), pp. 209–27.

ward morality in which the evil are punished and the good receive their just deserts. As Lloyd-Jones writes: "In the first half of the poem, the companions of Odysseus are warned by Tiresias of what will happen if they slaughter the cattle of the Sun; in the second half, the suitors are warned first by the old man Halitherses and later by the prophet Theoclymenus of what will happen if they persist in their wooing of Penelope. . . . It is true that the human characters sometimes blame the gods for their misfortunes, but the poet, unlike the poet of the *Iliad,* never in his own person blames the gods. . . . The survival of Odysseus and his triumph over the suitors are the reward of *aretē.*"[4]

In Lloyd-Jones' view, even if the *Odyssey* does not signal an "advance," it nonetheless expresses an "unquestionable difference" in moral climate from the *Iliad.*[5] If so, however, the new morality of the *Odyssey* poses a difficulty for the view of poetics described in the previous chapter. For the hallmark of morality is its *certainty:* the evil deserve punishment, and in the view of Lloyd-Jones and others, are duly punished in the *Odyssey.* Similarly, the good should be rewarded, and the *Odyssey* obligingly reunites its virtuous characters. A poem celebrating the reward of virtue and the punishment of vice is premised on the belief that the world works in a readily comprehensible way and would seem to posit the transcendental and objective truth that I have argued the *Odyssey* seems in fact to deny.

By way of addressing this apparent contradiction—between the *Odyssey* as a poem celebrating the certainties of reward and punishment, and the *Odyssey* as a poem immersed in the contingent and opaque—I begin by noting that, as Clay has emphasized, Zeus himself does not deny that the gods are responsible for some human misfortunes. "On the contrary," she writes, "his speech suggests the existence of two sources of evil: one that is fated and comes from the gods, and another that is over and above what is fated, a kind of evil men bring upon themselves."[6]

Moreover, as Clay has pointed out, the two conceptions of the gods' role in human affairs find expression throughout the poem, in which characters speak now of the gods sending evils without regard to the sufferer's deserts, and now of the gods punishing the wicked.[7] Even within the opening scene, Zeus's words do not go unchallenged. Ath-

---

[4] Lloyd-Jones, *Justice of Zeus,* p. 29.
[5] Ibid., p. 30.
[6] Clay, *Wrath of Athena,* p. 217.
[7] Ibid., pp. 221–26, where Clay has assembled a number of passages illustrating that "characters in the *Odyssey* simultaneously entertain two quite different views of the gods without, however, considering them to be inherently contradictory."

ena has no objection to Zeus's sentiments concerning Aegisthus, but she points out that Odysseus' sufferings are hardly explained by any misdeeds he may have committed: Odysseus "suffers sorrows" (*pēmata paskhei*, 1.49) as a prisoner on Calypso's island even though he has never failed to tend and honor the gods (see 1.45–62). Hermes will later describe Odysseus as "the most woeful" of men (*oïzurōtaton*, 5.105), and Athena's words seem to imply that he is someone to be pitied, for he has not deserved, as Aegisthus did, the evils he suffers. Indeed, all the gods, except for Poseidon, feel pity for Odysseus (*eleairon*, 1.19).

Rather than an authoritative pronouncement justifying the ways of the gods to men, Zeus's words emerge from this scene as defensive and self-serving. Just as on Ithaca every statement was liable to refutation and attack, so on Olympus, it appears that no statement can hope to command universal approval. The "web of interpretation", therefore, is not so much a feature of mortal life that distinguishes it from the gods, but rather a denial of *any* transcendental point, for not even Zeus's words are unimpeachable. Thus, it seems clear that the *Odyssey* cannot be taken as a straightforward "moral tale", since Zeus's attempt to impose on men some of the blame for their own evils leaves untouched the other ills that mortals do not bring about by their conduct. Even more strikingly, Zeus's example of Aegisthus is immediately countered by the case of Odysseus, who does not at all fit into Zeus's picture of human folly and the evils it brings about. Yet, to say that the *Odyssey* is not a simple morality tale does not explain what place and importance such moral sentiments have in the narrative. To suggest an answer to this question, I consider one of the most striking supplication scenes in the *Odyssey*.

II

It is a hallmark of the new moral tone of the *Odyssey* that supplication takes on an air of moral obligation. Not only is Zeus thought to protect suppliants,[8] but, as hosts in the *Odyssey* say, "all strangers and beggars are from Zeus."[9] In his office as Zeus Hiketēsios ("Zeus of the Suppliants"), he "punishes whoever errs" (*tinutai hos tis hamartēi*, 13.213–14). A suppliant is entitled to the same esteem as one's own brother.[10]

[8] See, e.g., 6.207–8; 7.165;9.270–71; 14.283–84.
[9] See 6.207–8; see also 17.475.
[10] See 8.546.

Thus, Odysseus' formal supplication of Arete when he arrives among the Phaeacians evinces a far more moralistic coloring than do analogous scenes in the *Iliad*. Odysseus wraps his arms around Arete's knees, and while all those assembled in the royal banquet hall look on in astonishment, he begs (*litaneuen,* 7.145):

> Arete, daughter of godlike Rexenor,
> After many toils, I come before your feet and knees,
> And these banqueters—may the gods grant them
> A happy life, and may each bequeath his children
> His wealth and the honor given him by the people.
> Send an escort to take me to my fatherland
> At once, since I suffer woes far from my friends.
>
> (7.146–52)

The different spirit typically animating the ceremony of supplication as it appears in the *Odyssey* is immediately apparent in the courtly reception the Phaeacians extend to their visitor. An adviser of the king, Echeneus, stirs Alcinous from his amazed silence and reminds him that it is "not beautiful and not fitting" (*ou. . .kallion oude eoike,* 159) to leave the suppliant lying on the ground. Echeneus bids the king seat the stranger and have wine prepared for a libation to Zeus, who watches over "suppliants who must be revered" (*hikatēisin aidoioisin,* 165).

The belief that Zeus watches over the suppliant ensures that the suppliant's plea is felt as imposing a moral obligation on the person supplicated. The suppliant does not merely seek to rouse shame (*aidōs*) in the other—a goal which, as presented in the *Iliad,* he may or may not succeed in achieving. Rather, as Echeneus says, suppliants are *aidoioi*—ones who *must* be revered. The quality of reverence—that is, the ability to arouse shame in others—is somehow inherent in the suppliant's very status as a suppliant in the *Odyssey* and contributes to the poem's distinctively moral tone.

A moral description does not capture every aspect of supplication as it appears in the *Odyssey,* however. At least as characteristic of the *Odyssey*'s presentation is the distinctive nature of the suppliant's misery. For what typically drives the suppliant in the *Odyssey* is hunger, referred to bathetically as the *gastēr,* or "belly." I argue below that the suppliant's hunger to an important extent undermines the morality surrounding the reception of the suppliant, as it is confidently expressed by characters in the *Odyssey.* Just as significantly, however, the suppliant's *gastēr* suggests the reasons why moral sentiments hold an important place in the *Odyssey* and furnishes a guide to the proper understanding of such sentiments.

In response to Alcinous' broad hint that the stranger may in fact be a
god in disguise, Odysseus hastens to insist that he is no divinity but
rather the most wretched of men:

> Alcinous, don't be misled. For not at all am I
> Like the immortals, who rule the broad heavens,
> In body or in nature, but like mortal men.
> Whoever you know bears woe especially—
> His equal am I in sorrows.
>
> (7.208–12)

But Odysseus adds something more to the declaration of his mortality:

> And many more evils could I speak
> All that I suffered by the gods' will.
> But let me eat, despite my grief,
> For nothing more doglike than the stomach
> Exists, which forces me to remember it
> In spite of my distress and the sorrow in my heart.
> So do I have sorrow in my heart, but always
> It bids me eat and drink, and everything
> I have endured I forget, in order to obey its demands.
>
> (7.213–21)

Odysseus' response to Alcinous is structured as a series of sequential
diminutions: 1) I am not a god; 2) I am a wretched mortal; and 3) I am a
creature of fleshly appetites, and therefore unable to dwell in memory
on my wretchedness. The first of these statements sets forth a view not
unlike that which Sarpedon described in his famous speech in *Iliad* 12:
Odysseus is neither immortal nor unageing; he is not a god. Odysseus'
emphasis on his wretchedness, in the second of the above statements,
recalls the pity Zeus feels for Achilles' divine horses and his comments
on the wretchedness of mortals: "There is nothing more woeful than
man, of all the things that breathe and move across the earth" (*Il.*
17.446–47). The third statement, however, is distinctive of the *Odyssey*,
for it describes an aspect of human wretchedness virtually unknown in
the *Iliad*—namely, that it cannot aspire to tragic grandeur and is rooted
in the vulgar and unremitting demands of the body. Pietro Pucci has
written illuminatingly on the importance of the belly in the *Odyssey*.
For Pucci, *gastēr* is the source of the characters' instinctual life and
reflects a provocative conception of the human being. Because "Odyssean man" is an appetitive creature, ruled by his hunger, Pucci writes,
he "lives under the empire of necessity and accordingly under the
phantasmatic, upsetting effects of *gastēr*. He endlessly returns to famil-

iar pleasures; he never ceases to disguise his kaleidoscopic self; he fights constantly to fill his belly and lose everything, for he obeys a master whose orders are incompatible, vicarious, and without reference."[11] Hunger is distinguished above all by its *insistence:* it emerges from the *Odyssey* as the most immediate and compelling of all motives. On the *gastēr's* account, humans are obliged to suffer buffets and blows (see 17.283) and, paradoxically, not to regard their safety or well-being. Thus, compelled by its *gastēr* the lion braves the winds and rain to attack a cow or sheep or stalk a deer (6.130–34).[12] As Pucci has shown, the *Odyssey* often recasts formulae so that the *Iliad's* references to heroic *thumos* become descriptions of *gastēr*.[13] The effect of this is at least in part a debunking one, in which the tragic sublimity of the *Iliad's* characters is revised as a pedestrian human need. Perhaps the most striking example of this is one that Pucci does not discuss. In Book 17, Odysseus assures Eumaeus that he can deal with the suitors; or more precisely, that he can deal with them because he *must* be able to do so:

> There is no hiding the growling stomach—
> Dire thing! which gives many evils to men.
>
> (17.286–87)

Again, after Antinous has struck him with the flung stool, Odysseus speaks of the suitor's effrontery:

> But Antinous has struck me on account of my wretched stomach—
> Dire thing! which gives many evils to men.
>
> (17.473–74)

In these passages the belly, which gives evils to mortals (*hē polla kak' anthrōpoisi didōsin,* 17.474), is substituted for Zeus himself, who doles out evil and good lots to mortals in Achilles' story (*Il.* 24.527–33). In the *Odyssey,* the cause of the evils imposed on mortals is immanent in the individual, who is necessarily held in the thrall of his appetites. The stomach is expressive, more generally, of necessity: that is, of mortal

[11] See Pucci, *Odysseus Polutropos,* p. 182. See also the discussions of: Jean-Pierre Vernant, "At Man's Table," in *The Cuisine of Sacrifice among the Greeks,* ed. Marcel Detienne and Jean-Pierre Vernant, trans. Paula Wissing (Chicago: University of Chicago Press, 1989), pp. 57–61; Marylin B. Arthur, "The Dream of a World without Women: Poetics and Circles of Order in the *Theogony* Prooemium," *Arethusa* 16 (1983): 97–116; and Jasper Svenbro, *La parole et le marbre: Aux origines de la poétique Grecque* (Lund: Studentlitteratur, 1976), pp. 54ff.

[12] On these lines, see Pucci, *Odysseus Polutropos,* pp. 157–64.

[13] Ibid., pp. 157–64 and 173–80.

life as lived in a world that does not regard the person's will or well-being. As Vernant has remarked, the *gastēr* "indicates the human condition in its totality. . . . The *gastēr* represents the ardent, bestial, and wild element in man, that internal animality that chains us to the need for food."[14]

In this case as elsewhere, the *Odyssey* seems at pains to avoid any hint of transcendence. Achilles' parable of the jars was an account of the yoke of necessity laid on mortals, but the evils came from a transcendent source outside the shifts and alarms of human life. Not so in the *Odyssey,* where the forces that consign the mortal to a life of duress and insecurity are themselves a part—an "organic" part, so to speak—of that life. Similarly, when Odysseus tells Eumaeus "on account of the destructive stomach, well-benched ships are fitted out for the barren sea to bring evils on one's enemies" (17.287–89), the reference is most naturally to pirates, but as Pucci has pointed out, it can refer to the Trojan War. Here, as elsewhere, the *Odyssey* seems deliberately to undercut the sublimity of the Iliadic characters by insisting that people are necessarily appetitive creatures and, as such, rooted in the vulgar concerns of daily life. In effect, the *Odyssey* is denying the paradoxical transcendence implicit in the Iliadic warrior's heroic, larger-than-life grief. An appetitive creature is compelled to disregard the memory of tragic sorrows by the insistence of his belly (7.215).

Odysseus' complaint in Book 7 of the *Odyssey* inevitably recalls the confrontation between Odysseus and Achilles in Book 19 of the *Iliad.* There, Achilles insisted on remembering griefs, and was sublimely indifferent to the demands of the stomach. Odysseus, in turn, urged the importance of "remembering drink and food," which, as developed by Odysseus in that scene, became a profound defense of the warrior society and its values. *Odyssey* 7 plainly sets *Iliad* 19 on its head: Achilles' heroic sublimity is replaced by a story of the grating baseness of human motivations. Odysseus betrays an Achillean wish to remember his griefs, without, however, achieving Achilles' sublime indifference to the body's demands.

As presented in the *Odyssey,* therefore, supplication not only calls forth moralistic views of the gods' role in human affairs, it counterposes against them a view of the individual as hungering and compelled throughout his life to satisfy his hunger by whatever means possible. Such a view not only debunks the heroic stance of the *Iliad,* but inevitably calls into question the attitude toward the world re-

[14] Vernant, "At Man's Table," p. 59.

flected in the moral assurances of the Phaeacians. For while the moral view of the world is inevitably one of clean and well-settled distinctions, appetitive beings must seek to satisfy their hunger through cunning, stealth, and deceit; in short, such creatures are necessarily bound to uncertainty.

Before addressing the relevance of hunger to the moral sentiments expressed by characters in the poem, I consider first the implications of *gastēr* for the poetics of the *Odyssey*. For, as Pucci has argued, two poetics are implicitly contrasted in Odysseus' response: that of hearts that remember griefs, and the poetics of bellies that forget griefs.[15] It is the latter that seems more distinctive of the *Odyssey,* where poetry is not simply human speech but, more particularly, the speech of beings with insistent needs that cannot be disregarded with the heroic disdain that Achilles (for example) seems to have for them.

This Odyssean "belly" poetic has startling affinities with blame poetry, which as Gregory Nagy has shown, is correlated with imagery that dwells on the devouring of meat.[16] Thus, the blamer is said to "fatten himself" on his blame; he is *margos,* or "gluttonous."[17] Similarly, the ravenous Odysseus verges on being a "blame poet" who debunks others' pretensions to nobility; his insistence on his hunger in *Odyssey* 7 undermines the sublimity of the *Iliad's* praise of the Achaean warriors, especially as this finds expression in the portrayal of Achilles' attitudes in *Iliad* 19. Insofar as it resembles blame poetry, the *Odyssey* is like the quarrelsome speech characteristic of such poetry and reflects a view of language as used in quarrels—multifarious, unreliable, and intended to impress. In *Iliad* 20, Aeneas had characterized wrangling words:

> Flexible is the tongue of mortals; it has many words
> Of all kinds, a great rangeland of words here and here.
> The word you speak—such is what you'll hear.
>
> (20.248–50)[18]

---

[15] See Pucci, *Odysseus Polutropos*, p. 175. William G. Thalmann, *Conventions of Form and Thought in Early Greek Epic Poetry* (Baltimore: Johns Hopkins University Press, 1984), pp. 143–46, discusses song and belly as antithetical and polarized features of the banquet: on the one hand, song is an adornment of the table's abundance; in contrast, the belly is what hungers to be fed from it. As Pucci has convincingly shown, however, the urgency of the belly's demands is significant for an understanding of the poetics inherent in the *Odyssey*.

[16] See Nagy, *Best of the Achaeans*, pp. 225–26.

[17] Nagy cites Pindar's description of Archilochus as a blame poet "fattened [*piainomenon*] on his hates" (*Pyth.* 2.55–56), and of his own praise-poetry as providing the envious a "relish" (*opson*) to eat (*Nem.* 8.21). See also his discussion of the Iros-episode (*Od.* 18.1–19) in *Best of the Achaeans*, pp. 229–30.

[18] On the translation of *nomos* as "rangeland" see Ford, *Homer: The Poetry of the Past*, pp. 66–68.

Aeneas' description of wrangling words is suggestively like the *Odyssey* itself. For the *Odyssey*, too, is "flexible" (*streptē*) and opaque: the very opposite of that lucid transparence that seems to characterize the *Iliad*. Words spoken by characters within the *Odyssey* do not reliably represent their true meaning, but are tactical moves intended to secure the speaker's position in a given situation: very often, what characters in the *Odyssey* say—rather like what quarrellers say—is largely a function of what they hear. As an utterance of appetitive creatures, poetry is inherently unreliable, since what is said must always be referred to the speaker's sense of his best advantage. Thus when Odysseus returns, Phemius is as willing to sing in a way that pleases his new master as he had been to gratify the suitors (see 22.344–53).

Moreover, the *Odyssey* makes the point that narratives spreading another's renown have their source in the narrator's having been the beneficiary of the other's largess (see 14.402–5, 17.418, and 19.332–34). The wanderer is the means *par excellence* in the *Odyssey* of disseminating the host's renown. Thus, when the disguised Odysseus is begging from the suitors, he promises Antinous that, should the young man be generous, he will spread his renown across the boundless earth (*egō de ke se kleiō kat' apeirona gaian*, 17.418). A. T. Edwards remarks, "The *Odyssey*. . .differ[s] from the *Iliad*. . .in regarding *xeiniē* [hospitality] as a source of *kleos*."[19] Yet one effect of this new source of *kleos* is to undermine the reliability of "fame." For the wanderer is by no means a disinterested observer. The very theme of the wanderer's report—the host's hospitality—is a reason for being skeptical about what he says, since his praise necessarily has an element of self-seeking in it. As Eumaeus tells the disguised Odysseus, for example, Penelope does not credit the stories told by wanderers (*alētai*), because they are unwilling to speak true things (*alēthea*) but rather say whatever they think will most ingratiate them with their host and so secure a more generous reception (see 14.124–25). The acoustic similarity of "wanderer" (*alētēs*, 14.124; see also *alēthēn*, "I have wandered," 14.120), and "truth" (*alēthea*, 14.125) seems to affirm a close linkage between the two. The wanderer speaks "*alēthea*": the Greek word is translated "true things," but, in its root sense, the word means "things not forgotten" (from *a* + *lanthanomai*).[20] The affinity between the guest and renown shows the pertinence of this etymological sense: the wanderer ensures

---

[19] Edwards, *Achilles in the "Odyssey,"* p. 74.
[20] On *alētheia*, see Thomas Cole, "Archaic Truth," *Quaderni Urbinati di Cultura Classica* 13 (1983): 7–28; and Detienne, *Maîtres de vérité*, pp. 15–27. The homophony of *alēthēn* ("I have wandered") and *alētheia* has been noted and commented on by Goldhill, *Poet's Voice*, p. 38.

that his hosts' excellences are not overlooked and that their fame is perpetuated.

Yet this etymology further suggests that "true things" are not at all perspicuous or easily judged. Penelope appreciates that wanderers, because they depend on their hosts for food, have every reason to lie. Penelope therefore resists the "linguistic guarantee" linking "wanderers" (*alētai*) and "truth" (*alētheia*): even the clearest possible report must be doubted, because the wanderer is not a disinterested source. To credit what the wanderer says would be to mistake the world for the kind of place where meanings are easily and transparently present, and where the individual is not required to scrutinize and be skeptical. The narratives of the wanderers, as appetitive beings, are necessarily opaque and indirect, and finally impenetrable—the very opposite of accounts that reliably and transparently reflect a world where the righteous are surely rewarded and evil-doers are just as surely punished.

Thus, Odysseus' speech about *gastēr* offers a key to the poem's distinctive vision of an opaque and unknowable world. The *gastēr* does not, however, simply undermine or subvert the moral view of the world. Rather, *gastēr* has the peculiar property of making moral considerations *relevant* to humans, while at the same time making moral judgments *inherently uncertain*. That the belly makes moral distinctions relevant can be appreciated if we compare the Iliadic warrior to the characters in the *Odyssey*. The main characters of the *Iliad* represent only a tiny segment of humanity: they are aristocrats, predominantly male, and typically warriors. Moreover, these characters are in general motivated only by the most sublime considerations. It goes without saying, for example, that the warriors in the *Iliad* willingly risk their lives daily in the battlefield in order to win "unperishing renown" (*kleos aphthiton*). They represent the very best of humanity; their ruin and death thus evince in the clearest way possible the shape of human fate.

Hence, Achilles' insight at the conclusion of the *Iliad* is that of a highly schematized character. He is the best of the Achaeans in every way—the most feared on the battlefield, the most staunchly insistent on his own honor, and the most passionately distraught at the death of a companion. There is nothing vulgar or pedestrian about him. He is the son of a goddess, and beyond such lowly physical considerations as eating. His relationship to Patroclus is ardent and intense, yet apparently unrelated to sexual passion.[21] The canons of morality are in an

---

[21] On the question whether Achilles and Patroclus were lovers, see above, Chapter 3.

important way irrelevant to Achilles. Even though he intends his withdrawal to cause the death of his comrades-in-arms, no one condemns
him as a murderer or traitor. It would distort the *Iliad* to blame
Achilles' perverse intractability for Patroclus' death, notwithstanding
the fact that by refusing Agamemnon's gifts he set in motion the chain
of events leading to the death of his companion. The important thing
about Achilles is the intensity of his passions. What makes Achilles
such a compelling figure, in spite of his highly unrealistic sublimity,
is precisely this intensity. Achilles enables the listener to experience
the tragedy of loss at once more powerfully and more understandingly than is possible in actual life. He is emblematic of mortal fate—
that is, of griefs as inherent in his or anyone's life. Achilles is considerably simplified, but that simplicity gives his passions a clarity
—and his understanding of them a lucidity—that is seldom available in
lived life.

The "artificiality" of Achilles—his impossible loftiness—means,
however, that the audience's experience of his misfortune as something "inflicted" cannot constitute a practical understanding of griefs.
Achilles has been simplified to the point where moral considerations
scarcely apply to him: *his* insight into sorrow as a part of human fate,
therefore, cannot suffice for actual persons. Those who listen to the
story of Achilles' wrath are more complex creatures than Achilles.
They respond not only to Achilles' searing passion, but to Odysseus'
more commonplace advice that "one cannot grieve with the stomach"
(*Il.* 19.225).

Actual persons have bellies: they must take nourishment; they need
to work in order to eat. Most are not warriors, and seek to avoid death
for as long as possible. They are not heroic and have not devoted their
lives to securing a "deathless renown." Moral categories are surely
relevant to creatures such as these. The ills they suffer are not, after all,
simply "inflicted" on them, as though there were no way to avoid
them, but are to some extent self-inflicted, since they spring from the
person's own conduct. Hesiod makes especially clear the link between
moral considerations and the scarcity that is the most fundamental
condition of mortals construed as "bellies." Thus, as Hesiod advises his
wayward brother Perses:

> The gods have hidden their sustenance from men:
> For easily, in a single day, could you obtain by work
> Enough to sustain you in idleness for a year. . . .
> But Zeus, angered in his heart, hid it all away.
> (Hesiod, *Works and Days,* 42–44, 47)

Because of the scarcity Zeus has inflicted on mortals, they must inevitably engage in some struggle or strife (*eris*): that is part of the human condition. Mortals must also choose, however, between the "good" *eris* and the "bad": that is the moral choice which their condition imposes on them. (See *Works and Days*, 11–24.) Strife in the *Works and Days* resembles the *gastēr* in the *Odyssey*, because it is a condition imposed on mortals and bringing in its train the need for moral choice.[22]

In this light, we can appreciate that morality itself—more particularly, the need to distinguish between right and wrong, and the need to believe that wrong-doers will be punished—is itself a sign of the mortal condition, for it grows from the individual's subjection to physical needs and from the scarcity of the resources to satisfy those needs. Morality is paradoxical, like so much else in the mortal world, for it is necessitated by those very conditions—scarcity and appetite—that undermine the certainty of moral judgments.

As emerges from the Phaeacians episode, morality is a phenomenon associated with the time after the golden age and bears the characteristics of the post-lapsarian era. The Phaeacians clearly still live (or believe that they live) in a golden age,[23] one of whose hallmarks is that mortals and immortals banquet together (see, e.g., Hesiod fr. 1.6–7 MW). At one point, Alcinous wonders aloud if the stranger is a god:

> But if he is one of the immortals come down from heaven
> Then this is some new contrivance of the gods,
> Since formerly they always appeared to us face-to-face
> When we sacrificed our glorious hecatombs,
> And dined by our side, seated at our tables.
>
> (7.199–203)

By referring to his hunger when he responds to Alcinous and by insisting that he is not a god Odysseus is in effect introducing his host to the post-Promethean age of scarcity and hunger, and indeed, the Phaeacians' reception of Odysseus will prove costly and destructive for them (see 13.125–83).[24] This age, in which mortals are "bellies," con-

---

[22] See Kevin Crotty, *Song and Action: The Victory Odes of Pindar* (Baltimore: Johns Hopkins University Press, 1982), pp. 42–47.

[23] ξυναὶ γὰρ τότε δαῖτες ἔσαν, ξυνοὶ δὲ θόωκοι/ἀθανάτοις τε θεοῖσι καταθνητοῖς τ'ἀνθρώποις (Hes. Fr. 1.6–7 MW). On the significance of the "golden age" for the Phaeacians episode, see Pierre Vidal-Naquet, *The Black Hunter: Forms of Thought and Forms of Society in the Greek World,* trans. Andrew Szegedy-Maszak (Baltimore: Johns Hopkins University Press, 1983), pp. 15–38. On the fellowship of the table between gods and mortals, see the discussion by Thalmann, *Conventions of Form and Thought,* pp. 100–102.

[24] On the petrification of the Phaeacians' ships, and the history of scholarly attempts to address it, see Peradotto, *Man in the Middle Voice,* pp. 77–80.

strained by their appetites, began when Prometheus deceived Zeus, and secured for mortals the edible parts of the sacrificial animal (Hesiod, *Theogony* 535–37). Of Prometheus' famous trick, Vernant writes: "When [Prometheus] set all the meat aside for the mortals, Prometheus made them a fool's bargain. To keep in the sacrificed animal all of what can be eaten implies that one becomes a *gastēr* oneself, that one begins an existence in which life can only be sustained or strength restored by stuffing one's paunch, time and again, just as the flesh and entrails of the ox are stuffed in the *gastēr*."[25]

As Vernant shows, Greek sacrifice and culinary practices are used mythically to explain the mortal condition—specifically, our condition as creatures who are constrained to satisfy our appetites. The banquet, which is the setting for Prometheus' trick and the definitive alienation of mortals from gods, is also used to express the morality necessitated by the new dispensation. Although gods and mortals no longer share banquets, gods are believed to eat with mortals in secret, by way of policing them. Thus, later on Ithaca, one of the suitors remonstrates with Antinous for his outrageous behavior toward the disguised Odysseus:

> Antinous, this was not well done, to strike the wretched wanderer.
> Destructive man! And what if he is a god from heaven?
> Indeed, gods come in the shape of all kinds of men,
> And roam through cities in different forms,
> Looking upon men's insolence and justice.
>
> (17.483–87)

In a world believed to work morally, the gods are thought to ensure, by their very presence, that mortals behave in an upright way. The gods remain among mortals in the post-Promethean era but are no longer clearly seen, nor indeed could they be. Only by remaining secret can the gods truly judge of mortals' characters. After the intimacies of the golden age, this distinctive presence of the gods as overseers of moral conduct bespeaks the gods' real absence from the life of mortals and the ambiguity of morality: a world that reliably conforms to moral laws is also beyond mortals' ability truly to know and grasp.

III

I have tried to show that the belly—and the conditions of scarcity that make the belly's demands onerous and distracting—make moral

---

[25] Vernant, "At Man's Table," pp. 60–61.

considerations necessary, for there is a commendable and a culpable way of satisfying one's hunger. Yet, at the same time, moral judgments are inherently uncertain, since they are made in a world where any such certainty is beyond mortals' reach. Properly understood, morality does not reflect a world-view at odds with a tragic vision of the mortal lot as one steeped in obscurity, since the very need to make moral distinctions, and the clinging uncertainty of these judgments, are themselves instances of the mortal condition. While moral considerations are undoubtedly necessary, therefore, they are not sufficient for a full appreciation of these characters and of the fates that befall them. A full understanding of events in the *Odyssey*—of the reasons why this or that person has suffered—often eludes the characters themselves. Their tendency is inevitably to explain events in a way that both edifies and reassures. Wherever possible, they see evil events as punishment from the gods for the person's evil deeds. Yet such narrow explanations of events are regularly misleading in the *Odyssey* and promote a dangerous complacency.

The most striking and significant example is Odysseus' response to Polyphemus after he has made his escape from the Cyclops' cave. Odysseus claims that the Cyclops brought on his own mutilation as a punishment for his misdeeds:

> Cyclops, he was no weakling, the man whose companions
> You ate in your hollow cave by strength and force.
> Only too surely were your evil deeds bound to catch you,
> Villain! since you did not scruple to eat the guests
> In your house: so Zeus and the other gods have repaid you.
>
> (9.475–79)

On the strength of his moral convictions, Odysseus makes bold to reveal his true name:

> Cyclops, if any of mortal men
> Asks about the shameful blinding of your eye,
> Tell them Odysseus, sacker of cities, blinded you,
> The son of Laertes, who dwells in Ithaca.
>
> (9.502–5)

Odysseus' ill-judged disclosure of his name results not from moral weakness, but precisely from the strength of his moral convictions. Odysseus is brought to boast over Polyphemus and to speak his own name because he views Polyphemus as justly ruined. Because the Cyclops' actions have surely, in Odysseus' view, earned him the anger of the gods, he can no longer pose a threat. He has been decisively crushed: it is—Odysseus therefore thinks—an occasion to boast. Of course, Odysseus is wrong. It seems clear that the evils Odysseus suffers after escaping the Cyclops arise because Polyphemus curses Odysseus upon learning his true identity:[26]

> Hear, dark Poseidon, shaker of the earth:
> If I am truly yours and you boast to be my father,
> Grant that Odysseus, sacker of cities, not return home—
> Laertes' son, who dwells in Ithaca.
> But if it is fated that he see his friends and reach
> His well-built house and his fatherland,
> Let his return be late and evil—after his companions' death,
> On a foreign ship, and let him find sorrows in his house.
>
> (9.528–35)

Polyphemus' curse outlines the action of the rest of the poem: the deaths of Odysseus' companions during his voyage homeward and the suitors' infestation of his house. In calling down these curses, Polyphemus carefully repeats Odysseus' name and the elaborate epithets which Odysseus himself had used in vaunting over Polyphemus' misfortune.

Notwithstanding Zeus's complaint that mortals blame the gods (1.32–3), therefore, mortals do in fact find others morally culpable—especially when they have just inflicted some injury on those others. Thus, Odysseus' vaunts over Polyphemus contain the judgment that Polyphemus is the cause of his own death, even though Odysseus was admittedly the physical cause of the Cyclops' blinding. Similarly, as Zeus suggests in laying down his challenge in the opening scene, Aegisthus had been the cause of his own death, even though Orestes wielded the blade that took his life. Anyone familiar with Aegisthus' deeds (his seduction of Clytaemnestra and his murder of Agamemnon) would judge that he "deserved" to die—in effect, that he caused his own death. As a result, Orestes has won renown, not censure, "amongst all men" (see 1.298–300).

Odysseus conceives of his deed as like Orestes'. He believes that anyone who heard of Polyphemus' deeds ("not scrupl[ing] to eat the

---

[26] That Odysseus' proclamation of his name enables Polyphemus to call down a curse on him is discussed by Goldhill, *Poet's Voice,* p. 33; Peradotto, *Man in the Middle Voice,* pp. 140–42; and Segal, "*Kleos* and Its Ironies." For a different view see George E. Dimock, *The Unity of the "Odyssey"* (Amherst: University of Massachusetts Press, 1989), p. 113, who argues that by taking vengeance and proclaiming his name, Odysseus succeeds in bringing Polyphemus to respect the gods.

guests in [his] house," 9.478) would agree that the Cyclops deserved just what he got. Odysseus' deed, like Orestes', should win him a broad-ranging renown; and so, he cries out his name, and bids Polyphemus tell it to all who ask. In fact, Odysseus' view of the situation is dangerously narrow and ill-considered. Odysseus cries out his name spontaneously, moved by his fury at Polyphemus (*kekotēoti thumōi*, 9.501). In his anger, Odysseus fails to appreciate the danger inherent in his confidence that all will blame Polyphemus for his behavior. For Poseidon will not think that his son's mutilation was merited: his sympathies are with his son, and his anger is reserved for any who would cause him physical harm.

It is true enough that no one would blame Odysseus for doing what he had to do to escape from Polyphemus' cave. Even Poseidon, whose anger follows Odysseus all the way home to Ithaca and then beyond, scarcely blames Odysseus, or judges him to be morally reprehensible; rather, he is simply and irreparably angry at Odysseus because he has maimed his son. Odysseus wrongly assumes, however, that because no one will blame him, all will praise him. Odysseus is too insensitive to the repercussions of what he has done and seems unaware of the necessary limitations on judgments such as his. Odysseus has, essentially, offered an interpretation of an act of violence—he asserts that the maiming of Polyphemus was just. Inevitably, however, there will be those—in this case, Poseidon—who look upon the result of violence as a catastrophe, even violence befalling one as villainous as Polyphemus. Indeed, there is a certain ineptitude in Odysseus' judgment that Polyphemus has been punished because he violated the codes of hospitality. To eat human flesh is so horrific as to be utterly beyond such codes. To accuse Polyphemus of "not scrupling" (*ouk hazeo*, 9.477) to eat "his guests" (*xeinous*, 477) is an unwarranted importing of one culture's ethics into another realm, where such ethics can have no meaning.

The story itself, as Odysseus tells it to the Phaeacians, undermines the interpretation Odysseus seeks to give it during his escape. Odysseus' escape from Polyphemus' cave is a tribute to Odysseus' inventiveness and self-restraint: in the most fearsome conditions he is able to consider coolly and calculate his best course. Odysseus emerges from the account he gives the Phaeacians as a man who can lie convincingly and maim dispassionately. Unaided by the gods and relying only on his wits, Odysseus manages to blind a monster and make his escape. The story Odysseus tells, then, concerns his own cunning intelligence.[27]

---

[27] The nested narrative of the Cyclops is apparently a sophisticated version of a widespread and morally uncomplicated folktale. On the affinities of the Polyphemus episode with folktales, see Justin Glenn, "The Polyphemus Folktale and Homer's Kyklōpeia," *Transactions of the American Philological Association* 102 (1971): 133–81; and the

During his escape, however, he offers Polyphemus a different explanation of the events in the cave: they were the result not of his own unsurpassable cleverness but of just punishment by the gods (9.479). This interpretation is simply not sufficient to the story he has told the Phaeacians, for it ignores Odysseus' responsibility for contriving and executing his gruesome stratagem.

In claiming that "Zeus and the other gods" have repaid Polyphemus, Odysseus seems to be trying to make the world a more secure place than it really is. For the gods have been notable by their absence during Odysseus' adventures in the Cyclops' cave: it was left to Odysseus' unaided resources to devise some method of escape. Odysseus' judgment, then, is self-serving, for by means of it he seeks to mitigate the sheer horror of what has befallen him and his companions. As against the Cyclops' unpitying brutality—which has reduced Odysseus' men to things and fodder—Odysseus wishes to see a world where evil deeds are surely punished.

In the *Odyssey* sound judgment appreciates its own limitations and a judgment that blithely assumes its indisputability is, to that extent, unstable. Odysseus makes his momentous mistake because, in his anger, he can look at Polyphemus only from his outraged point of view. He does not consider how Polyphemus' blinding might look to others—how, indeed, some might not at all care about the harm done to Odysseus and be concerned solely with the evil that has befallen the Cyclops.

A different way to make the same point is this: Odysseus, in his judgment of Polyphemus, is insensitive to the events as a "tale of griefs." To see the events as a tale of insolence punished is to mitigate to some degree the horror of the experience. It is also, however, to overlook the kind of thing violence is, and the effect it must inevitably have on at least some onlookers—for example, Poseidon—as a destruction that is to be lamented and, if possible, avenged.

IV

Moral pronouncements in the *Odyssey* should not be taken as an indication of the poet's outlook. As the story of Odysseus' escape from Polyphemus suggests, moral judgments are but one more example of statements—like oracles, or like the wanderer's assertion of eyewitness

---

discussions in Denys Page, *The Homeric Odyssey* (Oxford: Clarendon Press, 1955), and in Ludwig Radermacher, "Die Erzählungen der *Odyssee*," *Sitzungsberichte der Kais. Akademie der Wissenschaften in Wien, Philos.-Hist. Kl.* 178 (1915): 1–59, pp. 13–16.

knowledge—that seem authoritative and trustworthy but are not. Mortals are constrained to make moral judgments about the worthiness of their own conduct and that of others. Yet it is one sign of the mortal condition that such pronouncements cannot achieve the certainty and security they claim. In order to be a convincing account of why someone has suffered evils, a story must embrace not only moral choice but the concrete situation in which the choice is made, that is, what the person involved might regard as "necessity." The account must seek not merely to praise or to blame but also to show the moral agent's vulnerability to the circumstances imposed on him. Only such an account can do justice to mortals as creatures of the belly, whose moral choices are made within, and indeed occasioned by, the constraints of necessity. There are not many such accounts in the *Odyssey*, which more often portrays characters who fail to accommodate the necessary ambiguity of moral explanations in their accounts of events. One narrative that affords a beautiful and compelling account of evils befalling mortals, however, is Odysseus' tale of his companions' dire hunger and their fateful slaughter of the cattle of the sun.

Odysseus' account of their death is distinguished by the complexity of the causes that lead to his companions' destruction. Odysseus presents their story, I will argue, as a "tale of griefs," in which the companions make their fateful decision because of the distressed circumstances that have been sent by the gods. His version implicitly corrects the condemnation of the companions that we find in the prologue to the poem: "For they died by their own gross folly, The fools, who ate the cattle of the Sun" (1.7–8). The companions emerge, in Odysseus' narrative, as ordinary men tested beyond their strength, rather than as fools who blithely ignore the gods' express warnings. From the beginning of Odysseus' account of the companions' death, he makes clear that the gods have kept them all hopelessly marooned on the island of Trinacria, where the Sun's cattle graze. So, when Eurylochus opposes Odysseus' suggestion that they simply sail past the island, Odysseus recognizes that a "*daimōn* was planning evil things" (12.295).[28] Gales from the south then prevent Odysseus and his men from getting away from the island, until "hunger wearied their stomach" (332). A god also sends sleep to Odysseus, so that he is not present when the companions make their fateful decision (12.335–39).

The companions' decision to kill and eat the cattle, as presented by

---

[28] One reason why Odysseus might detect an evil-planning deity in Eurylochus' insolence is that Eurylochus' words—stressing the need to respect the natural rhythms of day and night and to heed the body's fatigue (12.279–93)—are similar to those that Odysseus himself had once urged on Achilles (see *Il.* 19.230–37).

Odysseus, is ultimately foolish but not mindless. They do not ignore the possible results but expressly weigh the consequences of slaying the cattle against those of refraining. Eurylochus' speech, in which he sets forth the outcome of each course, is the crucial part of Odysseus' account. As presented by Odysseus, Eurylochus says:

> Hear my words, companions in suffering evils:
> All deaths are hateful to wretched men,
> But the most piteous is to die of hunger and meet one's fate.
> Now come, let us take the best of the Sun's cattle
> And sacrifice to the gods in the broad heavens.
> Should we reach Ithaca, our fatherland,
> Immediately, a rich temple to the Sun
> We will build, and place there ornaments many and precious.
> But if, angered over his long-horned cattle,
> He wishes to destroy the ship, and the other gods agree—
> Then I prefer to die quickly swallowing water
> Than suffering long torments on a desert isle.
>
> (12.340–51)

Although Eurylochus' arguments are wrong, they are nonetheless compelling: he urges his companions to compare two ways of dying and to choose the lesser of two evils. Eurylochus' reasoning is the same as that of Ajax, in the *Iliad,* urging his comrades on to renewed fighting:

> Better to live or die in a moment
> Than to suffer long torments in the dreadful slaughter.
>
> (*Il.* 15.511–12)

Both Eurylochus and Ajax urge their fellows to take an immediately decisive action rather than to "suffer long torments" (*streugesthai, Il.* 15.512 and *Od.* 12.351). That Eurylochus' advice follows a heroic model only underscores the irony of this passage: Eurylochus' advice is ultimately but not obviously pernicious. It is compellingly persuasive, as its similarity to Ajax's battle-cry would indicate. Thus, far from rushing blindly to commit a forbidden act, the companions make a fateful decision—a wrong one, but one born of their distress. The story of the companions' death, in other words, is to a large extent a story of evils imposed by the gods and the companions' hapless effort to react to their extreme circumstances. Eurylochus seeks to articulate good reasons for killing the cattle, yet so in the grip of circumstances is he that his reasoning can only be spurious and leads to disastrous results. Thus, circumstances have overwhelmed the companions. They emerge as ordinary mortals—not heroes—who died simply because they were not heroically self-controlled and able to reason clearly while starving. Their death is at once "beyond fate" (for they have brought it on themselves by their foolish choice) and yet "fated" (for their death shows the overwhelming power of the gods, which is apparently massed against the companions). As told by Odysseus, the story of the companions' death is a story of the "destructive belly." It is a tale of griefs—a story of evils imposed by the gods on mortals—but one which accommodates a sense of human agency.

Odysseus' narrative of the companions' deaths reflects an understanding of evils which, later in the poem, he encapsulates for Amphinomus, one of the more benign suitors:

> Nothing frailer than man does earth nourish,
> Of all that breathes and moves across the earth.
> For he thinks that he will never suffer an evil
> While the gods give him strength and movement.
> But when the happy gods send catastrophe,
> He bears it unwillingly with an enduring heart.
> The mind of earthly men is whatever
> The father of men and gods brings on that day.
>
> (18.130–37)

Man is the frailest of creatures partly because he has the capacity to be the strongest. Thanks to his mind, or *noos,* he is capable of wisdom and genuine freedom in his choices and actions. For the most part, however, the *noos* simply reflects the person's immediate circumstances, and the mortal merely behaves as circumstances dictate. The companions may have thought they were deliberating; in fact, however, their hunger had pretty much destroyed their power to think correctly.

People make wrong choices and act badly—in a way that genuinely merits others' blame—but they do so because they are wholly contained within their circumstances. The companions, who are starving and so "choose" a possible swift death over what seems certain slow death, act wrongly (and so deserve our blame), but they act wrongly because they fail to disengage themselves from their immediate circumstances. Because they are totally immersed in the rigors of their distressing situation, they become the victims of their circumstances. Thus, pity and blame are at once appropriate in responding to the companions; they are at the same time moral agents and mortals.

V

The slaughter of the suitors by Odysseus may seem at first glance to be an emphatic vindication of the moral vision of the world, in which the evil-doer is surely vanquished. Indeed, in granting Phemius' and Medon's pleas that their lives be spared, Odysseus seems to point the moral: he spares them so that they may tell others "how much better good deeds are than evil deeds" (*hōs kakoergiēs euergesiē meg' ameinōn,* 22.374). Similarly, he seems to pronounce judgment on the suitors. When Eurycleia begins to cry out in triumph at the sight of the suitors' newly-slain corpses, Odysseus quickly silences her:

> Old woman, keep your joy to yourself, and do not cry out.
> It is not holy to boast over the slain.
> The gods' fate and their own wicked deeds have defeated them.
> They honored no one among men,
> Neither evil nor good, whoever approached them.
> And so, they met their fate through their own gross folly.
>
> (22.411–16)

Although Odysseus sounds like a judge pronouncing sentence, his attitude toward the suitors' deaths is significantly different, for example, from his treatment of the Cyclops, where his confidence that the gods had punished Polyphemus for his evil deeds led him to triumph over his victim and to proclaim his real name. Here, by contrast, Odysseus understands that the kinsmen of the slain will be grieved by the suitors' deaths and will in turn seek to be avenged.[29] He therefore bids Eurycleia (literally, "wide fame") to keep these events wrapped in silence.

"It is not holy (*hosiē*)," Odysseus says, "to boast over the dead." *Hosiē,* as Benveniste has shown, means "that which is permitted to men by the gods."[30] Hence, Odysseus' words seem to envision a moral universe in which the gods have laid down what is, and what is not, permitted. Equally important, however, is the novelty of Odysseus' proposition. Throughout the *Iliad,* the death of an enemy on the battle-

---

[29] See 23.118–22, 361–65.

[30] Benveniste, *Vocabulaire,* vol. 2, pp. 198–202. See also Henri Jeanmaire, "Le substantif *Hosia* et sa signification comme terme technique dans le vocabulaire religieux," *Revue des études grecques* 58 (1945): 66–89, p. 72; and M. H. A. L. H. van der Valk, "Quelques remarques sur le sens du nom *Hosia,*" *Revue des études grecques* 64 (1951): 417–422, p. 418.

field was the occasion par excellence for boasting. War was, precisely, an affair of boasting: the warrior fought in order to see if he would afford a vaunt to some one else or another to him (*Il.* 12.328).

Although the slaughter of the suitors, with its battle account, is the most Iliadic part of the *Odyssey,* it is paradoxically a battle in which *kleos* may *not* be won. Instead, the suitors' death must be kept shrouded in silence; indeed, it must be kept secret *because* it is a battle. If the suitor's death were a transparent work of justice that everyone—townspeople and kinsmen—would necessarily condone, there would be no need for secrecy and the deed could be openly announced. Odysseus, however, is scarcely the dispassionate dispenser of justice. Before the overt hostilities begin, he cries:

> Eurymachus! Not if you should return all my patrimony—
> Everything you now have or ever laid hands on,
> Not even then would I keep my hands from slaughter
> Until all the suitors have paid for their transgression:
> It's up to you—either fight
> Or fly, to see if you escape death and fate.
> But I think none of you will escape deep destruction.
>
> (22.61–67)

Odysseus' frenzy marks what follows as a battle scene, in which—as Redfield has argued—warriors become less than human, "monstrous and impure."[31] His fury has an elemental quality that likens it to that of Achilles, refusing Hector's plea:

> Dog, do not beg me by my knees and my parents.
> Would that I had the heart and power
> To eat you raw for what you did.
> Nobody will keep the dogs from your head,
> Not if ten and twenty-fold ransom
> They set before me, and promise more besides;
> Not if Dardan Priam should decree that you
> Be saved by gold—not even then will your mother
> Lay you to rest and bewail the son she bore.
> No! dogs and birds will eat you entirely!
>
> (*Il.* 22.345–54)

Thus, the slaughter of the suitors seems to court comparison with the battle books and to set them on their head, for in the *Odyssey,* war is what must *not* be made famous. As I have noted above, the poem seems

[31] Redfield, *Nature and Culture,* p. 201.

to reinterpret the warring of the *Iliad* along less sublime lines and to view it as motivated essentially by the belly. The battle scene in *Odyssey* 22 bears this out, for it is caused by the suitors' rapacious appetite. The battle thus embodies that "evil strife" (*kaka eris*) Hesiod describes in the opening verses of his *Works and Days* as "foster[ing] evil war and contention" (*Works and Days*, 14). The *eris* embodied in the slaughter is to be kept silent, on this reading, because it is of that lowly or evil kind that Hesiod describes.[32]

At a deeper level, however, there is a convergence between the view of war as it is presented in the *Iliad* and the war in Odysseus' house. In the *Iliad*, war emerged as an inescapable condition of mortal life. The heroic ethic was, in effect, an acknowledgment of the inexorable nature of strife: the warrior sought, by courageously facing death, to wrest something of permanence from the transiency of mortal life. In the slaughter scene war also emerges as an inescapable condition of mortal existence, for violence is the only means at Odysseus' disposal to secure his place within his household. Odysseus does not—indeed cannot—rise to some transcendent height to condemn the arch-deceiver Antinous but must meet him on his own ground. Odysseus not only outwits Antinous but outdoes him in ruthlessness. Antinous had planned to murder Telemachus but let himself be overruled by the other suitors; Odysseus, on the other hand, plans and executes the deaths of over a hundred of the islands' finest youths. Odysseus' vengeance bears a striking and troubling resemblance to Aegisthus' ambush of Agamemnon and his companions while they sat at table.[33]

In both the *Iliad* and the *Odyssey* war and strife are the limiting conditions of mortal existence. Even though Odysseus decisively puts an end to the suitors, his vengeance does not at all signal the return to some earlier state where right and wrong were readily distinguished. Odysseus returns not as a judge of universally recognized authority but as a trickster, able by wit and subterfuge finally to undermine the enemies in his house and to escape the wrath of their kinsmen. The bloodshed and uncertainty attending strife ensure that no act of vengeance will be universally acknowledged or condoned as just. Thus, Odysseus' vengeance does not end with an epiphany of good van-

---

[32] On the connections between Hesiod and the slaughter scene in the *Odyssey*, see Dieter Kaufman-Bühler, "Hesiod und die Tisis in der *Odyssee*," *Hermes* 84 (1956–57): 267–95.

[33] See Edwards, *Achilles in the "Odyssey,"* chap. 1, on the ambush (*lokhos*) motif in the *Odyssey* and, in particular, pp. 35–38, on the slaughter of the suitors as an ambush. Edwards' discussion makes clear the parallels between Odysseus and Aegisthus.

quishing evil, but with Odysseus demanding that it be kept silent. Odysseus' silencing of Eurycleia reflects his understanding that the revenge has only an equivocal claim to justice, at least insofar as others are unlikely to acknowledge it uniformly as just. His understanding of the griefs that the slaughter will inflict on the families of those slain leads to his insistence that the situation be shrouded in obscurity.[34]

Michael Nagler has recently suggested that Odysseus' violent slaughter of his own people is the "central problem" of the *Odyssey*.[35] Nagler argues that the proem, by insisting on Odysseus' innocence in regard to the companions' deaths, is in effect insisting on his innocence in the matter of the suitor's deaths. That is, the *Odyssey* is saying that even though Odysseus was the *instrument* of the suitors' deaths, he was not the *cause* of their deaths, which the suitors brought upon themselves. On this reading, Odysseus' speech to Eurycleia is a kind of washing of the hands by Odysseus, who insists that not he, but the gods and the suitors themselves are responsible for their deaths.

The slaughter is, indeed, one of the most deeply troubling aspects of the *Odyssey*. It seems to me to distort the *Odyssey*, however, to argue that the poem draws our attention to these unsettling elements in Odysseus' revenge, only to insist that they are not troubling at all. Instead, the *Odyssey* seems deliberately to emphasize the disturbing features, by stressing, for example, the differences in the degree of culpability that exist among the suitors. Antinous and Eurymachus are the most purely villainous, but the poet takes care to point out not only the essential decency of two other suitors, Amphinomus and Leodes, but also the fact that their decency did not save them from death.[36] It is characteristic of the ironic mode of the *Odyssey* that the sanest plan for resolving the suitors' crime is put forth by Eurymachus, one of the most villainous suitors, who argues that Antinous, the one person to blame (*aitios*, 22.48), has now died, and the pilfering of Odysseus' household can be made good by restitution. He asks Odysseus to "spare your

---

[34] Indeed, the *Odyssey* regularly points out the grieving caused by deaths, however justified the death was and however blameworthy the person killed. Notwithstanding Antinous' culpability, his father Eupeithes mourns him and tries to prompt others to seek vengeance (24.426–37). Similarly, Poseidon is angered at the blinding of Polyphemus and does not consider that Polyphemus hardly deserved better than he got. Finally, even Aegisthus—whose death seems to be universally regarded as just—was mourned and given his funeral rites rather than being abandoned for the dogs to eat (see 3.253–61). Thus, no act of violence in the *Odyssey*, however justified, ever quite achieves a consensus concerning its justice.

[35] See Michael N. Nagler, "Odysseus: The Proem and the Problem," *Classical Antiquity* 9 (1990): 335–56, p. 354.

[36] See, e.g., 18.119–56 (Amphinomus); 21.143–47 (Leodes); 22.310–25 (Leodes).

people" (*su de pheidao laōn / sōn*, 22.54–55), and promises to give "bronze and gold, until [Odysseus'] heart is warmed" (22.55–59). Here, as in Book 2, Eurymachus has a remarkable capacity to use moral judgments to baffle our sense of where right lies. For his words are, in a sense, true: the suitors' crime does indeed largely affect Odysseus' property and could be repaired without violence. Eurymachus captures what is morally troubling about the slaughter, but in doing so, he reduces moral qualms to mere sophistry, since he of all people is scarcely in a position to reprove Odysseus. Far from simplifying the moral issues, therefore, the *Odyssey* is at pains to show how complex and unsettling they are.

Nor, I think, does it do justice to Odysseus to construe his speech to Eurycleia as a simple denial of responsibility. To read his speech that way not only suggests that Odysseus learned nothing from the Polyphemus episode, but also ignores the insight that characterized his account of the companions' death—namely, that death for misdeeds is only partly a function of the evil-doer's character. Rather, Odysseus seems to understand the troubling features of his slaughter, and to give expression—above all, by his call for silence—to his understanding of the complexity of the suitors' deaths.

More precisely, Odysseus expresses the viewpoint not of the victor but of the slain. For it is the loser, typically, who sees past the other's moment of victory and bids him not to boast about his success. This point of view finds eloquent expression even within the *Iliad*. So, for example, Patroclus, as he lay dying, had sought to silence Hector's boast by the assurance that Hector's days, too, were numbered (see *Il.* 16.852–54). Patroclus denied that Hector was in fact the cause of Patroclus' death: "Destructive fate and Apollo have killed me, and, among men, Euphorbus: you are but the third cause of my death," (*Il.* 16.849–50).

Odysseus' injunction against boasting, like Patroclus' dying speech, attributes the suitors' death to causes other than Odysseus—"the gods' fate and their own wicked deeds" (22.413). Odysseus implies that he is only a third cause of the suitors' death. Yet Odysseus is not seeking to shift responsibility onto the suitors and thereby to deny his own; rather, he insists on the complexity of the causation of the suitors' deaths. Odysseus is well aware that he has killed the finest of the local youth—the "bulwark of the city"—and that he will have to confront the suitors' kinsmen, angered at the deaths of their brothers and sons (see 23.121–22, 361–65). In contrast to his attitude after blinding Polyphemus, Odysseus is under no illusion that all will condone the deed as just and praiseworthy. Thus, Odysseus' judgment of the evils that have befallen the suitors—their bloody deaths—proceeds from a broadened perspective which incorporates the loser's view as well as the victor's.

While Odysseus says that it is not holy to boast over the slain, his attitude is not simply one of piety, but rather evinces that same breadth of understanding that informed his response to the companions' deaths. Indeed, the suitors—apart from Antinous and Eurymachus and perhaps one or two others—are reminiscent of the companions in point of fecklessness. As we have already seen, what Odysseus tells Amphinomus, one of the suitors, about the frailty of mortals is equally true of the companions: mortals are the most wretched of creatures partly because they are for the most part incapable of seeing past their immediate situation. Their *noos*, which seems able to reason actively, in fact merely reflects their circumstances. Odysseus' insistence on silence reflects his understanding that his own acts, too, do not transcend their circumstances, and are subject to various and conflicting responses by those who observe them or hear of them. Odysseus' vengeance on the suitors is just saved from being reprehensible by the modesty of his claims concerning it, and his appreciation of what is ambiguous and equivocal in it.

VI

I have argued in this chapter that the *Odyssey* presents morality as a part or consequence of the mortal condition: moral judgments in the poem must be sensitive to the ambiguous play of fate and choice in human behavior. The *Odyssey* can be read as implicitly answering Zeus's opening complaint that men unjustly blame the gods for the evils that they bring upon themselves. Zeus's complaint was an attack on poetry as an account of human fate—that is, of the evils imposed on men by the gods. Poetry, Zeus implied, could not provide an adequate understanding of human griefs, for to a large extent these sorrows are brought about by mortals' own folly—a cause that *aoidē*, as a song of mortal fate, ignores. The *Odyssey* shows, however, that *aoidē* does not necessarily exclude tales of human folly, but that such folly can be only understood within the larger considerations of the evils that are part of mortal life. Such inherent evils are an aspect of our physical existence: man is a creature of the belly. Thus, the fated (*moira*) and that which is beyond fate (*hyper moron*) do not come in separate packets. Moral choice is necessarily made from within each person's circumstances and cannot be understood unless those circumstances are taken into account. To be a satisfying account of the evils that befall its characters, then, a narrative must accommodate the complexity of causes, the better to capture the felt importance of death and grief. It is the hallmark of Odysseus' account of the suitors' deaths that he achieves this and avoids the trap of construing his revenge in too narrowly moral a way.[37] Similarly, it is in large part because Odysseus is sensitive to the variety of possible responses to the suitors' deaths—because he understands that not all will hail it as a work of justice—that his revenge is successful.

The complexity of causation that informs the accounts of the companions' and the suitors' deaths is characteristic of epic *aoidē* in general. Dodds presented Agamemnon's apology to Achilles in *Iliad* 19 as an instance of this characteristic "over-determination."[38] "I am not the cause" (*ouk aitios eim'*, *Il.* 19.86), Agamemnon says, of taking Briseis from Achilles, "but Zeus and my fate and the Fury." Agamemnon is not seeking to deny responsibility, for in fact he is offering Achilles generous restitution for the offense offered him. Agamemnon's apology, as Dodds argues, reflects the characteristic multiplicity of causes in the *Iliad* and is not a sophistic ploy or piece of special pleading.

Over-determination is not only a characteristic of the *Iliad's* narrative, but is indispensable to song, insofar as it is a tale of human fate. Characters in the song's narrative necessarily act and are the "causes" of events. Only if causation is sufficiently complex and encompassing will an individual's action not be felt to exclude fate. Not only Agamemnon's act, for example, but the gods and fate, too, must have a role in the offense offered Achilles, if the story is to be one of human fate, rather than one of Agamemnon's folly. Moreover, complex causation better accords with the sense, fundamental to *aoidē,* that death and the experience of grief are of crucial importance. To assign a death to a single cause—for example, the victim's own previous folly—is in some way to diminish its importance. The death is too readily ex-

---

[37] The remarks by Peradotto, *Man in the Middle Voice,* p. 133, are illuminating. Peradotto refers to the "ambivalent attitude toward human action expressed, almost as if it were a programmatic statement, in Zeus's remarks, early in book 1 of the *Odyssey,* about the contending explanations of human suffering." Peradotto continues: "Are mortals fully developed agents who must be held responsible for their actions, or are they for the most part passive objects of divine activity, or, what may be closer to the tonalities of the whole text when all its contending voices are averaged out, do they feel themselves immersed in the action in such a way that, at least at times, 'doer' and 'done to' become inadequate categories, drawing a sharp line, legislating a boundary, where none is felt?"

[38] Dodds, "Agamemnon's Apology," in *Greeks and the Irrational,* pp. 1–27. See also Albin Lesky, "Göttliche und Menschliche Motivation im Homerischen Epos," *Sitzungsberichte der Heidelberger Akademie der Wissenschaften,* Phil. Hist. Kl. 4 (1961): 1–52.

plained thereby, and the painfulness of death is removed by rational demonstration.

Aoidē is an understanding of grief because it takes the emotion seriously on its own terms. Unlike the moral judgment that Zeus seems to call for in the prologue to the *Odyssey*, epic *aoidē* does not try to refer human suffering to a single cause or to remove its sting by seeking to dissolve it ultimately into its causes. Rather, it treats sorrow on its own terms, as something felt to be inflicted, not something deserved or avoidable. Only because it takes suffering seriously on its own terms can song offer an understanding of the experience. It enables that experience to be at once felt and observed; one can both be within an emotional situation and outside, able to view the situation with a certain objectivity. From that perspective, one may be able to judge the hero's responsibility for his own distress, but such judgment will not detract from the power of the hero's experience of grief.

Because song deals with evils by accommodating the complexity of their causes and therefore captures the importance of human suffering, its account of why men suffer evils is a more satisfying and more adequate account than blaming alone can be. Song does not necessarily exclude human folly, but neither does it diminish the importance of grief by reducing evils to the deserved and, therefore, untroubling consequences of peoples' own blameworthy conduct. The death of the companions is a striking example of the *Odyssey's* art: the companions are shown to be at once blameworthy and pitiable. They died because of their own "gross folly," as the prologue has it, but their deaths are not the less sad or deserving of pity for that.

VII

Aoidē, which in the *Iliad* had taken for its province only a tiny fraction of humanity, embraces more of life in the *Odyssey.* It is not the one-time wrath (*mēnis*) of the greatest of heroes that is "destructive," but the hunger that drives everyone—both the warrior and the beggar. Thus, Odysseus speaks of the "destructive belly" (*gastera oulomenēn,* 17.286–87) a phrase that invites comparison with the announced theme of the *Iliad*—Achilles' "destructive wrath" (*mēnin. . .oulomenēn, Il.* 1.1–2). Odysseus, on the verge of reentering his home again after an absence of twenty years, speaks—as it were—a prologue to the adventures he expects to find there:

> I am not unlearned in beatings and blows
> My spirit is hardy, since I have suffered much

On the waves and in war. Let this be added to those.
It is impossible to hide away the craving stomach—
Destructive thing!—that brings many evils on men:
Because of it, well-benched ships are equipped
For the barren sea, to bring evils to enemies.

(17.283–89)

This "prologue" to the battle books of the *Odyssey* puts the poem in self-conscious relation to the *Iliad,* offering the "destructive belly" as a theme to match the "destructive wrath" of Achilles. The *Odyssey* expands the scope of song from quasi-divine wrath to include the lowly appetites; indeed, it suggests that those appetites underlie more sublime-seeming motivations like *mēnis.* The *Odyssey* points to this expansion by applying the noble epithets of the *Iliad* to the everyday objects it has introduced to song. A phrase like the "destructive belly" is deliberately oxymoronic, juxtaposing the sublime and the bathetic. This juxtaposition is deeply characteristic of the *Odyssey,* a poem self-consciously engaged in broadening the scope of epic song. A word like "*oulomenē,*" which seems appropriate for sublime concepts, is now paired with the base things to which sublime concepts are ultimately reducible: not "wrath," then, but the "stomach" is *oulomenē.*

Aoidē derives its importance and its compelling beauty from the memories and aspirations of its listeners. Man's fate, which emerges with such crystal clarity in song, is only glimpsed dimly in life as it is lived. That is the source of song's power: it articulates in a concentrated and pellucid way what must be felt only vaguely and in a diffuse way in actual life. The compelling emotional effect of *aoidē* rests, however, on the listeners' own experiences of grief, and on their ability to see in the poem a vehicle to express feelings they have toward their own lives. The *Odyssey* reflects this deep affinity between song and audience by setting an epic hero in an everyday world, and by applying the noble epithets of epic songs to the base appetites which constitute a major portion of human desires and which are, in consequence, the source of so much misery. The *Odyssey* is not merely the story of Odysseus' return home; it is about *aoidē's* return to the homely. As I hope to show in more detail below, the *Odyssey* is in large part a poem about the connections between the poem and its audience.

CHAPTER 8

Supplication and Narrative

I

In the midst of Odysseus' grand recital of his adventures, Arete, the queen of the Phaeacians, interrupts to invite the admiration of those assembled for the man she proudly, and with some emphasis, calls "*my* guest" (*xeinos . . . emos,* 11.338): "How does this man seem to you in shape and size and intellect?" she asks rhetorically, before bidding the Phaeacians to bestow their wealth upon him. Alcinous, too, takes up the queen's suggestion, and bids Odysseus stay until the next day, so that the Phaeacians may accomplish their gift-giving. (See 11.352–54.) Odysseus' response to Alcinous' invitation seems unusually candid:

> Mighty Alcinous, famed among all your people,
> If you should bid me wait here a year
> Until you provide an escort and give me shining gifts
> I would be willing to do so, and more profit would I have
> To return to my beloved homeland with full hands.
> For more revered and better loved would I be
> To all who saw me returning to Ithaca.
>
> (11.355–61)

What is striking about Odysseus' response is that he shows that he has every reason to lie or distort the truth in order to win the Phaeacians' good will. For if he can obtain their benevolence, Odysseus can better ensure his welcome home. Because Odysseus is still radically dependent on his hosts, his speech might be suspect and inherently unreliable since it is plainly motivated by his need to obtain the host's good will. Even though Odysseus has been fed and is no longer hungry, his response is what may be expected of an appetitive creature: the more Odysseus possesses, the more honored he shall be. Because Odysseus is a creature of the belly and because he relies so deeply on Alcinous and Arete's good will, Odysseus' speech might be expected to invite skepticism about its truth and, ultimately, about its value.

Yet Alcinous, far from being skeptical, hastens to reassure Odysseus that, notwithstanding his wish for greater wealth to ensure a warm welcome in Ithaca, the Phaeacians do not look upon him as in any way "like a cozener or a thief—the sort the dark earth nourishes in droves—who devise lies from thin air" (11.363–65). Far from being put on guard about Odysseus' words, Alcinous assures his guest that he finds them praiseworthy:

> Your words are well-shaped; you have a noble mind,
> And like a singer you spoke understandingly
> The Argives' dire griefs and your own as well.

> (11.367–69)

In the story of his adventures, Odysseus has made no secret of his ability to cozen and steal. His story of the blinding of Polyphemus, for example, is almost a celebration of Odysseus' cleverness at deceit and at getting the upper hand. Notwithstanding the Polyphemus episode, however, Alcinous finds in Odysseus' narrative, which is characterized by the "shapeliness" of his words (*morphē epeōn,* 367), proof of his guest's "noble mind" (*phrenes esthlai* 367).

The fact that beautiful speech should reassure Alcinous—rather than putting him on his guard against a possible deception—may seem to reflect the Phaeacians' naïveté.[1] Yet earlier in the story, Odysseus himself had also deemed *morphē epeōn*—the beauty or shapeliness of speech—to be the sign of a person of noble mind. Thus, in rebuking a young Phaeacian prince (who had insulted the still unrecognized stranger), Odysseus contrasted the handsome youth's foolish speech with that of the person, less impressive to look at, whose words "a god crowns with shapeliness" (*morphēn epesi stephei,* 8.170).[2] The words of such a speaker evince "grace" (*kharis,* 8.175) and the beauty of his speech makes him preeminent at the assemblies (8.172). Even should he be unprepossessing in his appearance, says Odysseus, the people look upon him as a god when he makes his way through the city (see 8.173). Such is certainly the effect that Odysseus has had upon the assembled Phaeacians. While he has told his narrative, they have sat

---

[1] See, e.g., Thalmann, *Conventions of Form and Thought,* pp. 172–73.
[2] See Walsh, *Varieties of Enchantment,* p. 7.

"in silence . . . without a word" (*akēn . . . siōpēi*, 11.333), "entranced" (*kēlēthmōi . . . eskhonto*, 11.334).

Odysseus' words have the same effect on the swineherd Eumaeus, who is skeptical when his guest assures him that Odysseus is about to return (14.363–65) but even so is struck by the beauty of the stranger's speech:

> As when a man beholds a singer, who from the gods
> Has learned to sing words sweet to mortals:
> They yearn to hear him when he sings;
> Thus did he enthrall me, as we sat together.
>
> (17.518–21)

Eumaeus' skepticism about the truth of what the stranger reports does not extend to the stranger's character as reflected in his speech. "Sir, the tale you tell is blameless; not once have you said anything profitless or inappropriate," he at one point tells the stranger (14.508–9), whom he elsewhere praises as "not foolish" (*oude . . . anoēmōn*, 17.273), and as speaking "appropriately" (*kata moiran*, 17.580).[3]

So too, the Phaeacians are right not to be skeptical about Odysseus: he is a genuinely great hero, fully deserving of their admiration and their gifts. However ill-starred his visit may ultimately be for the Phaeacians, there can be no doubt that he is a truly eminent guest.

It appears, then, that Odysseus' response cannot be adequately judged simply from the viewpoint of the *gastēr;* there must be another point of view from which to evaluate his words and, more generally, suppliant speech. In this chapter, I will argue that the excellence of Odysseus' language—the "noble mind" (*phrenes esthlai*) reflected in his words—consists in its active embrace of griefs. As Alcinous says, Odysseus is able to "speak skillfully the griefs of all the Argives and [his] own" (11.369). This skillful speaking of griefs reflects a particular orientation towards them—that is, an ability to stand apart from them sufficiently to transmute them into a public narrative that conveys to others a sense of what the griefs were like. Because this objectivity toward one's experience—and the ability to conjure it up for others— shows in one's speech and does not depend on the literal truth or falsehood of one's account, speech is a reliable indicator of the speaker's character. In the *Odyssey* a person is assessed less on the basis of the veracity of his account than on the inherent quality of his storytelling.

---

[3] That Odysseus' lying tales present an accurate characterization of who he is, is argued by Katz, *Penelope's Renown*, p. 8; and P. Walcot, "Odysseus and the Art of Lying," *Ancient Society* 8 (1977): 1–19.

This is not an aesthetic criterion so much as an ethical one: an excellent narrative bespeaks a praiseworthy ability to stand apart from one's own painful experience.

A corollary of this argument is that the *gastēr* is not the sole instinctual source of the characters' behavior in the *Odyssey*. Pucci has rightly stressed the importance of the *gastēr* for an appreciation of the *Odyssey*, and, in particular, the troubling view of individuals as immersed in their contingent circumstances and driven, more or less blindly, by their appetites. As appetitive creatures, mortals have only a tenuous claim to a stable identity, since they vary with their fortunes and can scarcely remember or desire past their immediate need. Odysseus' false name "Nobody" (*Outis*) in the Cyclops episode is disturbingly appropriate for other characters as well—for instance, the companions and the suitors—whose sense of themselves depends on the vagaries of the moment. As a poem of the "destructive belly," the *Odyssey* undermines attempts to impose neat distinctions and clean moral precepts. Pucci describes the poem as involuted, complex, and "undecidable."

Important as Pucci's emphasis on the belly is, however, I believe it is finally insufficient as a model for understanding the *Odyssey* and its characters. The Phaeacians' response to Odysseus, I think, suggests where the insufficiency lies, since it would unduly diminish Odysseus' grand narrative to see it solely as a means of securing wealth and passage home, and therefore as unreliable. Despite Odysseus' ulterior motives, the narrative is impressively shaped and of extraordinary interest—the features that most intrigue the Phaeacian audience. The "shapeliness of [Odysseus'] words" (*morphē epeōn,* 11.367) is immediately apparent to his listeners and is distinct from the individual storyteller's sense of the advantage to be gained from telling his tale. Narrative—the possibility of narrative—reflects an aspect of the mortal above and beyond his appetites and the evils suffered or incurred on account of them. Narrative flows from the ability to remember past one's immediate circumstances; it is the sufferer's coming to grips with his past. While it cannot ultimately claim to transcend human speech, *aoidē* is nonetheless human speech at its most masterly in its ability to transform griefs into a kind of celebration of mortality. Thus, the action of the poem cannot be understood unless we appreciate the sufferer's ability actively to encompass and understand his mortal nature, which is the ultimate cause of his suffering. This ability ensures that mortals are not merely creatures of the belly and are formed by memories and desires apart from their immediate appetites.

To substantiate these remarks, I begin by considering the contrast between Odysseus' attitude toward his sufferings as expressed in his suppliant speeches in Book 7 and in Book 9. Upon his first arrival at the court of Arete and Alcinous, Odysseus thought of his griefs as oppressive and as a dead loss, whose effect had been to deprive him of his identity. One reason why Odysseus refused to speak his name in response to Arete's question was, as Mattes showed, that his bitter experiences had reduced him to something less than his full heroic self: in his wretched state, he was scarcely capable of claiming the full dignity of being "Odysseus, son of Laertes."[4] Odysseus' failure to name himself conveys the power of evils to obscure the person and suggests how dependent identity is on circumstance.

The contrast with Odysseus' attitude toward his griefs in Book 9 is striking. There, not only does he speak in a way that commands universal admiration, but he does so particularly in regard to his sorrows:

> But your spirit inclines to ask about my griefs
> So I may groan, sorrowing the more.
> What shall I speak first, and what next?
> The gods in heaven have given me many griefs . . .
>
> (9.12–15)

Odysseus' reference to his many griefs is no longer, as it was in Book 7, an insistence that he is the most wretched of mortals. Rather, it serves now as introductory foil to his impressive and long-delayed naming of himself: "I am Odysseus, Laertes' son, the fear of all men for my tricks, and my fame reaches the heavens" (9.19–20). The depth and number of his griefs now contribute to the stranger's eminence as one who has seen and known much. Odysseus' reference to his many sorrows is a preamble to his long story, which the Phaeacians enthusiastically praise, precisely as a tale of griefs. Alcinous commends Odysseus: "like a singer (aoidos) you spoke understandingly (epistamenōs) the Argives' dire griefs (kēdea), and your own as well," (11.368–69). Later on, he expressly bids Odysseus to continue his story or, more precisely, to "speak your griefs" (ta sa kēdea muthēsasthai, 11.376). In describing Odysseus' narrative as a tale of griefs (kēdea), Alcinous takes up Odysseus' own understanding of his narrative. Odysseus characterizes

---

[4] See Wilhelm Mattes, *Odysseus bei den Phäaken* (Würzburg: Trilsch, 1958), pp. 129–40. S. Besslich, *Schweigen—Verschweigen—Übergehen. Die Darstellung des Unausgesprochen in der "Odyssee"* (Heidelberg: C. Winter, 1966), p. 62, adds that Odysseus not only acts out of his own inner need but is cannily taking the measure of the Phaeacians. For a thorough discussion, see Bernard Fenik, *Studies in the "Odyssey"* (Wiesbaden: Steiner, 1974), pp. 5–60. See, more recently, Alice Webber, "The Hero Tells His Name: Formula and Variation in the Phaeacian Episode of the *Odyssey*," *Transactions of the American Philological Association* 119 (1989): 1–13.

his "return home" as "having many griefs" (*noston . . . polukēdea*, 9.37) and, when he picks up his narrative again, he promises to tell the Phaeacians other things "even more pitiful (*oiktroter'*) . . . the griefs of my companions" (*kēde' emōn hetarōn*, 11.381–82).

The difference between these scenes in Books 7 and 9 is partly the difference between hunger and satisfaction: because Odysseus has eaten, he can look upon his griefs from a certain remove. Indeed, Odysseus begins his grand recital by paying homage to the joys of the table (9.2–11). Yet the difference between Books 7 and 9 cannot be merely a difference between an empty and a full stomach, since Odysseus still fails to speak his name even after eating (see 7.167–78). Rather, Books 7 and 9 represent two orientations toward the past and show different understandings of the place and significance of suffering in Odysseus' life.

The central moment in the change from the earlier attitude to the later comes during the athletic contest in Book 8, when the young Phaeacian princes challenge the stranger to a game. After initially refusing, Odysseus nonetheless boasts of his athletic skills, when one of the youths, Euryalus, speaks slightingly of them. Such is the semantic overlap between athletics and warwork, however, that the exchange about games (ἄθλοι) is inevitably one about Odysseus' military past. Thus, at one level, the exchange is a straightforward piece of quarreling:

> Euryalus: "I do not liken you to one skilled at *athloi*."
> Odysseus: "You talk like a fool."
>
> (8.159–66)

The word ἄθλοι, however, which can mean "ordeals" or "trials" as well as "games,"[5] lends the passage a significance deeper than the overt quarreling. Odysseus' response to Euryalus virtually forces the semantic ambiguity on us:

> ἐγὼ δ' οὐ νῆϊς ἀέθλων,
> ὡς σύ γε μυθεῖαι, ἀλλ' ἐν πρώτοισιν ὀΐω
> ἔμμεναι, ὄφρ' ἥβη τε πεποίθεα χερσί τ' ἐμῇσι.
> νῦν δ' ἔχομαι κακότητι καὶ ἄλγεσι· πολλὰ γὰρ ἔτλην,
> ἀνδρῶν τε πτολέμους ἀλεγεινά τε κύματα πείρων.

[5] See, e.g., the description of Helen's weaving in the *Iliad*: πολέας δ' ἐνέπασσεν ἀέθλους / Τρώων θ' ἱπποδάμων καὶ Ἀχαιῶν χαλκοχιτώνων ("She wove in many ordeals of the horse-taming Trojans and the bronze-clad Achaeans.") (*Il*. 3.126–27). See also Nagy, *Pindar's Homer*, pp. 137–40, who cites *Il*. 8.363 and *Il*. 19.133; and *Od*. 11.622–24.

I am not ignorant of games [ordeals],
As you say. No! among the first I think
I was, while I had youth and strength.
But now hardship and woes have me in their grip; I have borne
    much,
Traversing the wars of men and the harsh seas.

(8.179–83)

Odysseus means to contrast his former athletic skills with his current wretchedness. So close are athletics and battle, however, that Odysseus inevitably expresses two different attitudes toward his past: he is "held" by evils and woes, but it is a point of pride that he is not ignorant of "ordeals." Grief is at once something that oppresses him and a part of what makes Odysseus who he is: it is an achievement and part of his excellence.[6] It is significant that immediately after this, Odysseus, having given proof of his skills, is praised and enters into a far greater rapport and mutuality with the Phaeacians than had been the case.[7] He enjoys the Phaeacians' demonstration of their acrobatic dancing and listens enthusiastically to the court poet's comic song of Ares and Aphrodite.[8]

The linguistic clues in the contest scene in *Odyssey* 8 point forward to Odysseus' grand recital in Books 9–12 and his new orientation toward his griefs. The shapeliness of Odysseus' narrative bespeaks his "noble mind" (*phrenes esthlai*) because in his narrative his sufferings cease to be things imposed on him and become distinctive of his personality. Ultimately, narrative emerges from Odysseus' grand recital as an active appropriation of the mortal condition and its sorrows, which are embraced as being truly who and what one is. Through narrative, the griefs can be shared with others, and it is by this dynamic link between speaker and audience that Odysseus becomes not only more distinctively himself but more recognizably praiseworthy. His narrative transforms what had been private sorrows into public excellences.

The narrative progression in *Odyssey* 7–9 bears a suggestive resem-

---

[6] Odysseus' griefs and his athletic skills are also conflated by a pun on the word *peirōn*: Odysseus says, "I have endured much, passing through [*peirōn*] the wars of men"; yet even so, Odysseus announces, "I will try [*peirēsom'*] the contests" (8.182–84). See Dimock, *Unity of the "Odyssey,"* p. 97, who points out the pun and writes that, by "associating Odysseus's painful career with trial by games," the play on words "suggests that that career too is a kind of contest and a way of showing his excellence."

[7] Having shown his superiority in athletics, Odysseus is praised by Athena in disguise and rejoices to find a "gentle companion" (*enēea hetairon*) in the crowd (8.200).

[8] On Odysseus' participation in the Phaeacians' contest, see Herbert Eisenberger, *Studien zur "Odyssee"* (Wiesbaden: Steiner, 1973), pp. 122–24.

blance to the movement in the *Iliad* from Achilles' complete immersion in his griefs to his obtaining perspective on them. Achilles' attainment of perspective on his own experience was marked by his climactic ability to speak *about* them, as distinguished from uttering exclamations of pain and anger under their thrall. Achilles' ability finally to generalize from his own grief to another's was embodied in his feelings of *eleos* and his attempts to explain to Priam the source of griefs as inherent in mortal life. The *Odyssey* traces a similar development in Books 7–9, but with a characteristic self-consciousness by which the hero's emergence from his sorrows is expressed by his ability to narrate his story.

Odysseus' active disposition toward the evils of the mortal condition finds expression not only in his grand narrative of *kēdea*, but in his first appearance in the poem, when he explains why he seeks out Penelope. For, like a narrator embracing the griefs he has suffered, Odysseus willingly accepts the evils he knows must lie in store for him if he returns to Penelope. As he says to Calypso:

> Lady goddess, do not be angry with me. I myself know
> All [you say]: that wise Penelope is less
> Impressive than you in shape and size to look upon,
> For she is a mortal, while you are immortal and unageing.
> Yet even so I wish and hope every day
> To go home and to look upon my day of return.
> If a god breaks me on the wine-dark sea
> I have a heart that has borne with sorrows before.
> I have already suffered much and labored much
> On waves and in war. Let this be added to those.
>
> (5.215–24)

The story of Odysseus' return shows that mortals do not simply endure the evils imposed on them by the gods; they assimilate them and look upon them as a part of themselves. In rejecting Calypso for Penelope, Odysseus deliberately welcomes the numberless griefs that Calypso has warned him will ensue. In one sense, Odysseus chooses Penelope "in spite of" the griefs that reunion with her will cost him. In a deeper sense, however, because Penelope is hardly extricable from such griefs, Odysseus' choice of Penelope over Calypso is an embracing of the mortal world over a life of untroubled ease. The very difficulties that reunion with Penelope necessarily entails are part of what make her a fitting object of Odysseus' desire.[9]

[9] See Dimock, *Unity of the "Odyssey,"* pp. 67–70.

Odysseus is the opposite of the Iliadic warrior, insofar as the latter was motivated by his wish for an "undying renown." Mortality, in the *Iliad,* was something thrust on the individual and frustrated his deepest desires. The warrior's hope for "undying renown" was, at bottom, the wish to salvage something from a transient world. Were the Iliadic warrior to be offered an immortal and unageing existence like that which Calypso offers to Odysseus he would renounce his life as a warrior, since the fighter's career makes sense only as a means of securing a kind of immortality (see *Il.* 12.322–28). Yet even the prospect of an immortal life fails to prevent Odysseus from returning to Penelope and Ithaca. Here again, as in so many other ways, the *Odyssey* expresses a refusal of transcendence: its hero's desires are fully contained within the mortal world.

That Odysseus' desire for Penelope grows from his sense of himself as a mortal emerges most clearly from the Nekyia and from Odysseus' encounter with the shade of his mother Anticleia. Odysseus vainly attempts to embrace his mother's empty shadow just as Achilles tried to embrace Patroclus' ghost (*Il.* 23.99–107). The grief that Achilles and Odysseus each feel, however, has significantly different effects. Achilles must simply relinquish the thought of embracing his companion, and his final understanding of grief is that it must be "let go" (24.549–51). The shade of Anticleia, in contrast, expressly refers Odysseus' frustrated effort to embrace his mother to his subsequent reunion with Penelope:

> Alas, my son, unfortunate beyond all men!
> Persephone, Zeus's daughter, is not deluding you:
> No, this is the way of mortals once they die.
> Their strength has no flesh or bones,
> After the fire's blazing strength
> Consumes them and the spirit abandons the bones,
> And the soul like a dream takes wing and flies away.
> But now, as quickly as possible, yearn for daylight, and know
> All this, so you may tell it hereafter to your wife.
>
> (11.216–24)

As the painful and beautiful scene with Anticleia makes clear, Odysseus undertakes to be restored to Penelope in the full awareness that the day must come when they, too, will lack flesh and bones. Odysseus' sense of the importance of his desires is not "in spite of" his mortality, then, but derives its very urgency from his deeply assimilated sense of his mortal limitations.

What Zeus misses in his opening question, "Why do mortals blame the gods . . . ?" (1.32) is the value that mortals set on the griefs they endure. Zeus construes mortals as enduring passively what is inflicted on them. Odysseus' willing embrace of griefs for the sake of Penelope, however, suggests that one reason mortals suffer evils is because they choose to, doing so from an achieved sense of themselves as mortal persons who are constrained to suffer. Such a choice is a praiseworthy thing, the very opposite of that blind foolishness that leads the person to continue in a course of action even after he has been told of its destructive consequences. Although Odysseus, like Aegisthus, could be said to have "brought his griefs upon himself" (for he chooses to return to Penelope even though Calypso has expressly warned him of the sorrows that will result), yet he is wholly unlike Aegisthus, for his deliberate choice rests upon a praiseworthy sense of who he is.

Sense cannot be made of sorrow unless this embracing of griefs is taken into account. Odysseus is neither an evil-doer who gets his just deserts nor a victim of evils inflicted on him for no reason. He is an emblem not of human fate but of human desire: Odysseus "endures" or "suffers" evils, but he does so willingly, for the sake of obtaining his deepest wish. The good that Odysseus seeks is not the kind of value that is somehow larger than the individual—something for which he might be willing to sacrifice his life. Penelope is desirable precisely because she reflects Odysseus to himself, not because she is bigger or better than he is. (We may contrast "unperishing renown" for which a warrior willingly surrenders his life.) While Odysseus is willing to encounter numberless troubles in order to be restored to Penelope, it would make no sense for him to die for her.

From this perspective, we may get a new insight into Odysseus the trickster. Martial prowess is inappropriate in Odysseus' encounters with opponents, for such prowess rests ultimately on indifference to one's own death, while Odysseus' sense of the good (as something mortal, unique, and irreplaceable) demands that he remain alive. Odysseus' "tricksterism"—his cleverness at staying alive and getting home —thus grows from his assimilated sense of himself as a mortal who desires mortal things.[10]

In order to attain his desire, Odysseus must be *kerdaleos* (13.291)— literally "profitable"—able to achieve a desired result. The word also

[10] On the figure of the trickster, see Robert D. Pelton, *The Trickster in West Africa* (Berkeley: University of California Press, 1980); Laura Makarius, "Le mythe du 'Trickster,'" *Revue de l'histoire des religions* 175 (1969): 17–46; and Paul Radin, *The Trickster: A Study in American Indian Mythology* (New York: Greenwood Press, 1956).

conveys a sense of cunning and inventiveness—an ability to find new and unexpected uses for things.[11] So, for example, Odysseus sees in Polyphemus' cudgel a means of blinding the Cyclops, and he sees in Polyphemus' animals a clever way to make his escape from the cave. The person capable of such invention is *poikilomētis*, "of dappled wit" (13.293). This inventiveness requires a mind whose ability to calculate and devise is not affected by circumstances like scarcity or hunger. Odysseus immediately rejects the urge to kill Polyphemus for his horrifying acts, because to do so would doom Odysseus and his men to death in the Cyclops' sealed cave. He has discretion (cf. *epētēs*, 13.332), wit (cf. *ankhinoos*, 13.332) and firm-mindedness (cf. *ekhephrōn*, 13.332).

John Peradotto has given a stimulating reading of Odysseus' trickster qualities, especially as summed up in Odysseus' alias—*Outis* or "Nobody"—in the Cyclops episode. Odysseus as the unconventional trickster "Nobody" is a "secret base for open predication, . . . and thus presents a paradigm for a view of the self as capable, dynamic, free, rather than fixed, fated, defined."[12] For Peradotto, Odysseus' name, though ostensibly false, is in fact deeply appropriate to Odysseus as a figure for narrative itself: "In the final analysis, it refers in a sense to no one, to nothing, but nothing in the rich sense of the zero-degree, which signifies not simply nonbeing, but potentiality, what it means for the empty subject of narrative to take on any predication or attribute."[13] Peradotto presents a buoyant, hopeful—almost utopian—vision of an undefined and limitless self. Yet Peradotto's portrait scarcely seems to fit Odysseus. The definitionless individual Peradotto describes seems perfectly empty and without content: without memory, without deep and abiding desires, without loyalties or commitments. This is far indeed from the Odysseus who undertakes to return to Ithaca and Penelope. From this perspective the undefined self loses some of its utopian luster and begins to resemble a "creature of the belly," in Pucci's more somber formulation: subject to immediate impulses, and driven here and there by circumstances. Peradotto seems to miss the "manyness" that is a feature not simply of a trickster like Odysseus, but of all the characters in the poem, who are as multifarious as the changing circumstances that shape them. "Manyness"—the lack of definition and the splintered sense of self—is scarcely the hopeful phenomenon in the *Odyssey* that Peradotto so engagingly describes.

[11] See Hanna M. Roisman, "*Kerdion* in the *Iliad:* Profit and Trickiness," *Transactions of the American Philological Association* 120 (1990):23–35.

[12] Peradotto, *Man in the Middle Voice*, p. 169.

[13] Ibid., p. 170.

For Peradotto, "character"—in the sense of regular attributes that can be named—emerges largely as something imposed on the free play of potentiality by society, whose practice of naming defines and confines the person. He presents the *Odyssey* as a dialogic text that moves between a tragic view of self as defined and fated, and a folklore view of the self as endless potentiality. The problem with this formulation, however, is its too neat polarization of freedom and necessity. Peradotto's view of the freedom of the individual is so devoid of content as to be indistinguishable, finally, from a fatal subjection to circumstance. In the *Odyssey,* however, the individual is not reducible to circumstances, precisely because the store of memories and desires—the personality's contents—shape the individual from within. In a sense, there is an element of necessity in this shaped individual, since desire, as presented in the *Odyssey,* is partly an acknowledgement of the person's mortal condition. That acknowledgement, however, reflects an *active* orientation toward one's mortality—a willingness to embrace it and to achieve what is possible within its confines. Rather than a simple polarity between freedom and necessity, I have sought to describe a willing embrace of necessity: a freedom that results from an understanding of the mortal world and a canny ability to achieve one's deepest desires within it.

Thus, Odysseus as the trickster par excellence in the *Odyssey* is characterized by his ability to maneuver his way through the world in order to obtain what he desires in it. He is distinguished by the immanence of his wishes—their containment within the boundaries of the mortal world—and by the resourcefulness of the means he uses (pluck, ingenuity, wit) to achieve them. While Odysseus' trickster nature may seem to be at odds with the moral sentiments expressed by the characters, I would argue that it reflects Odysseus' praiseworthy understanding of his mortality and the importance of his desires, notwithstanding their transiency. Odysseus' trickiness tends to undercut a confident view of the world as a morally structured place where evil deeds are reliably punished by the gods. Nonetheless, Odysseus is not an amoral character, since his trickiness grows from the assimilation of his mortality into his deepest wishes.

As the motivation for his actions in the poem, Odysseus' desire for Penelope stands apart from the "hunger" that we have discussed already as a deep motivating force for characters in the *Odyssey*. To be sure, the belly (*gastēr*) and desire are alike in that each causes the person feeling them to be deeply engaged in the world and to grapple with the obstacles between him and his satisfaction. Odysseus' desire, however, is for long-term goals—the distant homeland and the absent spouse—

and therefore requires him to be at the same time disengaged from his immediate circumstances: if he is to reach home, for example, Odysseus must not act on the hunger pangs he feels while stranded on Trinacria. This ability to remain at a remove from one's immediate situation finds expression in Odysseus' ability to "remember" his *nostos*. The conflict between "forgetting" home and "remembering" it runs throughout Odysseus' tales of his adventures.[14] To "forget" the day of return is to be subject to one's immediate situation; such is the danger presented by the lotus or Circe's drug, or less magically, the pleasures of repose afforded by Circe's hospitality (10.472). By refusing to "forget" his *nostos,* however, Odysseus escapes confinement to this immediate circumstances.

Among the Phaeacians, then, as indeed throughout his adventures, Odysseus is prompted by the same motivation—the strength of familial and intimate ties—that drives suppliants in the *Iliad.* Yet what seems tragic in the *Iliad*—the fated impossibility of finally being reunited with one's loves—appears in the *Odyssey* as a more active disposition: a fundamental sense of one's place in a mortal world. Odysseus' efforts to win the Phaeacians' benevolence, especially in the vivid narrative of his griefs, are an important part of his exertions to reach Ithaca.

I began this chapter by distinguishing between Odysseus' dependency as a suppliant on his hosts, which suggested that skepticism was an appropriate response to his words, and the internal properties of his story, which offered a trustworthy guide to his character. We can now appreciate, however, that Odysseus' motives in telling his story are of a piece with the shapeliness of his speech. For Odysseus' desire to be restored to home and family, which prompts him to try and obtain the Phaeacians' good will, reflects an understanding of himself as mortal. Similarly, the tale of griefs he tells grows from his understanding of sorrow as a formative element of who he is.

The *Odyssey* identifies what is praiseworthy in suppliant speech: namely, the suppliant's ability to obtain others' goodwill by a lively account of griefs that makes them compellingly present to the listener. Thus, Odysseus' narrative in Books 9 through 12 is an especially clear linking of supplication and poetics. The Phaeacians' enthusiastic acclaim of their guest not only marks this as a particularly successful supplication, but shows the connections between suppliancy and skillful narrative.

---

[14] See 9.97, 102; 10.236, 472; 12.41–44; and 12.137; cf. 1.57. See also M. J. Apthorp, "The Obstacles to Telemachus' Return," *Classical Quarterly,* n.s., 30 (1980): 1–22, pp. 12–13.

II

That mortals are not wholly identified by the evils thrust on them is shown most clearly by the ability to delight in griefs. Characters in the *Odyssey* remember their sorrows, conjure with them and reflect on them, and in the end shape them into compelling narratives. In doing all this, they "delight" in their sorrows, and make them delightful, too, for others to hear. The key text is Eumaeus' narrative of how he came to be a slave (15.390–484). Eumaeus expressly links the *kēdea* recounted in narrative with the pleasure or "delight" that the narrative gives to its listeners.

Eumaeus tells Odysseus, "One delights (*terpetai*) even in griefs, once they are past" (15.400). Yet as Odysseus' desire to nurse his griefs when he first arrives on Scheria attests, the past does not come about solely by the passage of time but through a person's orientation toward it. As we saw in considering the *Iliad,* the past can be remembered either passionately or objectively: how it is remembered is a function of the person's ability and willingness to attain perspective on it. In the *Odyssey* perspective is achieved when characters narrate their griefs.

As Eumaeus' words suggest, narrative is distinguished by its ability to endow the mortal condition with pleasure: through it, the listeners can embrace or welcome mortality, as a part of what and who they are. For the delight one takes in song has most deeply to do not with the shapeliness of the plot or elegance of diction, but with the destruction or ruin as shaped in song. "Let the two of us, remembering, delight in baneful griefs!" is Eumaeus' deliberately paradoxical way of introducing the story of his enslavement as a young boy (15.399–400). "For a man delights even in sorrows once they are past, whoever has suffered much and wandered much," (15.400–1).

The narrative of Eumaeus—"the godlike swineherd"—is one of the highlights of the *Odyssey,* and is an evocative demonstration of narrative as an embracing of and delighting in grief. We must ask, first, what is delightful in Eumaeus' griefs? The central figure in his story is the Phoenician woman who was his nurse when he was a toddler—a young prince in his splendid native land (see 15.403–14). Eumaeus' Phoenician nurse, rather like Odysseus' companions, is a person doomed by her lot to act viciously. For she too had come from a prosperous family and had been kidnapped and sold into slavery (15.425–30). She was tall, beautiful, and wise (418), and the trusting Eumaeus ran about at her feet (451). Eumaeus' misfortunes began when a ship of Phoenician traders arrived on his island. One of the merchants seduced the nurse and, learning of her Phoenician origins, offered to restore her, for a price, to her family (420–23; 431–33). The nurse made the merchants swear an oath to bring her home (435–36). She enjoined silence on them (440–45), and promised them payment—which was to include her young charge, Eumaeus, for the Phoenicians to sell into slavery (448–53). After the Phoenicians had sold all their wares, the trader signalled the nanny, who stole the young boy and three cups (465–70). The story draws to a quick conclusion: Artemis slew the woman after she had absconded out to sea with the merchants and the kidnapped Eumaeus. The Phoenicians dumped her in the water to be food for the seals and fish, and they sold Eumaeus to Odysseus' father Laertes (477–84).

The Phoenician woman remains nameless, but her plight emerges clearly and poignantly in Eumaeus' story. Reduced from a life of privilege to one of slavery, she cannot aspire to the simplest human emotions—the desire to return home—without falling into the blackest crime. Despite her beauty and wisdom—qualities Eumaeus expressly points out—she betrays a vulgar and conniving side after her seduction by the Phoenician merchant: she knows enough to require her countrymen to swear an oath that they will do what they have undertaken. She has her escape all thought out, apparently: it is she who instructs the crafty Phoenicians what to do. The Phoenician woman lived in an extraordinarily harsh world that trafficked in children; having been badly used by the world, she now seeks to use its harshness to attain her own—surely very modest and sympathetic—purposes. She can attain these purposes, however, only by conniving with mercenaries and meeting them on their own venal level.

"Zeus takes away half a man's excellence," Eumaeus says on another occasion, "when the day of slavery comes upon him" (17.320–23). Eumaeus' story of his Phoenician nurse shows in what way this statement is true. Because their circumstances have changed profoundly, the recently enslaved no longer have the wherewithal to act on their simplest desires: they must behave deviously to achieve their deepest wants. The mind or *noos* of the slave—like that of most people—reflects what "Zeus has brought on for the day" (cf. 18.136–37). The Phoenician woman is both a villain and a victim. It is precisely the excellence, however, of Eumaeus' story that he engages our sympathies for some one as heartless as his nurse. Eumaeus' story, like Odysseus' tale of the companions' death, offers a compelling portrait of how human evils come about—how they are neither simply imposed nor simply deserved.

Eumaeus is able to delight in the griefs he recounts because they are now "past" (see *meta*, 15.400). Yet in what sense are Eumaeus' griefs in the past if he is still enslaved? Indeed, Eumaeus' situation is substantially the same as the Phoenician woman's: he, too, was stolen at an early age from a life of prosperity and privilege, and sold into slavery. It is clear that the Phoenician woman did not look upon her griefs as "past" but bitterly regretted her enslavement and hoped one day for her freedom. The similarity of Eumaeus' and the nurse's histories shows that the mere passage of time does not establish a "time after." Rather, Eumaeus has *made* the events past by understanding them. Eumaeus' story about the nurse's attempt to escape suggests that narrative is his own means of coping with enslavement and that it grows from his ability to distance himself sufficiently to gain perspective on it. His narrative—the very fact that he tells this story—stands in tacit but striking contrast to the nurse's own inability to come to terms with her misfortune and her desire to escape it at any cost.

Eumaeus' ability and willingness to understand his story is, in terms of the *Odyssey,* a reflection of his "noble mind" (*phrenes esthlai* 11.367). Indeed, I would suggest that Eumaeus' story reflects his understanding more than it does his powers of recollection. Specifically, it seems unlikely that Eumaeus, a mere toddler at the time of the recounted events, could have known or understood all that passed between the merchant and his nurse. His narrative may initially seem to be that of an eyewitness who merely reports events he once saw; but the events narrated seem too sordid, and the machinations too complex, to have been absorbed by a child.

The narrative proceeds, I suggest, from the adult Eumaeus' mature reflections on what he saw and heard. The narrator supplements back into the narrative what he understands, from his newly gained perspective, must have happened. This reading of Eumaeus' story may derive some support from a similar feature that characterizes Odysseus' account of the companions' death. For the judgment implicit in Odysseus' story of the sun's cattle—that the companions' death was caused at once by the gods and by their own decision—seems to be the product of mature deliberation by Odysseus rather than a simple reporting of events Odysseus saw and participated in. Because he had been put to sleep by the gods, Odysseus was not an eyewitness to the crucial part of the story, the companions' fateful efforts to reason out the best course of action. It is especially in their deliberations that the companions emerge as complex beings—fools who are, however, not wholly blameworthy. (See 12.335–39.) Yet, Odysseus heard of Eurylochus' speech only later—he tells the Phaeacians—from Circe, who had the story in turn from Hermes (12.389–90).

Homer is not nodding here, despite the apparent awkwardness of these lines.[15] The point, I believe, is that Odysseus' account of the companions is the product of his later insight into what was tragic about their deaths. It is worth noting that, had Odysseus recounted only what he had personally witnessed, the companions would emerge solely as *nēpioi* who died because of their own "reckless folly," just as they were presented in the prologue. In such a version, Odysseus could relate his command to his men not to eat the cattle; then, his fateful sleep, and, finally, his return to find that the companions had slaughtered the cattle, notwithstanding his command. Such a version could only make the companions seem like fools who blindly ignored the warnings of the gods. Their deaths would seem richly deserved—untroubling and untragic. Odysseus can "do justice" to the companions, therefore—bring out the horror and pity of their deaths—only at some cost to verisimilitude: he is not a narrator who can narrate these events on his own knowledge. Yet the breach of verisimilitude would not make Odysseus' story untrustworthy, even if Odysseus had not invoked the authority of Hermes and Circe. For the account that results from such a breach ultimately is truer to our experience of death as something catastrophic.

Similarly, Eumaeus could not make the Phoenician nurse a sympathetic character if he spoke strictly as an eyewitness—that is, as the three- or four-year old who trusted her and was betrayed by her. Eumaeus' narrative is not a transcript of the past, in which the older Eumaeus merely reports events witnessed in his very early childhood, but a constructing of the past from his reflections as an adult on the events of his tender years. His noble mind transforms his own experience as a slave into an understanding account of his nurse's. Eumaeus must stand as himself an exception to the general rule he announces: "Zeus takes away half a man's excellence, when the day of enslavement comes upon him" (17.322–23). His narrative is a most eloquent demonstration of Eumaeus' nobility. Rather than nurse the bitterness of his personal catastrophe, as, apparently, the Phoenician woman did, Eumaeus has found in his own experience a means of understanding the lives of others and, in particular, that of his own nurse. Eumaeus can delight in his griefs because he has achieved an understanding of them. As a means of affording a paradoxical delight in *kēdea*, narrative reflects an embracing of one's past sorrows. The stories told by Odysseus and Eumaeus show that griefs are not simply imposed on a mortal during his life but are actively construed in narrative.

[15] Clay, *Wrath of Athena*, p. 25.

III

The relationship between Odysseus and Eumaeus bears surprising, but unmistakable, parallels to that between Achilles and Priam in the final book of the *Iliad*. These parallels serve as much to contrast the *Odyssey* and the *Iliad* as to show the similarities between them. More particularly, elements of *Iliad* 24 that conveyed the nature of pity and its power to illuminate the pitier's own griefs are used in the *Odyssey* to show the power of narrative to embody and convey a sense of grief. Here, as elsewhere, the *Odyssey* uses traditional elements in a way that reflects back, self-consciously, on the narrative mode of epic poetry.

I look first at the parallels linking the Eumaeus scenes with *Iliad* 24. After Eumaeus has completed his story, the disguised Odysseus declares himself moved and remarks:

> Zeus has given you a good thing besides the evil,
> Since after your toil, you came to the house of a gentle man,
> Who gives you food and drinks;
> Caringly you live a good life.
>
> (15.488–91)

Odysseus' response to Eumaeus' story is suggestively like what Achilles told Priam in the final book of the *Iliad,* for Priam, too, is said to have received both good and evil from the jars beside Zeus's throne. As we have seen, it is characteristic of the *Odyssey* to apply lofty conceptions to the mundane and everyday: thus, for example, even a swineherd may be called "godlike" and, like the king of Troy, may be said to receive good and evil things from Zeus.

Furthermore, the mutuality of Achilles' and Priam's accounts of their sorrows—and their *philotēs* based on the ultimate similarity of the experience of grief—finds expression here in the mutual narratives by Odysseus and Eumaeus of "all that [they] endured" (see 14.361–62 and 15.486–87). When Odysseus finishes his false narrative, Eumaeus says in response:

> Ah! sad guest! you stirred my heart deeply
> With all the things you say: your sufferings and wanderings.
>
> (14.361–62)

Similarly, after Eumaeus' story of the Phoenician woman and his enslavement, Odysseus cries:

> Eumaeus, you stirred the heart in my breast deeply
> With all the things you say—all the sorrows you suffered.
>
> (15.486–87)

The mutuality of their grief and their admiration recalls the encounter of Achilles and Priam but does so in a scene in which the power of narrative to convey the experience of grief predominates. While Achilles achieved an understanding of grief, the narratives of Eumaeus and Odysseus show the mastery that comes from such understanding— an expertise reflected above all in narratives imposing a shape on experience and making it possible for listeners, too, to understand what the experience was like. Their narratives show the delight inherent in the ability to encompass and shape the past. In the *Odyssey*, a narrative that recurrently denies the possibility of transcending the flux and opacity of mortal existence, narrative itself emerges as a kind of highly circumscribed transcendence, which consists in the ability actively to construe griefs and to delight in forming them into expressive narratives.

Epic narrative itself, or *aoidē*, is a paramount instance of mortals' ability to achieve this very local kind of transcendence. Thus, the court singer Demodocus has, like Eumaeus, received both a good thing and an evil from the gods (8.63; cf. 15.488). Homer says of Demodocus, "The Muse loved him exceedingly, and gave him a good thing and a bad: she took away his eyesight and gave him sweet song" (8.63–64). Eumaeus' narrative helps explain the relationship between the Muse's "exceeding love" for Demodocus and her infliction of blindness on him: the evil that Demodocus endured was a condition for the great good—"sweet song"—the Muse bestowed. Eumaeus' mastery of grief through narrative suggests that only by acquainting Demodocus with sorrow did the Muse make it possible for him to sing understandingly and compellingly about grief—so that his narrative of the sacking of Troy, for example, conveys in the most authentic and emotionally piercing way what the experience was like.[16]

In treating narrative itself as an expression of understanding, the *Odyssey* makes explicit what the *Iliad* had implied: epic poetry (*aoidē*) is

---

[16] Demodocus' blindness therefore is completely different from the harm inflicted on Thamyris by the angered Muses (*Il.* 2.594–600). The Muses wholly deprive Thamyris of his ability to compose song: they "took away godly song and made him forget his skill at the cithara." The Muses are also said to make Thamyris *pērōn*—a word, G. S. Kirk writes, that evidently implies "damaged" or "mutilated," but cannot mean "blind," since that presented no impediment to the poet's composing song. See Kirk, *Commentary*, note on 2.599–600. On the tradition of blindness and the poet, see R. G. A. Buxton, "Blindness and Limits: Sophocles and the Logic of Myth," *Journal of Hellenic Studies* 100 (1980): 22–37, p. 27. See also Clay, *Wrath of Athena*, pp. 11–12.

a reflection of the understanding of the experience of griefs. The *Odyssey* presents itself as a self-conscious example of what every song is. So, for example, though the *Iliad* tells a tragic story, its narrative represents a praiseworthy mastering of the experience of griefs and makes the *Iliad* a splendid accomplishment. The *Iliad* can delight its listeners, notwithstanding the tragedy of the story it tells.

The *Odyssey*, too, is a tale of griefs or *kēdea*. Although it is the story of a hero's successful return home, reunion in the *Odyssey* is above all a time for tears for the long separation from the loved one. Return may be said to put an end to absence, but Odysseus' physical presence at long last serves to crystallize for those who are reunited the painfulness of the years apart. So when Odysseus and Telemachus embrace, their sorrow is likened to that felt by parent birds mourning their lost nestlings:

> Telemachus
> Draped around his noble father and wailed, shedding tears.
> In both of them arose the desire for lament.
> They wept piercingly, more shrilly than birds,
> Vultures or buzzards with crooked talons whose children
> Hunters snatched before they grew their wings:
> So did they shed piteous tears from their eyes.
>
> (16.213–19)

The reunion of Odysseus and Telemachus is described as though it were in fact a bereavement. Indeed, reunions in the *Odyssey* are characteristically occasions for wailing and tears (see 19.471–72, 21.223–24, and 22.500–501, 23.232, 241), and typically awaken in those reunited the "desire for lament" (*himeros gooio*, 16.215; see also 22.500–501). The *Odyssey*, then, is a tale of griefs, since even its happiest moments of reunion are nonetheless filled with the sadness of past and future separation, but it is also a tale of the active understanding that encompasses grief: it relates not only Demodocus' tale and Odysseus' weeping, but also Odysseus' stunning narrative of his adventures. The *Odyssey* is in some measure *about* song as a praiseworthy act of understanding. It seeks to encompass other songs: it is a poem about the understanding of understanding. Other songs afford a vivid experience of the suffering of griefs, but the *Odyssey* draws attention to the very power of narrative and of song to convey such an experience. Epic songs are largely tragic in the view they present of evils inflicted on mortals by the gods. The *Odyssey*, although telling a tale of sorrows, is nonetheless comic, for it draws attention to the praiseworthy accomplishment that the ability to speak one's griefs understandingly represents.

Zeus's opening criticism—to the extent that it challenges the ability of song truly to convey an understanding of the world—receives an answer over the course of the *Odyssey*. For *aoidē* does not blame the gods for human evils, but at its deepest embraces those evils as constituents of human life. Far from providing an escape from the evils of mortal life, song affords its listeners an internal human perspective on what the experience of evils is like.[17] *Aoidē* deepens the experience of grief so that it is felt not simply as a frustrating intrusion, but as an essential part of one's experience—a part of who and what one is. Delight is the experience, through song or narrative, of grief as woven into the very fabric of mortal life.

[17] The interpretation I offer here may seem to be contradicted by Hesiod, *Theogony* 53–55, where Hesiod says that the Muses—the daughters of Memory (Mnēmosunē)—bring "forgetfulness (*lēsmosunēn*) of evil and a respite from cares." To the extent that Hesiod is actually claiming that the sad person is inevitably cheered and distracted from his griefs by song, the *Odyssey* seems to offer a different view. It stresses, for example, that Penelope is not at all soothed by Phemius' song, nor is she made to forget her sorrows (see 1.337–44). There seems no need to suppose, however, that by *lēsmosunē* Hesiod refers to an oblivious cheeriness that affords no perspective or illumination of the listener's situation, even of his distress. The *Works and Days* is the clearest proof that Hesiod understood song to be capable of edifying its listeners. *Lēsmosunē* is best taken as a step back from the listener's immersion in daily cares. It is a "forgetting" of what is immediately pressing and distressful. Similarly, Achilles in Book 24 of the *Iliad* could be said to "forget" his grief in accepting ransom for Hector's body, but he "forgets" or releases only the adamant grief that had tormented him. His "forgetting" thus enables a more objective and more illuminating kind of "remembering."

CHAPTER 9

Song and *Philotēs*

The mutual understanding between Achilles and Priam in *Iliad* 24 was possible only on the periphery of the warrior society. Based on *eleos* and the memory of grief, their *philotēs* stood in contrast to the mutual ties binding the warriors—ties based on shame and a willingness to forget the dead. The *Odyssey,* like the *Iliad,* climaxes with an encounter between two characters who are able to speak at last with a mutual and deep comprehension. The late-night conversation of Odysseus and Penelope, finally reunited after Odysseus' return and the slaughter of the suitors, stands apart from the obscurity—the web of interpretation—that necessarily characterizes the rest of the world.

> After the two of them had delighted in love's friendship
> They delighted in words, speaking to each other:
> The god-like woman told all that she had endured in her home,
> Looking upon the horde of destructive suitors
> Who, on her account, had slaughtered much—
> Cattle and sheep—and drawn much wine from jars.
> As for god-like Odysseus: all the griefs he had caused
> Others and all he had himself endured, sorrowing,
> He told. She delighted to hear, nor did sleep
> Fall on her eyelids before he spoke everything.
>
> (23.300–9)

I

The reunion of Penelope and Odysseus and their mutual delight in each other's company and words shares several features with the meeting of Achilles and Priam in the last book of the *Iliad*. Both meetings take place at night, in a secluded place, and surrounded by danger. In the *Iliad*, the danger is that the Achaeans would kill Priam if they learned of his presence in their camp; in the *Odyssey*, it is that the kinsmen of the slain suitors would attack Odysseus if they learned about the slaughter. Furthermore, it is a remarkable feature of both the *Iliad* and the *Odyssey* that the hero's greatest martial feat is praised in secrecy and hiding. Priam's supplication, as we have seen, is the most prestigious honor that could be bestowed on Achilles, yet it is the very opposite of that public acknowledgment that is the usual hallmark of "renown." Similarly, Odysseus' nearly single-handed defeat of over one hundred of the islands' finest youths is surely one of his greatest military feats,[1] but is kept scrupulously hushed. Here, as elsewhere, we may see the *Odyssey* as making more explicit what was implied in the *Iliad*. For the finale of the *Iliad* seems tacitly to invert *kleos* by making its most glorious celebration something that must go unseen and unheard by the Achaean hosts. The *Odyssey*, in contrast, brings to the surface this paradoxical nature of the hero's *kleos* as one which shrouds its inception in silence.

The inversion of *kleos*—tacit in the *Iliad*, more explicit in the *Odyssey*—is not simply a matter of paradox. At its heart is the necessarily private nature of that intimate *philotēs* that grows between Achilles and Priam and that binds Odysseus and Penelope. The climactic *philotēs* between the two enemies in the *Iliad* was based on a shared understanding of griefs and reflected the transformation of passionate grief into a more tempered and wiser sadness. In this chapter, I will argue that the "love's friendship" (*philotētos . . . erateinēs*, 23.300) that Odysseus and Penelope share is similarly based on a mutual sense of grief for their years apart and of the suffering they endured in order to be restored to each other. The encounter of Odysseus and Penelope—as fleeting as that between Achilles and Priam—is a privileged moment of respite in which the obscurity of the world is not so much banished as briefly transformed into the mutual clarity felt by two people who have achieved a mastery of the ambiguous world.

As with the reciprocal narratives of Eumaeus and Odysseus, the encounter of Odysseus and Penelope recasts the final book of the *Iliad* in a primarily narrative context. Odysseus' and Penelope's mutual delighting in one another's words follows immediately on their delight in love's friendship. Love-making and narrative are alike the occasions for "delight" ("the two . . . had delighted" *tō . . . etarpētēn*, 23.300; "the

---

[1] Cf. *Il.* 4.382–400 and *Il.* 5.800–13, recounting the story of Tydeus, who like Odysseus defeated singlehanded a whole party of ambushers, with Athena's help.

two delighted . . . speaking" *terpesthēn* . . . *eneponte,* 23.301). This delight is distinguished, above all, by its mutuality, a feature emphasized by the use of the dual number.[2] Neither Odysseus nor Penelope is exclusively the storyteller or the listener, since each listens and narrates.

The *philotēs* between Odysseus and Penelope, I shall argue, is ultimately a model for the relationship between the poem and its listeners. *Aoidē,* as presented in the *Odyssey,* participates in the obscurity of the world. It does not illuminate the world from some transcendentally authoritative or divine coign of vantage, but rather, by its ability to convey imaginatively what the experience of the obscure world is like. Conceived in this way, epic *aoidē* is not easily and immediately available to its audience. To the extent that song affords an understanding of the world—as distinguished from a knowledge of it—it requires an understanding response, one that appreciates its nature as a tale of griefs and grasps the mastery of the experience of grief that skilled narrative embodies. It is this relationship between *aoidē* and its listeners that is captured in the mutual narratives of Odysseus and Penelope.

Here, too, the meeting of Odysseus and Penelope seems to take up and elaborate suggestions inherent in the meeting of Achilles and Priam. As Françoise Frontisi-Ducroux has argued, the climactic supplication in the *Iliad* is rife with suggestions of the relationship between the poet and his audience.[3] In the course of their meeting, she writes, Achilles and Priam both attain to a perspective on their own lives like that which the gods regularly have as the "divine audience" of mortal events. I believe that the midnight discourse of Odysseus and Penelope is similarly redolent of the relation between poet and audience. The *Odyssey,* however, here as elsewhere, avoids transcendence—doing so, finally, in regard to its own listeners, who are not put in a god-like position at all, but in the essentially human, vulnerable, and ignorant position of a Penelope or an Odysseus. Far from affording its listeners a

---

[2] On the distinctions in the use of *terpesthai* and, in particular, between the alpha- and epsilon-forms of the root, see Joachim Latacz, *Zum Wortfeld 'Freude' in der Sprache Homers* (Heidelberg: Winter, 1966), especially pp. 217–18. The distinction Latacz draws between the pleasurable satisfaction of physical needs (as, for example, weeping—expressed primarily by the α-stem) and the pleasure taken in "higher" needs (curiosity, pleasure in story-telling—expressed primarily by the ε-stem) seems to be illustrated here by the use of *etarpētēn* (Odysseus' and Penelope's pleasure in love-making) and *terpesthēn* (their pleasure in storytelling).

[3] See Frontisi-Ducroux, *Cithare d'Achille,* pp. 67–70, 73. See also Griffin, *Homer on Life and Death,* pp. 179–204. Since, as Griffin writes, an important aspect of the gods' response to the mortal spectacle is pity for mortals' suffering, the divine audience in the *Iliad* resembles a human audience.

reliable knowledge of all that will happen, the *Odyssey* is an obscure poem which, in a final twist, tricks even its audience.

II

It is Penelope's glory—and a theme for "broad fame" in its own right—that she ensures the enduring vitality of Odysseus' *kleos*. Thus, the shade of Agamemnon praises Penelope, thanks to whom Odysseus' fame will never die (see 24.196–97),[4] and prophesies that a "gracious song" (*aoidēn . . . khariessan*, 24.197–98) will exist for "wise Penelope": the *Odyssey* is the very song that Agamemnon's shade anticipates.[5] Penelope's name has, indeed, become synonymous with fidelity, as Agamemnon's shade predicted that it would. On the other hand, as scholars have recently begun to note, it is strange that this should be so. For throughout the poem, Penelope's conduct is hard to decipher; while not inconsistent with a resolve to remain faithful to Odysseus, it seems equally to suggest a willingness at least to countenance remarriage with one of the suitors.

So, for example, Penelope's famous ruse of the shroud has the apparently counter-productive effect, as the suitor Antinous points out, of keeping the suitors in the house. The ruse enables Penelope to postpone a decision indefinitely (see 2.89–110), but at the same time entails giving the suitors cause to hope (see 2.96–103). Penelope tells the story of her stratagem to the disguised Odysseus (19.138–56), and the ghost of the suitor Amphimedon relates it to Agamemnon's shade (24.123–146), but none of these accounts clears up the problem that Antinous points out, that Penelope's behavior perpetuates the suitors' stay in her house.[6] Another example of Penelope's puzzling behavior occurs in Book 18, where she appears in the great hall to warn Telemachus against the suitors, but fails to carry out the task she has set herself, and instead rebukes the suitors for failing to give her gifts.

---

[4] The Greek text reads τῷ οἱ κλέος οὔ ποτ' ὀλεῖται / ἧς ἀρετῆς. I adopt here the translation suggested by Nagy, *Best of the Achaeans*, pp. 37–38: "The *kleos* of his [Odysseus'] virtue will not die."

[5] As John Finley shrewdly observes, "That comes near making our *Odysseia* a *Penelopeia*." See John H. Finley, Jr., *Homer's "Odyssey"* (Cambridge: Harvard University Press, 1978), p. 3.

[6] On the motif of the shroud, see Radermacher, "Erzählungen der *Odyssee*," pp. 32–35. What we may see in the *Odyssey* is a sophisticated, ironic comment on a received story about the faithful wife's behavior: why does the faithful wife contrive actually to keep the trespassers on the premises? It is part of my argument that the question goes unanswered: Antinous is never decisively refuted.

Finally, and perhaps most notoriously, Penelope announces a contest in Book 19 and promises to marry whichever one of the suitors wins, even though the guest, who is almost certainly Odysseus, has promised her that Odysseus' return is imminent.

In each of these instances, Penelope's strategems arguably serve the purpose of keeping the suitors at bay by appearing to take seriously their claim to be suitors. Just as arguably, however, Penelope flirts with the idea of remarriage. Her appearance among the suitors in Book 18, for example, strikes the disguised Odysseus favorably as a wily attempt by his wife to use the suitors for her own purposes and increase the wealth of her household (see 18.281–83). Odysseus' interpretation of Penelope's behavior seems insecurely based, however, since Penelope, whom he has not seen or spoken to in twenty years, here behaves very like a woman who intends to remarry. Rather like Halitherses' interpretation of the eagle omen in Book 2, Odysseus' understanding is not necessarily wrong, but we are made aware of the meagerness of the reasons supporting it.

Because we are never afforded an authoritative glimpse into her motives for acting as she does, Penelope remains, so to speak, absent from her audience—who are thus constrained to build up interpretations of her behavior and what it means. Penelope puts the audience of the *Odyssey* in a position similar to that which Odysseus' absence puts his household and the Ithacans in general. We are in a privileged position in regard to Odysseus, for we are told where he is, why he is there and what he is thinking about when he acts. We are not constrained to guess—as Penelope, Telemachus and the others are—about what Odysseus' absence may portend. Penelope, however, is presented in a way that requires the audience to make just such interpretive leaps as Odysseus' absence requires of those he left behind. She seems almost a figment of the text—a compound of gestures but ultimately without a stable and centered self to which the audience can confidently refer the gestures. Penelope—the "real" Penelope, the Penelope beyond or beneath the poses and tricks—is disturbingly absent.

The response to Penelope's obscurity on the part of interpreters has by and large been to offer explanations that attempt to reconcile her acts with what is assumed to be a given—Penelope's unswerving loyalty to Odysseus. More recently, however, Marylin Katz has argued against the validity of interpretations that attempt to impart to the text a simplicity that it cannot support. As Katz argues, such interpretations in effect deny, without any textual warrant, the troubling implications of Penelope's conduct. Critics' explanations rest upon the assumption of a perduring self existing beneath or beyond the ambiguous words or actions. This "self"—which is for the most part understood to be the "faithful Penelope"—is then used to exclude any untoward implications of her ambiguous behavior.[7]

Katz offers a reading that seeks to give full weight to the implications of Penelope's ambiguous conduct. In Katz's view, Penelope's situation places inherently contradictory demands on her. She is confronted with the essentially unresolvable dilemma of either staying where she is (thus causing the depletion of Telemachus' inheritance) or marrying one of the suitors (and thus proving disloyal to Odysseus). Penelope's actions are opaque and hard to understand partly because she may be pursuing either, both, or neither of these different courses of action at any given time. Penelope's behavior in Book 18, for example, promotes both options: her motherly advice to Telemachus expresses her wish to remain beside her son and keep everything safe (see 18.166–68); her dazzling looks and her call for gifts, on the other hand, suggest a movement toward remarriage. As Katz writes, "Thus, in the epiphany of Book 18, the two options consistently appear side by side, with Penelope herself articulating or representing first one, then the other."[8] More broadly, Penelope's dilemma is perhaps an instance of women's sociological ambiguity, in which the female is defined in terms of a male other—a son, a suitor, a husband.[9]

As she emerges from Katz's study, Penelope is characterized by considerable rifts and discontinuities; her portrait calls into question the very notion of character as a unitary and stable core from which a person's acts predictably and knowably proceed. The resultant indeterminacy of Penelope, in Katz's view, "undermines [the] notion of a coherent, essential self and presents us with a notion of the person as constructed . . . and ultimately brought into being as such by time, place, and circumstance."[10] As Penelope herself says, "The gods destroyed my excellence (aretēn . . . ōlesan) and my form and body when the Argives embarked for Troy, with my husband Odysseus among them" (18.251–53; cf. 19.124–26). Penelope's insistence on her subjection to circumstance is suggestively close to what Eumaeus says about slaves: "Zeus takes away half a man's excellence (hēmisu . . . aretēs apoainutai) when the day of enslavement comes upon him" (17.322–23). Penelope illustrates Odysseus' insight that "The mind of earthly men is whatever the father of men and gods brings on for the day" (18.136–

---

[7] Katz, *Penelope's Renown*, pp. 93–113.

[8] Ibid., p. 93.

[9] Marylin Katz, letter to author, August 27, 1993.

[10] Katz, *Penelope's Renown;* p. 94; see also Murnaghan, *Disguise and Recognition*, pp. 128–30, 135.

37). Katz's reading of Penelope adheres more rigorously than others' to the *Odyssey*'s view of the subject as shifting and multifarious, in accordance with the play of changing circumstances.

Thus, Katz argues that the division between semblance and being is so blurred in the *Odyssey* that ultimately it is impossible to sustain a distinction between the "real" Odysseus and a false pretender. In acknowledging Odysseus as her husband, Penelope is not retrieving an essential Odysseus from the past. Rather, her recognition of Odysseus is a "re-cognizing"—a fresh, new construction of a relationship. The *Odyssey* emerges from Katz's reading as a story less about marriage than re-marriage, for the affinity between Odysseus and Penelope consists less in the historical fact of their marriage years before, than in their current and on-going like-mindedness (*homophrosunē*).[11] For Katz, Penelope's re-marriage to Odysseus paradoxically incorporates features that had been associated with disloyalty to her husband—specifically, Penelope's willingness (implicit in the narrative) to entertain the thought of remarriage to one of the suitors. Thus, at one level, the ambiguity surrounding Penelope throughout the poem is never resolved, for she imports this ambiguity even into her recognition of Odysseus.

A central argument in Katz's study is that Penelope's recognition is "the culmination of a ritual of *xenia*" or hospitality.[12] "When Odysseus announces his return," Katz writes, "this revelation is not so much a replacement of disguise with truth . . . as it is a convergence of the persona of the *xeinos* with that of Odysseus, of the *xeinos* with the *kurios*."[13] Katz notes a homology, in the Greek world generally, between *xenia* and marriage, in that each involves the incorporation of a stranger into the household; moreover, each combines a measure of reciprocity and a differentiation in status.[14] Furthermore, the Phaeacians' clear interest in Odysseus as a possible husband for Nausicaa suggests a more immediate affinity between marriage and hospitality within the *Odyssey*: "a good *xeinos* makes a good husband."[15] In Katz's view, the affinity between the ceremony of *xenia* and marriage is perhaps the most fundamental way in which the *Odyssey* questions the relation between semblance and being.[16] It does so because the homology between the two institutions inevitably suggests that the spouse

[11] Katz, *Penelope's Renown*, pp. 170–82.
[12] Ibid., p. 175.
[13] Ibid., p. 156.
[14] Ibid., pp. 135, 175.
[15] Ibid., p. 135.
[16] Ibid., pp. 155–56, 193.

has much in common with the stranger. In addition, the intimacy between spouses ultimately cannot be distinguished cleanly from the rapport between host and guest.

As will become clear, there is much in Katz's reading that I accept: in particular, her argument that Penelope remains finally unknowable and that her tricks remain ambiguous—not easily reducible to a loyal wife's wily efforts or even to a rational person's attempt to maximize her advantages against stiff odds. As listeners, our plight is like that of the Ithacans in the opening books of the poem, in that we are never able to extricate ourselves from the "web of interpretation" in regard to Penelope. Nonetheless, I shall argue against Katz, in this section and the next, that we may properly speak of Penelope as a coherent entity. My point is not that there is some point of view from which we can confidently resolve all the apparent inconsistencies in Penelope. Rather, I seek to show that Penelope's ultimate unavailability to us does not leave her *simply* inscrutable, a *mere* absence.

As I sought to demonstrate in the previous chapter, characters in the *Odyssey* are not reducible to "creatures of the belly"—that is, beings utterly in the thrall of their immediate circumstances—because they are possessed of memories and desire for that which is especially beloved. Indeed, Odysseus' desire for the mortal Penelope suggests a canny awareness of himself as mortal. This awareness itself distinguishes him from one who unreflectingly acts on the spur of the moment and its demands.

I want to suggest, ultimately, that *mutatis mutandis,* the same is true of Penelope. Penelope is the fullest realization of the *Odyssey*'s vision of mortals as necessarily immured in their very particular circumstances but to view her solely as produced by her circumstances—that is, as finally incoherent—seems to me to impoverish the *Odyssey*. Still, this leaves open the question, what kind of coherence does Penelope evince? Katz is right that interpretations of Penelope have tended unduly to smoothe ambiguities out of the text and have too blithely assumed a consistent, edifying self—a faithful wife—hovering beyond the troubling signals of the text.

In this section, I argue that Penelope's coherence is not a denial of the formative role of circumstance but, to the contrary, an awareness of its pervasiveness in shaping what others say and do, and an ability to marshall and control her circumstances. Penelope's "self" emerges in the qualities that link her with her trickster husband—her mastery of appearance and her ability, finally, to trap Odysseus into a surprised and spontaneous exclamation that proves this stranger is and can only be her husband. Penelope is not simply a figure of indeterminacy; she actively embraces indeterminacy, insisting on it in the face of seemingly unmistakable signs. It is this active embrace that makes Penelope more than simply a creature who passively reflects her circumstances.

Penelope appreciates her own vulnerability to circumstance and deliberately conducts herself cautiously, so as to correct for the distortions of perspective brought about by any mortal's necessary immersion in circumstance. Thus, for example, in explaining to Odysseus her refusal to acknowledge him before she obtained proof of his identity, Penelope speaks of Helen, as one who could not see past her immediate situation:

> For neither would Argive Helen, Zeus's child,
> Have made love in her bed with a stranger,
> If she knew the brave sons of the Achaeans
> Would bring her back to her beloved fatherland.
> A god stirred her to do a shameless deed:
> Before that, she did not lay up in her heart that dire
> Folly [*atē*], from which sorrow first came upon us.
>
> (23.218–24)

As Monro comments, "the lesson would seem to be that men do wrongly from their ignorance of the future, and because they are led astray by higher powers."[17] More precisely, Penelope's point is that Helen was led to her fateful deeds because of her vulnerability to the gods and her inability to judge beyond the immediate satisfaction of her wants. Penelope understands that she is necessarily in the same predicament: it is difficult for any mortal to discern whether what seems compellingly right at any given moment is so in fact, or whether it merely appears that way because of the pressure of one's immediate circumstances. "Penelope's caution," writes Sheila Murnaghan, "stems from fear of her own susceptibility to desire."[18]

Penelope not only sees her own vulnerability to circumstance but, more importantly, appreciates that others are just as vulnerable. As we have seen, Penelope refuses to trust the narratives of wanderers (*alētai*), and insists that they cannot be relied upon to speak the truth (*alētheia*), because of their dependence on her goodwill (see 14.124–25). The skepticism reflects Penelope's awareness of the necessary role of circumstance—and the speaker's ineluctable sense of self-advantage—in shaping what gets said.

[17] D. B. Monro, *Homer's "Odyssey:" Books XIII–XXIV* (Oxford: Clarendon Press, 1901), note on 23.218–24. Katz, *Penelope's Renown,* pp. 183–84, sets forth the scholarship concerning these lines.

[18] Murnaghan, *Disguise and Recognition,* p. 142.

The most powerful example, however, of Penelope's resistance even to seemingly irresistible signs and of her deliberate embrace of indeterminacy is her response to the dream that she recounts for the benefit of her visitor, when the disguised Odysseus comes to see her by night in Book 19.[19] The most striking feature of this dream is that it purports to interpret itself: in the dream, an eagle, after killing Penelope's geese, tells Penelope that he is her husband Odysseus, who has returned and will soon visit death on the suitors (see 19.546–50). Penelope, however, rejects the self-interpreting dream, insisting that it is equally capable of being true (if it has issued from the gates of horn) or of being false (if it has proceeded from the gates of ivory) (see 19.560–67). Penelope's refusal to place any trust in the apparently transparent and perspicuous dream may seem to land her in a perfect impasse: she can say nothing whatsoever about it or what it may portend. Dreams are "not to be judged" (*akritomuthoi*, 19.560), she insists: there is no canon or standard by which to assess them. Penelope's refusal to impose a meaning on the dream does not, however, simply leave a muddle. First, in adopting a skeptical attitude toward it, Penelope rightly acknowledges that the world disguises itself and does not make itself easily and transparently available to the inquirer, as the self-interpreting dream purports to do.

More specifically, Penelope's rejection of the dream's interpretation of itself is an acknowledgment of the stranger's own lack of candor. Scholars have split on the question whether Penelope recognizes Odysseus in this scene.[20] According to one interpretation, Penelope subconsciously recognizes Odysseus, and hence responds warmly to the stranger but is not ready to recognize him consciously and formally.[21]

---

[19] On Penelope's dream, see, e.g., Katz, *Penelope's Renown*, pp. 145–47; Joseph Russo, "Interview and Aftermath: Dream, Fantasy, and Intuition in *Odyssey* 19 and 20," *American Journal of Philology* 103 (1982): 4–18; Anne Amory, "The Gates of Horn and Ivory," *Yale Classical Studies* 20 (1966): 3–57; Anne Vannan Rankin, "Penelope's Dreams in Books XIX and XX of the *Odyssey*," *Helikon* 2 (1962): 617–24; and Georges Devereux, "Penelope's Character," *Psychoanalytic Quarterly* 26 (1957): 378–86. On dreams in general in Homer, see A. H. M. Kessels, *Studies in the Dream in Greek Literature* (Utrecht: HES Publishers, 1973); and E. R. Dodds, *Greeks and the Irrational*, pp. 102–34. See also Arend, *Typische Scenen*, pp. 61–63.

[20] On the question whether Penelope recognizes Odysseus in Book 19, see Katz, *Penelope's Renown*, pp. 93–113; Murnaghan, *Disguise and Recognition*, pp. 135–39; Russo, "Interview and Aftermath"; Austin, *Archery at the Dark of the Moon*, pp. 211–36; Anne Amory, "The Reunion of Odysseus and Penelope," in *Essays on the "Odyssey*," ed. Charles H. Taylor, Jr. (Bloomington: Indiana University Press, 1963), pp. 100–21; and Philip Harsh, "Penelope and Odysseus in *Odyssey* XIX," *American Journal of Philology* 71 (1950): 1–21.

[21] See Amory, "Reunion," pp. 100–121.

Sheila Murnaghan, on the other hand, has recently argued that Penelope does not recognize the stranger because Odysseus has withheld
the information she would need in order for her to recognize him.[22]
Below, I will follow a modified version of Murnaghan's interpretation.
The stranger hints that he is Odysseus but still leaves Penelope without
enough information to decide.

Penelope is not, however, simply the victim of Odysseus' failure to
take her into his confidence. As John J. Winkler argued, there is a
distinctively active thrust to Penelope's character.[23] Thus, Penelope is
able to signal her own response to the stranger's opacity: her criticism
of the dream as possibly false, in spite of (or even because of) its
insistence that it is true, is a way of indicating her recognition that the
stranger may well be "speaking many false things like the truth"
(19.203). There are certainly reasons for Penelope to harbor this suspicion. Her guest has been able to recall details of Odysseus' clothing
from twenty years earlier (see 19.221–248). More, he has clearly impressed Penelope, who praises him for his unsurpassed wisdom
(19.350–53) and who seems disposed to linger with him and tell him
intimate details about herself—her keen sorrow for her missing husband and her dreams about him (19.508–99). Yet if this stranger is in
fact her husband, he has watched impassively while she wept at his
false account of Odysseus: Penelope's tears are evocatively compared
to the melting snow caps in spring that swell the rivers (19.204–9). Yet
Odysseus, though "he felt pity in his heart for his lamenting wife, yet
his eyes never moved, as though horn or iron stood there; he hid his
tears by stealth" (19.210–12). Penelope thus has reason to know that
the guest is not being candid with her. If he is not Odysseus, Penelope
does not know him and can scarcely stake anything on the words of a
total stranger; if he is in fact Odysseus, he nonetheless pretends not to
be and has looked on impassively and without declaring himself even
after she has given every proof of loyalty to him.

Rather than claim him as her husband (when he apparently does not
wish to be unveiled) or deny that he is Odysseus, Penelope describes
her quandary by means of her dream. Just as she cannot trust the
seemingly candid and unmistakable dream, so—she seems to imply—
she cannot trust the seemingly candid and unmistakable signs her guest
has given her (see 19.250). Penelope's rejection of the dream's nearly

[22] See Murnaghan, *Disguise and Recognition,* pp. 138–39.
[23] See John J. Winkler, *The Constraints of Desire* (New York: Routledge, 1990),
pp. 141–43. On Penelope as one who actively designs for herself a multiplicity of plots,
see also Patricia Marquardt, "Penelope *Polutropos,*" *American Journal of Philology* 106
(1985): 32–48.

irresistible message is her acknowledgment that the world does not deliver up its meanings easily or without a struggle. It reflects her recognition that the man before her has secrets that he is not confiding and her awareness that he is not wholly available to her. By neither affirming nor denying that her guest is Odysseus, Penelope is closer to Odysseus than if she had recognized him and proclaimed her recognition. When Eurycleia recognized the scar on Odysseus' leg and blurted out her master's name, she brought down on herself Odysseus' threat to kill her if she spoke (see 19.487–90). Penelope's reticence contrasts favorably with Eurycleia's unwelcome outspokenness. More important, however, it likens her to Odysseus, who is similarly able to keep his own counsel and to cloak matters in secrecy.

Penelope, therefore, is not simply the victim of another's refusal to give her the information she requires. She is able actively to construe the dearth of information and the ambiguity of the signals she receives; she does so precisely by telling the stranger of her dream and of the skepticism which she feels is the only appropriate response to it. Indeed, the very opacity of the dream and her visitor's secrecy afford scope to the intelligence that is one of Penelope's chief claims to fame. Antinous, for example, says that Penelope "understands beautiful deeds and noble character (*phrenas esthlas*) and stratagems (*kerdea*) such as no other heroine" (see 2.117–18); no one has ever known "thoughts" (*noēmata*) like Penelope (see 2.121–22). The failure of the world to make itself simply available to her is the occasion for Penelope's distinctive excellence: by its resistance the world makes Penelope's intelligence shine out all the more clearly. Her "noble character" is evinced above all in her "stratagems" and "thoughts."

In rejecting the dream's interpretation of itself, therefore, Penelope affirms her own proper excellence, as one who "understands" (*epistasthai*, 2.117) and is skilled at stratagems and thoughts. Penelope, in effect, insists on the listener's role and the importance of an active and critical intelligence that scrutinizes and tests what others say. The need for such intelligence arises from the hiddenness of the world—its refusal to deliver up its meanings easily. Given the world's opacity, the intelligence that criticizes, discerns, and penetrates is an excellence, and one on whose importance Penelope insists.

From this perspective, I would like to offer an interpretation of Penelope's dream—one that lays stress on Penelope's active ability to maneuver her way adeptly through the obscure and dangerous world. The dream that Penelope reports is as follows: twenty geese are calmly eating grain, and the dream-Penelope's heart is warmed (*iainomai*, 19.537) to look upon them. A large eagle then attacks the geese and kills them, leaving them strewn throughout the house. The dream-Penelope mourns them: she weeps and shrieks (*ekōkuon*, 541), and Achaean women encircle her as she weeps piteously (*oiktr' olophuromenēn*, 543), because the eagle has killed her geese. Next, the eagle addresses the dream-Penelope in a human voice, and bids her by name ("daughter of far-famed Icarius") to take heart, for the dream is to be accomplished (*tetelesmenon estai*, 547). The geese, he explains, are the suitors; "while I who was an eagle previously (*paros*), am now your husband returned, who shall visit upon the suitors their shameful fate," (548–50). We do not learn what the dream-Penelope's response was, for at that point in the dream, Penelope awoke (551). However, upon awakening, she went looking for her geese, and found them eating grain at the trough, just as they had before (552–53).

The disguised Odysseus, upon hearing Penelope's account of her dream, is impressed above all by its clarity. "Woman!" he cries, "it is impossible to go astray in interpreting the dream, for Odysseus himself says how it will end: destruction is imminent for the suitors" (555–57). Yet Odysseus' "reading" of the dream–accepting its own interpretation of itself—does seem to go astray: indeed, it is a poor reading, for it ignores Penelope's curious and unsettling response to the death of the geese-suitors, and latches on solely to the announcement of Odysseus' return.

The dream-Penelope's heart is "warmed" to look upon her geese.[24] The problem posed for interpretation is how—and, indeed, whether—to reconcile the "warmth" Penelope feels in her dream toward the geese-suitors with her loyalty to Odysseus. Critics have sought in various ways to give due weight to the troubling indication that Penelope was in fact attached, at some level, to the suitors. Thus, for example, Peradotto has recently cited with approval Georges Devereux's argument that "a rapidly aging women, denied for some twenty years the pleasures of sex and the company and support of a husband, would inevitably be unconsciously flattered by the attentions of young and highly eligible suitors."[25] Katz describes the narrative of the latter part of the poem as one in which Penelope "moves steadily, though ambivalently, toward remarriage with one of the suitors."[26]

[24] On Penelope's warm feelings toward the geese/suitors, see Murnaghan, *Disguise and Recognition*, p. 131, and the literature cited in her note 14; see also Katz, *Penelope's Renown*, pp. 145–54; and Peradotto, *Man in the Middle Voice*, pp. 83–85.

[25] Peradotto, *Man in the Middle Voice*, p. 84, citing Devereux, "Penelope's Character." See also Russo, "Interview and Aftermath"; and Austin, *Archery at the Dark of the Moon*, pp. 122–24.

[26] Katz, *Penelope's Renown*, p. 148.

George Dimock argues that Penelope "somewhere inside her" partly "takes comfort in" the suitors[27] and John Finley writes that the geese "do not signify the suitors, in the sense of a flattering companionship, but the state of half-orderliness that had been her comfort."[28]

Such interpretations are unsatisfying for several reasons. First, even supposing that Penelope's "warmth" of feeling toward the geese can be explained as sexual attraction, Penelope's attitude toward the animals seems markedly assertive and protective. Clearly, it is Penelope who "rules the roost" in her dream. We may compare, by way of contrast, the simile describing the naked Odysseus as he approaches Nausicaa on the beach.

> Like a mountain lion he went, trusting in his strength,
> Who goes through the wind and rain with fiery eyes.
> He goes after the cattle or sheep,
> Or after the wild deer; for his stomach orders him
> To try the flocks and approach their close-built home.
>
> (6.130–34)

The lion-simile obliquely suggests the assertive sexuality of Odysseus as he must appear to the young woman, who will, in fact, soon regard him as a potential candidate for her hand in marriage. The sexuality in the Nausicaa passage is more conventional, in that the young woman is presented—as least for the duration of the simile—as the passive recipient of the approaching male. To assume a sexual element in Penelope's warm feelings toward the geese leaves unexplained Penelope's remarkable dominance. It seems misleading, furthermore, to understand Penelope's warm feelings as reflecting her yearning for the "half-orderliness that had been her comfort."[29] There is nothing to indicate that Penelope in fact feels at all attached to her routine, nor is it apparent what the "half-orderliness" of her household consists in. It seems closer to the mark to say that her house is in an uproar: its master gone, its servants demoralized, and its stores seriously diminished by the suitors' invasion.

If we cast around for other examples of a woman associated with tame animals, the most striking instance is Circe, who tames the men who visit her house and turns them into domesticated animals. The wolves and lions that the companions discover around Circe's house do not rush at them or attack them but fawn on them like dogs at their

---

27 Dimock, Unity of the "Odyssey," p. 263.
28 Finley, Homer's "Odyssey," p. 19.
29 Ibid.

master's table (see 10.212–19, 230–44). Penelope's dream presents the suitors in a similarly tamed and domesticated way. They calmly eat grain, and the dream-Penelope is warmed (*iainomai*) as she looks on them (see 19.536–37). For she has tamed them and successfully deceived them for three years with her weaving ruse, pretending to take them seriously but in fact avoiding selection of any of them as her husband.[30]

The suitors, then, are in a way "geese"—Penelope's pets, whom she tames and whose threat she manages to contain by means of her superior intelligence. Onto this scene of relative calm and equipoise, comes the eagle-Odysseus, who bloodily slaughters the geese-suitors. The dream-Penelope mourns them as painfully as any mourning described in the *Iliad;* she "shrieks" and engages in a ritual lament with the Achaean women. The eagle's injunction to the distraught Penelope to "take heart" (*tharsos,* 19.546) in Odysseus' imminent return is as crude as the eagle's sudden bloody attack on the geese. It reduces Penelope from the mastery of one who watches over her tame geese to a passive status rather like that of the young girl Nausicaa. To announce suddenly, as the eagle does, Odysseus' return as her husband and master ignores Penelope's own mastery of the geese-suitors. More than that, it ignores Penelope's crucial role in "recognizing" Odysseus as her husband. As Murnaghan and others have pointed out, Odysseus is helpless to complete his homecoming without Penelope's acknowledgement of it.[31] On this reading, Penelope's lament betokens not an erotic longing for the suitors but her feelings for her own autonomy, by means of which she overcame the suitors and which is crucial to the successful completion of Odysseus' return home.

Penelope's rejection of the eagle-Odysseus' interpretation is also a rejection of a rescue that simply leaves her out of account. A dream that interprets itself and preempts the dreamer's understanding is like a husband who suddenly rescues his wife after twenty years. The self-interpretive dream tries to seal out or do away with the interpreting intelligence of the dreamer. The dream purports to represent a clean

[30] On the similarities between Penelope and Circe, see Nagler, "Proem and Problem," p. 342, who writes, "The crew members are undone by Circe (they literally turn into animals) just as when the suitors see Penelope their knees go slack and every one of them wants to sleep with her."

[31] See Murnaghan, *Disguise and Recognition,* pp. 122–23. Of Penelope's final trick—by which she conclusively establishes Odysseus' identity—one critic writes, "In effect she is saying, 'I know who you are, but I have the ability, in the way I make your bed, either to make you my husband or to keep you a stranger . . . You cannot take that power from me yet, or be master of my *oikos* until I choose." Victoria Pedrick, "The Hospitality of Noble Women in the *Odyssey*," *Helios* 15 (1988): 85–101, p. 96.

division between a past era and the present. "I who was an eagle before (*paros*), am now returned again as your husband" (19.548–49). Yet, as we have seen, the past is not simply a function of the unrolling in time of external events. Odysseus and Eumaeus created the past for themselves by distancing themselves emotionally from their griefs and so gaining perspective on them. The dream's purported inauguration of a new era, however, wholly ignores Penelope's role in creating a past. In short, the eagle cannot become Penelope's husband until she is ready to acknowledge him as such.

The dream-Penelope's distress, like the waking Penelope's rejection of her dream's interpretation of itself, suggests that the dream that dispenses with the interpreter is no boon. The self-interpretive dream, like the rescuing husband, is objectionable because it altogether leaves out of account Penelope's ability to assess and judge. Hence, in the face of the dream's self-interpretation and of the stranger's insistence that the dream's meaning is unmistakable, Penelope insists that the dream could be false. Penelope's rejection of the meaning that the dream claims for itself is an affirmation of her own role in taming the suitors so that, among other results, she is still waiting for Odysseus when he returns.

III

To summarize the argument so far, Penelope is incompletely understood as one essentially in the thrall of her immediate situation, for she understands the fundamental importance of circumstance in shaping her own and others' beliefs and actions. Even in the face of seemingly unmistakable signs, Penelope insists on their opacity and their resistence to easy interpretation. Penelope's skepticism is, at the same time, an insistence on her own role in interpreting the world and coming to understand it. Penelope remains a hidden figure throughout the *Odyssey,* but in explaining her response to her dream, she suggests that her own obscurity is an appropriate response to an elusive and tricky world.

In this section, I consider how Penelope shows her mastery of the shifting world through her ability actively to manipulate appearances and, by her cunning, to create the circumstances that shape and partly constitute those who deal with her—the suitors, her son, her husband. For example, immediately after rejecting the dream's apparently unmistakable meaning, Penelope proposes the contest of the bow: a course of action that gives an appearance of finality, but that in fact concludes nothing and serves instead to keep the situation fluid and ambiguous. Thus, it seems clear—as Leodes, one of the suitors, in fact, says—that none of the suitors will be able to win the contest (see 21.152–62). The contest can remain just that—another episode in Penelope's outwitting the suitors, a demonstration of the suitors' worthlessness. If, however, Odysseus is in fact on Ithaca and so chooses, the contest can also set the stage for the bloody vengeance foretold in the dream.

Just how canny is Penelope being here? Murnaghan points out that the inherent duplicity of Penelope's action does not appear to be of her own devising. The result is not simply an "exhilarating twist" but a "disturbing use of chance for the resolution of the plot."[32] Such an absence of deliberate "plotting" is, indeed, disturbing, yet seems altogether appropriate in a poem that denies the existence of some transcendant viewpoint from which we may know the world. Penelope is not like the Iliadic Zeus, who sets forth the line that the ensuing narrative will take (see *Il.* 8.473–77 and *Il.* 15.49–77). It would misconstrue the narrative to see her as an arch-plotter and designer of narratives. Nonetheless, it is significant that, working from within her situation of imperfect information, Penelope finds means that in fact avoid a premature resolution and keep the situation fluid until matters can be clarified.

Penelope's power to create the circumstances others find themselves in is nowhere clearer than in the trap she lays for Odysseus, where she craftily elicits the spontaneous and unstudied exclamations that demonstrate to her satisfaction who the stranger is. After Odysseus has made his presence known at the contest and has finally rid his house of its invaders, Penelope elicits by means of a deceit the proof she needs that he is indeed her husband Odysseus.[33] When Odysseus, exhausted from battle and seemingly disheartened at Penelope's apparent coldness to him, bids Eurycleia to prepare his bed, Penelope seems to assure Odysseus that she has in fact already acknowledged him and turns to give the serving woman instructions:

> Strange fellow! I am not haughty or disdainful,
> Nor am I overwhelmed: well do I know the kind of man
> You were when you left Ithaca on the long-oared ship.

---

[32] Murnaghan, *Disguise and Recognition*, p. 134. It is noteworthy that the slain suitor Amphimedon, in attributing the slaughter to a joint plot by Odysseus and Penelope, resists an explanation that accepts the role of accident in directing the course of events.

[33] On Penelope's outwitting of Odysseus, see Winkler, *Constraints of Desire*, pp. 129–61.

Now, Eurycleia, hurry and prepare his bed.
Outside the sturdy chamber he once built,
Put the bed there and spread the bedclothes—
Fleece and covers and colorful blankets.

(23.174–80)

Odysseus' shock and surprise at Penelope's off-hand command to prepare the bed outside the room, and his spontaneous description of
carving the bed from an immovable tree-trunk (see 23.183–204) give
Penelope the decisive proof she needs that the man standing before her
is—can only be—Odysseus. Penelope, through her deceit, has man-
aged to make Odysseus speak artlessly: his unpremeditated words have
a directness and candor that make them far more reliable than any
planned speech could be. By falling into Penelope's trap, Odysseus
reveals who he is more surely than he could by any speech he might
make or proofs he might adduce.

Penelope's trick suggests an answer to the question posed at the
beginning of this chapter: what kind of consistency do Penelope and
Odysseus evince? Her ruse is pointless unless it establishes that the
stranger is the authentic Odysseus. As a result of Penelope's stratagem,
there is conclusively revealed the same irreplaceable individual to
whom Penelope was married years before. Penelope's trick, in short,
rests on some sense of a perduring self. At the same time, however,
Penelope elicits the speech she needs to hear and establishes the stranger's identity by reducing Odysseus to a creature in the grip of his
immediate circumstances. Even more than what Odysseus says, his
very consternation—his surprise, anger, and grief—at what he un-
suspectingly thinks is a dire change of affairs since his departure, is
itself the most conclusive proof that he is none other than Odysseus.
Odysseus is "troubled" (okhthēsas, 23.182) by what he hears and Penelope's speech is "painful to his heart" (thumalges, 183). Only Odysseus
would find Penelope's apparently innocent speech so deeply disturbing.[34] Anger, as Peradotto and Dimock in particular have pointed out,
is the preeminent response to the trickster: it is, so to speak, the trickster's trademark (see 19.392–409).[35] Odysseus' spontaneous dismay,
therefore, is at once a sign of Penelope's expertise in deceit and proof
that the stranger can only be Odysseus. Her trickery—her ability to

[34] See Peradotto, *Man in the Middle Voice,* p. 160: "Perhaps nowhere does Odysseus
show himself less master of the situation, his *mētis* matched and for the moment neu-
tralized, than in his confrontation with Penelope."
[35] See Peradotto, *Man in the Middle Voice,* pp. 128–34; and Dimock, *Unity of the
"Odyssey,"* pp. 256–58.

obfuscate and baffle—is evidenced in Odysseus' pained outcry. Yet this same spontaneous outcry is the irrefutable proof Penelope needs that this man is undeniably Odysseus.

Penelope, then, achieves the clarity she requires—the absolute certainty that the man before her is Odysseus—but she achieves that clarity by recognizing the opacity of the world and by embracing its ambiguity—in other words, by being a trickster. Penelope's glory is that she manages to transform the opacity and ambiguity of the world into a moment of lucidity and to make possible that time of absolute rapport and mutual candor and delight that she and Odysseus share soon after. Such rapport and candor are inseparable from Penelope's skill at outwitting even the wily Odysseus. Odysseus has observed Penelope deceiving others. He "rejoiced" (*gēthēsen*) to see her demand gifts from the suitors and charm them with her sweet but insincere words (18.281–83). Only when he has himself been taken in by her tricks, however, and felt baffled and defenseless, can Odysseus really get the proper measure of Penelope. The experience of being deceived is, paradoxically, a clarifying experience for Odysseus, for it most abundantly reveals the seriousness or importance which Penelope attaches to her desire for her husband, and her unmatched ingenuity in procuring the satisfaction of her desire. To be outwitted by her reveals to Odysseus, as nothing else could, Penelope's excellence.

IV

I have suggested that the reunion of Odysseus and Penelope in *Odyssey* 23 bears a marked and significant resemblance to the supplication of Achilles by Priam in *Iliad* 24. Central to the likeness between the two scenes is the distinctive nature of the *philotēs* that finds expression in both. The bond between Penelope and Odysseus, like the *philotēs* that grows up between Achilles and Priam, rests on a common experience of grief and on an ability to master that experience.

This affinity between the marriage of Odysseus and Penelope and the *philotēs* of Achilles and Priam, while perhaps initially surprising, nonetheless emerges naturally from what we have seen concerning supplication. For the appeal of a suppliant like Priam is precisely to the memory of those intense familial ties such as exist between husband and wife. The *philotēs* between Achilles and Priam was based on the mutual memory of such ties and their importance. The reunion of Penelope and Odysseus is in its own way a "memory" of such ties. As Penelope says,

> The gods have made sorrow our companion
> And begrudged us each other's company
> delighting in youth and approaching the threshold of old age.
>
> (23.210–12).

Penelope and Odysseus have come to know each other, paradoxically, by their prolonged absence from each other. The intimacy they enjoy upon being reunited, and which finds expression in their reciprocal narratives, rests upon the evils that they have separately endured and have surmounted with similar cunning and resourcefulness. Their reunion is thus partly a reflection on—a "memory" of—the intimacy and intensity of the ties binding husband and wife.

As shown above, Katz has argued that the ceremonial elements in the relationship between Penelope and Odysseus are crucial to the "blurring" in the *Odyssey* of the line between "seeming" and "being." *Xenia,* or hospitality, she writes, brings about a relationship "through efficacious words and deeds."[36] The gestures and words that constitute hospitality do not reach such problems as the "real" identity of the other person, but address only *what kind of person* she or he is. To the extent that the reunion of Odysseus and Penelope grows from the ceremony of hospitality, Katz argues, their marriage (or, better, their re-marriage) does not involve a retrieval of an essential self from twenty years previous, but a fresh re-construction of a new relationship.

Katz's formulation of the re-marriage of Odysseus and Penelope is an attractive one. Nonetheless, I believe that she overstates her case in arguing that ceremony—and, in particular, hospitality—blurs the division between semblance and reality. Katz bases her argument on the socially creative power of ceremony: its ability to confer a new "reality" on its participants. As I have argued, however, a ceremony like supplication—or hospitality, to which supplication is closely allied—draws its meaning on any given occasion from the specific purposes of those invoking it. For example, the interview between Penelope and the still disguised Odysseus in Book 19 of the *Odyssey* takes the form of a hospitality scene, and during it a new reality is inaugurated between the stranger and Penelope. Penelope assures the stranger, after he has accurately described Odysseus' clothes during a supposed encounter twenty years earlier: "Before I felt pity for you, stranger, but now you will be my honored friend" (19.253–54). Clearly, Odysseus has had a new status conferred upon him in the course of a hospitality ceremony. Just as clearly, however, these two consummate tricksters use the eti-

---

[36] Katz, *Penelope's Renown,* p. 193.

quette of hospitality for their own inscrutable purposes. Far from blurring the distinction between semblance and reality, the hospitality
scene in Book 19 seems to afford a powerful sense of the distance
between them: Odysseus and Penelope each act and speak in a way
appropriate to the ceremony of hospitality but their words are rife with
the implication of things not said. Penelope's interpretation of her
dream is a comment on this gap between reality and its representations.

I therefore disagree with Katz's view of ceremony as merging semblance and reality. I believe that supplication shows features of ceremony
that Katz's description overlooks. Supplication is, at one level, a powerful expression of the overwhelming importance of circumstance,
since it involves a drastic change from powerful and proud indepen-
dence to humiliating subjection. The source of supplication's power,
however, is the enduring self that asserts itself in the ceremony. The
suppliant is revealed as one who holds certain things to be especially
important and whose goodness persists through—and, indeed, is mag-
nified by—the dramatic change in circumstances. The suppliant,
moreover, appeals to this persisting self in the one who is supplicated,
inviting that person to remember the dearness of things—a memory
regularly suppressed in the on-going life of society. The *philotēs* between the suppliant and the victor does not fuse the two in a new,
ceremonial reality that blurs the contours of the individual. Rather, it
represents a heightened consciousness of oneself and the other as similarly situated in a mortal world.

This persistence of the self is really but another expression of the
individual's complexity. The Iliadic warrior is vulnerable to the shifts
of fortune in his search for prestige, and can, at any moment, fall from
victory to defeat. But the warrior is not wholly understood in terms of
his circumstances—his victory or his defeat—for he is not completely
described as an adherent of the warrior code. Conversely, the vaga-
bond in the *Odyssey* is a walking lesson to others about the shaping role
of fortune and circumstance in mortal affairs. Yet a noble wanderer
expects to be recognized as such by the wisdom he shows in understanding his experience to be illustrative of a mortal pattern.

It is on the basis of this common memory or understanding, rather
than upon the reality-conferring operation of the acts and words characteristic of hospitality, that the *philotēs* of Penelope and Odysseus is
founded. Each tells the other a tale of griefs (*kēde'*, 23.306). The mutual
delight the two take in their reciprocal narratives (see *terpesthēn*, 301;
eterpet', 308) signals that their griefs are now "past," if we recall Eumaeus' observation that people are able to delight in their griefs, once
they are past, 15.400. It is clear, however, that their griefs are past for

them only in the sense that the two have attained perspective on them. For Odysseus has already explained to Penelope that he must leave soon again to appease Poseidon: "Wife, not yet have we reached the last of our ordeals; there yet remains immense toil—great and difficult— that I must accomplish" (23.248–50).[37]

The reunion of Penelope and Odysseus is not a final conclusion to griefs—any more than was the encounter and *philotēs* of Achilles and Priam. Rather, it represents a privileged moment of respite, in which ambiguity is not banished so much as transformed for a brief while into the mutual clarity of two who have mastered and understand the ambiguous world. The simple frankness they achieve does not represent the end of an old era of obscurity and absence, and the inauguration of a transparent era of presence. Rather, it is like a brief flash or iridescence in which deceit and the experience of being deceived have become truly illuminating. In one of the most striking similes in the *Odyssey*, Penelope's joy upon her reunion with Odysseus is likened to the joy a shipwrecked man feels upon first seeing land (see 23.233–40). Penelope's story—less colorful, more private, and immersed in the domesticity that was the Greek woman's lot—is nonetheless essentially the same as Odysseus' own: a journeying through countless griefs to attain the beloved.[38]

Penelope can help Odysseus gain insight regarding his own experience only insofar as she insists on her own activity as one who interprets and judges. Were she to wait passively for rescue, Penelope would be wholly unlike Odysseus, whose life is one of constant struggle and strain toward his final goal. As one who insists, however, on interpreting and devising for herself, Penelope becomes an instance for Odysseus of that active and intelligent desire that has prompted him throughout, an instance he can view lovingly but in perspective. Because Odysseus is at once engaged with her and sufficiently disengaged to see with a certain objectivity, Penelope can serve as an occasion for Odysseus' self-understanding: she shows him who he is. Suggestive and illuminating for the reunion of Odysseus and Penelope and its significance is this passage from the Aristotelian *Magna Moralia*, 1213a10–26, arguing that self-knowledge depends on the knowledge of others:[39]

[37] On Odysseus' voyage to expiate Poseidon's anger, see Peradotto, *Man in the Middle Voice*, pp. 59–93, who examines Tiresias' prediction in Book 11 that such a voyage will be necessary—a prediction that remains unfulfilled in the *Odyssey*.

[38] On the complementarity and mutual mirroring of the sexes in the *Odyssey*, see Helene P. Foley, "'Reverse Similes' and Sex Roles in the *Odyssey*," *Arethusa* 11 (1978): 7–26. See also Russo, "Interview and Aftermath," especially p. 12.

[39] The translation is that given in John M. Cooper, "Aristotle on Friendship," in

The friend—if we figure a friend of the most intimate sort—will seem to be a kind of second self, as in the common saying, 'This is my second Heracles.' Since, then, it is both a most difficult thing, as some of the sages have said, to attain a knowledge of oneself, and also a most pleasant (for to know oneself is pleasant)—now, we are not able to see what we are from ourselves . . . ; as then when we wish to see our own face, we do so by looking into the mirror, in the same way when we wish to know ourselves we can obtain that knowledge by looking at our friend. For the friend is, as we assert, a second self. If, then, it is pleasant to know oneself, and it is not possible to know this without having someone else for a friend, the self-sufficing man will require friendship in order to know himself.

While it is true that Penelope puts aside her mask of deception and speaks candidly to Odysseus, it is perhaps more deeply true that her deceptive arts become themselves a revelation of who and what Penelope is. Her trick has shown the secrecy and resourcefulness that desire and the attainment of the desired object demand. Penelope reflects Odysseus to himself, for he has been prompted by a desire that complements Penelope's. This mutual mirroring—of those who understand the sorrows and obscurity of the world and who are adept at achieving their desires within its constraints—makes the reunion of Odysseus and Penelope an appropriate climax that resolves the action of the poem.

The reunion of Penelope and Odysseus is distinguished from the meeting of Achilles and Priam in *Iliad* 24 by the predominance in it of the active elements. Odysseus and Penelope have each suffered hardships—and, indeed, will continue to endure them—but the emphasis is placed on their ability to transform these into words and to delight in them. The characters' ability actively to encompass and understand their sufferings, which remained implicit in the *Iliad*, becomes explicit in *Odyssey* 23. The *philotēs* of Odysseus and Penelope, while based on the shared experience of griefs, also expresses their shared mastery of a world where love is inextricably tied to grief. Because the mutual narratives of Odysseus and Penelope figure so importantly in their reunion, this scene has implications for the poetics of the *Odyssey,* and, more generally, for the poetics of Homeric epic. I discuss these implications in the next section.

Essays on Aristotle's "Ethics," ed. Amélie Oksenberg Rorty (Berkeley: University of California Press, 1980), p. 320. Cooper's entire essay is well worth consulting. See also the discussion in Nussbaum, *Fragility of Goodness,* pp. 354–72.

V

Penelope's rejection of the self-interpreting dream is one of the poem's most striking images of the good listener's relation to the *Odyssey*. With its absent hero and its narrative opacity, the poem requires a listening that rejects the lucid transparence promised by what I have called song-as-knowledge: song that claims to convey what the Muses have seen and know. The *Odyssey* needs, instead, a listening that acknowledges the opacity of its narrative and the consequent need for interpretation. To insist on the importance of the listener is to reject the hope for speech that is authoritative, reliable, and transparent, and to embrace, like Penelope, the obscurity of the world.

In the Sirens episode, the *Odyssey* seems to offer a cautionary example of the dangers posed by song-as-knowledge and by the temptation to know simply by uncritical hearing. The Sirens claim the same powers that are attributed to the Muses as all-knowing goddesses. "We know all things—all the labors the Argives and Trojans endured in wide Troy by the gods' will," the Sirens tell Odysseus (12.189–90; cf. *Il.* 2.484–93). The pleasure they offer is expressly one of knowledge. The man who visits them "goes away in delight at knowing more," the Sirens deceitfully tell Odysseus (12.188). The destructiveness of the wish for knowledge through simple, uncritical hearing is conveyed by the sure death visited on all those who stay to listen to the Sirens' song.[40] Conversely, Menelaus' story of Proteus presents an image of good listening. For although Proteus is omniscient (4.385–86) he yields his knowledge only grudgingly: the one who would question him and learn must first wrestle with him (4.399–425). The struggle that Menelaus engages in with Proteus is an eloquent image of what the "good listener" does, and stands in striking contrast to the easy but fatal hearing that the Sirens seductively offer.

The reunion of Odysseus and Penelope captures another aspect of the relationship between the *Odyssey* and the good listener—namely, the rapport or *philotēs* that exists between them. Odysseus and Penelope are each of them good listeners. Among Demodocus' audience, Odysseus alone responds to the human grief suffusing the story of the sacking of Troy. So too, Penelope alone responds to the sorrow inherent in Phemius' tale of the returning Achaeans. Their reunion—when sexual pleasure mingles with reciprocal narrative and listening—

---

[40] See Pietro Pucci, "The Song of the Sirens," *Arethusa* 12 (1979): 121–32, and Ford, *Homer: The Poetry of the Past*, pp. 83–85.

expresses the intimacy between song and listener: song betokens an active apprehending of the experience of grief, and the listener responds both to the grief inherent in the narrative and to the mastery of the experience embodied in the well-formed story. Because good listening is itself a form of understanding, song and the good listener (like Odysseus and Penelope) mirror each other. The *philotēs* between song-as-understanding and the good listener is like the friendship Aristotle describes between two people who find in each other a second self.[41]

Philotēs can name the relation existing among members of a society—for example, the Achaeans' warrior society at Troy. Epic poetry, as a traditional song handed down from generation to generation, is associated with *philotēs* in this public or social sense, since it no doubt served, as Eric Havelock has argued, to strengthen the ties binding members of the community: it provided a common store of memories and taught a common set of values.[42] Epic poetry, therefore, has a pronounced sociological aspect and significance: it promotes the ties of *philotēs* binding the members of a society.

Yet, the argument so far suggests that more deeply, the *philotēs* between song and listener is closer to that between Odysseus and Penelope, or between Priam and Achilles, than it is to those ties of fealty and common purpose that bind the Achaeans in the Iliadic warrior society.[43] Like those examples of *philotēs*, the "friendship" between the poem and the good listener consists in the special and necessarily brief rapport between two who have mastered the experience of grief. The rapport arises from the ability of each to reflect and so illuminate the other.

That the *Odyssey,* as an instance of song-as-understanding, is not self-sufficient—but, rather, looks forward to and requires a good listener—emerges most strikingly from its ending. For the *Odyssey* does not offer a neat and satisfying conclusion to the story it relates. Rather than seeking to provide a lucidly transparent account of a neatly defined event in the past, the *Odyssey* offers a deliberately weak and ambiguous conclusion. As an instance of song-as-understanding, the

---

[41] See the passage from the *Magna Moralia* quoted above, which is as illuminating for the relationship between poem and listener as it is for the relation between Odysseus and Penelope.

[42] See Havelock, *Preface to Plato,* pp. 36–49.

[43] We might compare, too, as a model for the relationship between poet and audience, the ties between Achilles and Patroclus, especially as these find expression in Book 9 of the *Iliad,* where Achilles sings "the fames of men" and Patroclus attentively listens (*Il.* 9 189–91). See Frontisi-Ducroux, *Cithare d'Achille,* p. 12.

Odyssey participates in or embraces the ambiguities of the world, but the paradoxical result—as in the case of Penelope's embrace of ambiguity—is a revelation of what the understanding of such a world consists in.

Were the *Odyssey* to conclude with the reunion of Odysseus and Penelope, nothing would seem amiss. That meeting is strongly conclusive: Odysseus has at last attained his truest *semblable* and his heart's desire. The two delight in love and narrative; they do so in the marriage bed Odysseus had carved from a tree still rooted in the earth. Such an end is both passionate and stable; it celebrates the harmony of culture and nature. Surely, a story of a hero's return could have no more decisive and satisfying conclusion than this. Conclusiveness holds such a spell for us that we would gladly believe that Odysseus' slaughter of the suitors would be universally condoned, and that it would have no consequences other than the happy one of Odysseus' reunion at long last with Penelope.[44]

Yet, the *Odyssey* rejects such an ending in favor of an inconclusive and, from a strictly formal point of view, highly unsatisfying end. The story of the angered kinsmen is unwelcome after Odysseus and Penelope have been reunited: it seems like an unnecessary excrescence on a story that has already reached its climax and dramatic resolution. The *Odyssey* insists, in the face of our complacence—indeed, our insistence that endings be truly conclusive—that Odysseus' return was not universally hailed, and that the families of the slain suitors and the dead companions were aggrieved and sought satisfaction. The *Odyssey* does not present Odysseus as a uniquely and unquestionably important hero, one whose return brings about some momentous, worldwide pause. We are deliberately made aware of other persons pursuing other interests, indifferent or hostile to those of Odysseus.

The very untidiness of the *Odyssey*'s conclusion, which is so unsat-

---

[44] As is well-known, Aristarchus indicated that the *Odyssey* reached its boundary (*peras*) or fulfillment (*telos*) with the narration of Odysseus' and Penelope's reunion. See the scholia to 23.296. The arguments for and against the authenticity of the subsequent parts of the *Odyssey* are set forth in J. Russo, M. Fernandez-Galiano and A. Heubeck eds., *A Commentary on Homer's "Odyssey"* (Oxford: Clarendon Press, 1992), pp. 313–14, 353–55, and note to 23.297. Page, *Homeric "Odyssey,"* pp. 101–36, summarizes the case for concluding that Book 24 is indeed a later addition to the poem. See now Stephanie West, "Laertes Revisited," *Proceedings of the Cambridge Philological Society*, n.s., 35 (1989): 113–43. It is clear from the text that I agree with those who argue that Book 24 is not a dispensable addition, but an important part of the *Odyssey*. For arguments in favor of the authenticity of Book 24, see Dorothea Wender, *The Last Scenes of the "Odyssey"* (Leiden: Brill, 1978); see also Thalmann, *Form and Convention*, p. 232 n. 8 and p. 234 n. 28, who points out that the scholiasts may well have thought that the *Odyssey* "reached its goal" at this point, but not, necessarily, that it came to a stop.

isfying from a formal point of view, implies that the world does not have neat conclusions. The *Odyssey* would give itself the lie were it to suggest that Odysseus' return truly did bring about a conclusion—the end of his absence, the end of uncertainty, and a new era in which right and wrong are clearly distinct. The *Odyssey* violates the sense of an ending in order to be truer to the necessarily obscure and unending world.[45]

In offering a strongly conclusive ending, only to reject it in favor of an inconclusive and ambiguous finale, the *Odyssey* resembles its own story of Penelope's dream. In declining the dream's offer to rescue her from the opacity of the world, Penelope embraced that opacity and thus insisted on an active role for herself in construing and judging the world. In doing so, she came to resemble Odysseus and so could reveal him to himself. Similarly, the *Odyssey* deliberately refuses to rescue its listeners from the world's endlessness and inconclusiveness. Were the poem to end strongly with the reunion of Odysseus and Penelope, Odysseus would appear as an authoritative, heroic figure, whose return was hailed by all and inaugurated a new era of stable peace and enduring order. By rejecting such a conclusion, the *Odyssey* presents itself as a miniature instance of the obscurity of the world, and as such paradoxically becomes an illuminating poem: it better reflects the actual lives of its listeners and enables them to grasp the ambiguity of their own experience. The mutuality of the understanding listener and the understanding narrative is like the fleeting rapport between Odysseus and Penelope. The relationship between the *Odyssey* and the good listener affords the opportunity—the more precious for its brevity—to experience at once the unknowability of the world and the understanding of such unknowability.

This "friendship"—the intense but fleeting rapport between song and listener—happens because the *Odyssey* holds itself in abeyance,

---

[45] On the inconclusiveness of the ending of the *Odyssey*, see Peradotto, *Man in the Middle Voice*, pp. 59–63. Peradotto argues that the *Odyssey* can be "explained as the collision of, and attempted mediation between, two kinds of narrative ideology" (82)— on the one hand, "myth" (which Peradotto understands as essentially tragic) and, on the other hand, *Märchen* (which he takes to be essentially optimistic). The inconclusiveness of the *Odyssey* however, does not seem to me to be simply a "collision" of two modes, but rather a deliberate and highly effective mode of expressing the kind of world Odysseus and Penelope have each mastered. Ford, *Homer: The Poetry of the Past*, pp. 75–76, writes of a "gap between the multifariousness of experience and an account of it in speech. . . . The poet's problem is not simply the finitude of human existence; it is also an aesthetic problem, a difficulty with representation itself, with the project of recounting experience." Although Ford is talking about the *Iliad*, his words seem rather more applicable to the *Odyssey*, which, by its inconclusive conclusion, seems to situate the particular story it tells amidst an ongoing and unstoppable world.

retaining its autonomy and requiring listeners to exercise their own. From its very first lines, the *Odyssey* self-consciously fashions a relationship between itself and its listeners like that between friends. "Speak to me, O Muse, the man of many turns . . ." the poet sings (1.1). While the appeal is to the Muse, the request is like that posed by the host to the guest. Thus, the prologue continues:

> . . . the man of many turns, who wandered much,
> After he sacked the sacred citadel of Troy
> And saw the cities of many men and came to know their minds
> And suffered many griefs in his heart at sea . . .
>
> (1.1–4)

The central character of the poem remains unnamed throughout the prologue. In this way, the *Odyssey* differs from the prologue to the *Iliad,* which grandly names the hero and his patronymic in the very first line: "Sing, goddess, the wrath of Achilles, the son of Peleus" (*Il.* 1.1). It differs, too, from Odysseus' naming of himself to the Phaeacians. "I am Odysseus, son of Laertes—the fear of all men because of my deceits, and my renown reaches heaven" (9.19–20).

Commentators have argued that the absence of Odysseus' name in the prologue is a crystallization of Odysseus' absence through large spans of the poem and, more generally, of the opacity of the narrative—its resistance to clear and transparent meanings.[46] I agree, but would add that in its silence as to the hero's name, the prologue resembles the question that the host puts to his guest. Thus, the Muse is asked to say where the nameless man travelled, and what cities he visited, and what were the men like in those cities. Such were precisely the questions Alcinous put to his guest, Odysseus, before Odysseus has told the Phaeacians his name:

> Now, come and tell me truly:
> Where you wandered, what places you reached,
> And the men and the cities they inhabited,

---

[46] On the suppression of Odysseus' name in the prologue, see Peradotto, *Man in the Middle Voice,* pp. 114–17, who argues that the prologue plays epexegetically with the word *polutropos* ("of many turns") and, by stressing the multifariousness of the hero, does precisely the opposite of naming him. See also Pietro Pucci, "The Proem of the *Odyssey,*" *Arethusa* 15 (1982): 39–62, pp. 50–57; and Clay, *Wrath of Athena,* pp. 26–29, who make a similar point. On the structural elements of the Homeric prologue, see B. A. van Groningen, "The Proems of the *Iliad* and the *Odyssey,*" *Mededeelingen der Koninklijke Nederlandse Akademie van Wetenschappen,* Afd. Letterkunde, n.s. 9 (1946): 279–94 and S. E. Bassett, "The Proems of the *Iliad* and the *Odyssey,*" *American Journal of Philology* 44 (1923): 339–48.

Those who were harsh, wild and unjust,
And those who were hospitable and god-fearing.

(8.572–76)

The speaking of the Muse is to be like that of the stranger seeking hospitality and who wishes, through his narrative and its excellences, to enter into a friendship or *philotēs* with another. The prologue does not merely leave Odysseus unnamed, therefore, but alludes to the ceremonies of hospitality and looks forward to the introduction of the stranger to the host. This is not to say that the *Odyssey* fully discloses itself and its hero: no more does the stranger fully reveal himself in speaking skillfully his griefs. The good listener's relationship to the *Odyssey* is asymptotic: one can approach the *Odyssey* ever more closely but can never "touch" it—never wholly possess or know it. The *Odyssey* remains like a second self, autonomous, however intimate the rapport between the good listener and the song-as-understanding may become. This autonomy, which results from the poem's obscurity and resistance to easy intelligibility, reflects in an illuminating way the autonomy of its listeners.

Hence, in "speaking a man," the *Odyssey* does not do so directly and transparently, as though a man could be made wholly and simply available to others. To speak skillfully is not to pierce through to a reality existing behind the shifting appearances but to convey the inescapability of the play of appearance in human affairs. The *Odyssey* speaks Odysseus indirectly—through stories of Agamemnon's tragic return, for example, and through the story of those who go in search of Odysseus' "broad fame." In "speaking a man," the *Odyssey* employs different kinds of narrative, from the most exotic fantasy to the homeliest realism. The *Odyssey* deliberately eschews the homogeneity of the *Iliad*, and situates Odysseus within a far-flung and variegated world: it encompasses both aristocratic warriors and swineherds and presents both heroes sublimely conceived and corrupt youth. Odysseus is spoken, then, through an opaque, complex, and various narrative that requires a "second self"—a good listener—to grasp and understand the self that the *Odyssey* speaks.

As a poem that "speaks a man," the *Odyssey* self-consciously addresses the very speaking of him. For the *Odyssey* contains many "speakings" of Odysseus: Nestor, Menelaus, and Helen, for example, all speak of Odysseus in answer to Telemachus' earnest entreaties; Odysseus speaks about himself in response to Alcinous' question and tells several false but persuasive stories about himself on Ithaca; the suitors, and Eumaeus, too, speak about Odysseus. In the *Odyssey*, narrative does not transcend the narrated events (as, for example, the narrative of the *Iliad* does), but is itself a part of the narrative and, as such, subject like other activities to the vagaries of circumstance and the limitations of knowledge or perspective in the persons who narrate. The *Odyssey*'s speaking of Odysseus offers a refracted portrait, in which Odysseus is presented from a variety of perspectives, and the particular presentation serves the speaker's individual purposes.

Once again, the importance of the good listener for any song that aspires to "speak a man" is clear. For if the person cannot be "reported" objectively (that is, cannot be spoken without regard to the particular selves that observe and construe him), the speaking of the man must remain incomplete until some one listens to it and understands it. The narrative of the *Odyssey* is less a Muse-guaranteed and authoritative presenting of Odysseus, than it is a variety of efforts by several characters within the poem to "speak Odysseus"—to capture their own distinctive experiences of him. In eschewing the transparence of song-as-knowledge, the *Odyssey* offers a narrative, opaque and complex, that is an adequate vehicle for song conceived as the understanding of experience, rather than as the knowledge of events. The opaque narrative of the *Odyssey,* in more truly conveying the autonomous self, in turn reflects the listener's self. The listener's deepened awareness of his own autonomous self—a self that likens him to the hero who suffers, desires and understands—is the culmination, the *telos,* to which the *Odyssey* looks forward.

Conclusion

The family underlies the complexity of the individual, as presented in both the *Iliad* and the *Odyssey:* the intensity of the ties binding the warrior to father, wife, and homeland partly supplies the values of the warrior society with their emotional charge, and in the aftermath of war, helps ensure that the mortal, while inevitably vulnerable to the play of fortune, is not reducible to his or her immediate circumstances. The family is the focus of Achilles' memory in the *Iliad* and of Odysseus' desire in the *Odyssey*. It both prompts the suppliant's appeal and is the source of the emotions the suppliant hopes to rouse.

A final consideration of the family will afford some concluding insights into the relationship of the *Iliad* and the *Odyssey*. Far from offering escape from a strife-filled world, the family is itself distinguished by its considerable internal stresses and rifts. One of the most striking details in Phoenix's story of Meleager is the scene of Althaea, Meleager's mother, beating the ground and cursing her son after he killed her brother (*Il.* 9.565–72). While the *Odyssey* offers nothing so stark, the tension between son and mother—Telemachus and Penelope—is unmistakable. Telemachus more than once points out that Penelope's inability either to "say no to a hateful marriage" or "make an end" of it by marrying one of the suitors has resulted in the dissipation of what he pointedly calls "my household" (see 1.249–51; 16.126–28). Telemachus asserts that he can do nothing, however, to urge his mother to leave, for fear of her and his father's curses (see 2.130–37).

Athena plays on Telemachus' distrust of Penelope in order to spur him to hurry back to Ithaca from the Peloponnese. Athena deceitfully tells Telemachus that his mother is ready to marry Eurymachus and bestow the wealth of Odysseus' house on her new husband (15.14–19). Athena presents Penelope as utterly indifferent to Telemachus:

> For you know the heart in woman's breast:
> She wants to increase her husband's house,
> And no longer remembers or thinks of
> Her first children or her dead husband.
>
> (*Od.* 15.20–23)

Athena is lying, but her lies are persuasive because they reflect a tension inherent in the structure of the family: a woman was, to some extent, a stranger or *xeinos,* who had been incorporated into the house.[1] She is simultaneously insider and outsider, and the ambiguity of her status is reflected in her perceived ambivalence toward the child of her husband's house. Both the Meleager story and Athena's lies present a son's-eye view of the mother and reflect a suspicion of her divided loyalties. Just as Althaea calls down curses on Meleager (*Il.* 9.568–71), so does Telemachus fear his mother's curses, should he send her away (*Od.* 2.135).

Phoenix's account of his youth in *Iliad* 9 also emphasizes the enmity possible between father and son, and in particular the clash between the aging father's diminishing powers and the youth's burgeoning strength. As Phoenix tells Achilles, his own father Amyntor cursed him with sterility because of Phoenix's interference in Amyntor's affair with a mistress. The *Odyssey* too, draws attention to the inherent, "structural" tension between father and son, although it never permits any hint of actual antagonism to surface. It is clear that Telemachus is ready to take over the household and become its head. The *kleos* that Orestes achieved by avenging his father is dangled before Telemachus as a possibility in his own life.[2] The return of Odysseus, however, necessarily extinguishes any such ambitions, at least for the immediate future. Indeed, the *Odyssey* leaves unresolved the question what Telemachus' role in the house will be once Odysseus has returned.

The family's structural instability, where a number of deeply emo-

---

[1] On the woman as "outsider" in the patriarchal household, who is incorporated into the household through rituals centering on the hearth, see Katz, *Penelope's Renown,* pp. 135–37; Gould, "Hiketeia," pp. 97–98; Jean-Pierre Vernant, "Hestia-Hermes: The Religious Expression of Space and Movement among the Greeks," *Social Science Information* 8 (1969): 131–68, p. 136.

[2] On the connection between the *kleos* of Telemachus and of Orestes, see Katz, *Penelope's Renown,* pp. 66–72, who points out that for Telemachus, as for Orestes, the father's death would provide an occasion to show his own heroic capacities. Ibid., p. 68. See also Murnaghan, *Disguise and Recognition,* pp. 33–38, 156–59.

tional relations exist in potential conflict with each other, is the root cause both of Penelope's dilemma (whether to be true to her son or to her husband) and of Phoenix's catastrophe (for in honoring his mother's plea, he attacks his father's authority).

These structural tensions underlie, too, the misogyny that finds expression in the *Odyssey,* most strikingly, in Agamemnon's denunciation of Clytaemnestra. Precisely because the husband—Agamemnon or Odysseus—depends radically on the wife for recognition and restoration, she is his point of vulnerability. At one level, Clytaemnestra is a "bad" woman, and Penelope a "good" one. At another level, however, Clytaemnestra represents the fundamental instability of the family, which depends on two adults sharing the same wishes and aims.

Understood as an inherently unstable entity, the family can hardly serve as a final conclusion to the hero's journeying, for it is itself immersed in the tensions and ambiguities of the world. Hence, the *Odyssey* is not resolved by the restoration of a secure paternal authority once again on Ithaca. Even when he returns to his homeland and is restored to Telemachus, Odysseus is not "present" in the way Telemachus apparently had hoped he would be. As he appears to Telemachus, Odysseus is a chameleon-figure: old and bent when Telemachus first sees him but young and vigorous when he declares himself to be Odysseus (see *Od.* 16.172–212). His physical transformations reflect the vagaries of his life: "I am he," Odysseus says, assuring Telemachus that he is the astonished young man's father. "Having suffered evils and wandered much, I have returned in the twentieth year to my fatherland" (*Od.* 16.205–6).

Odysseus does not transcend such vagaries but physically embodies them in his transformation from weakness to strength. "No other Odysseus will come to you," he warns his son (*Od.* 16.204). Odysseus does not offer Telemachus release from the dangers of the world, nor does he restore for him the child's sense of security. The point is neatly made by a pun: "I am no god [*ou tis toi theos eimi*]," Odysseus says; "rather, I am your father [*alla patēr teos eimi*]" (16.187–88). The coincidence in sound of *theos* and *teos* gathers together god (*theos*) and mortal (*teos*), so that the contrast between them is pointed and striking.[3]

Odysseus, then, is never fully present to his son. The same was true of fathers in the *Iliad,* but what felt like tragic loss in that poem emerges here more as a challenge to the son to live up to the implications of his autonomy. When Odysseus ultimately challenges Telemachus not to shame the race of his fathers, the effect is different from when Glaucus'

---

[3] See Dimock, *Unity of the "Odyssey,"* p. 211; Goldhill, *Poet's Voice,* p. 10.

father similarly exhorts his son (*Il.* 6.206–10). "Telemachus," Odysseus tells his son as the two go off side by side to meet the angered kinsmen in battle, "now you will know—as you go where the best of battling men are distinguished—not to shame [*aiskhunein*] the race of your fathers—we who surpassed all others in strength and courage" (*Od.* 24.506–9). This scene is far different from those in the *Iliad* where the father sends his son off to war and imposes stringent codes of behavior on him. Odysseus and Telemachus are joint warriors. Laertes rejoices to see the day that his son and his son's son contend with each other in excellence (24.514–5). Odysseus' exhortation to Telemachus is an invitation to take up the same precarious existence as his father, having only the skills and cunning his father before him had with which to meet dangers.

The *Odyssey* brings us full circle. In the *Iliad*, fathers instilled in their sons that sense of shame that was such an important motivating force within the warrior society. The movement of the *Iliad*, however, was from shame as the emotional basis of the warrior society to pity as the basis for a friendship outside the *philotēs* of that society. Such pity constituted an understanding of loss as a necessary part of mortal life. It is just such a sense of himself as mortal and as one consigned to loss that characterizes Odysseus throughout the *Odyssey:* he seeks to be rejoined to Penelope to take up a relation that is expressly presented as transient and fleeting.

What Odysseus has to bequeath to his son is not the security of paternal authority, but a sense of the danger of the world and of the son's competence to be an autonomous being within that world. Coming at the conclusion of the *Odyssey*, the injunction not to shame the race of the fathers betokens the inability of one generation to shelter the next—to be an authoritative guide or to be wholly present and available to it. The father challenges the son to join the company of his ancestors, none of whom had anything more than the son has, and none of whom, consequently, can enable the son to avoid the obscurity and danger that comes with autonomy.

The instability of the family, as presented in both the *Iliad* and the *Odyssey*, suggests a kind of continuous oscillation: the two poems trace out between them the continuing cycle of the generations. The *Odyssey's* end—the father's injunction not to shame (*aiskhunein*) the race of the fathers—leads us back again to the *Iliad*, whose warriors are prompted by the father's injunction to feel shame and not to dishonor those who went before (see, e.g., *Il.* 6.209). The *Iliad*, in turn, traces the emergence of a sense of pity and an understanding of one's own experience of loss—an awareness that imbues the character of Odysseus throughout the *Odyssey*. Odysseus returns home only to leave again: his immediate departure reflects the view of the family not as final conclusion, but a phase or period in a constant oscillation between home and world, or between pity and shame.

Glaucus, in the *Iliad,* had compared the generations of men to the generations of leaves that bud and fall (see *Il.* 6.145–49). The regularity of this rhythm suggested to Glaucus the pointlessness of asking about another's background: the story of the generations, he suggested, was the essentially anonymous one of the leaves. The *Iliad* and *Odyssey* reflect the circularity of the generations, for the tradition handed down from father to son traces a circular progression from shame to pity and understanding, and from there, once again, to shame. Yet the two poems also show the eventfulness of this cycle: they rescue it from the anonymity of leaves. It is the peculiar merit of song that it captures at once the sameness of human experience and the significance of the individual's experience.

At the base of *aoidē,* construed as a tale of griefs, is the absence of the father: his inability to rescue the son or provide him with a "fatherly" world that reliably punishes the evil-doer and attends to the son's wishes. Even as a narrative about generations long ago, then, *aoidē* cannot offer knowledge—sure, authoritative, and reliable—but only understanding: a sense of the continuing story of each generation suffering its griefs and seeking somehow to come to grips with loss. As such, song can only tell its listeners what Odysseus tells his son: not to shame the race of their ancestors, but to embrace their mortal lot and employ their resources to achieve their best desires.

Bibliography

Adkins, Arthur W. H. "'Friendship' and 'Self-Sufficiency' in Homer and Aristotle." *Classical Quarterly* 55 (1963): 30–45.
Adkins, Arthur W. H. *Merit and Responsibility: A Study in Greek Values.* Oxford: Oxford University Press, 1960.
Amory, Anne. "The Gates of Horn and Ivory." *Yale Classical Studies* 20 (1966): 3–57.
Amory, Anne. "The Reunion of Odysseus and Penelope." In *Essays on the "Odyssey,"* edited by Charles H. Taylor, Jr., pp. 100–121. Bloomington: Indiana University Press, 1963.
Anderson, Ø. "Odysseus and the Wooden Horse." *Symbolae Osloenses* 52 (1977): 5–18.
Apthorp, M. J. "The Obstacles to Telemachus' Return." *Classical Quarterly,* n.s., 30 (1980): 1–22.
Arend, Walter. *Die Typische Scenen bei Homer.* 1933. Reprint, Berlin: Weidmann, 1975.
Arthur, Marylin B. "The Dream of a World without Women: Poetics and Circles of Order in the *Theogony* Prooemium." *Arethusa* 16 (1983): 97–116.
Ausfeld, C. "De Graecorum precationibus questiones." *Neue Jahrbücher Supp.* 28 (1903): 502–47.
Austin, Norman. *Archery at the Dark of the Moon: Poetic Problems in Homer's "Odyssey."* Berkeley: University of California Press, 1975.
Aycock, W. M., and T. M. Klein, eds. *Classical Mythology in Twentieth-Century Thought.* Proceedings of the Comparative Literature Symposium 11. Lubbock: Texas Tech Press, 1980.
Bassett, S. E. "The Proems of the *Iliad* and the *Odyssey*." *American Journal of Philology* 44 (1923): 339–48.
Beck, Götz. "Die Stellung des 24.Buches der *Ilias* in der Alten Epentradition." Inaugural diss., Tübingen, 1964.
Benveniste, Emile. *Le vocabulaire des institutions indo-européennes.* Paris: Editions de Minuit, 1969.

Besslich, S. *Schweigen—Verschweigen—Übergehen. Die Darstellung des Unausgesprochen in der "Odyssee."* Heidelberg: C. Winter, 1966.

Bethe, E. "Die Dorische Knabenliebe, ihre Ethik, ihre Idee." *Rheinisches Museum* 62 (1907): 438–75.

Blickman, Daniel R. "The Role of the Plague in the *Iliad*." *Classical Antiquity* 6 (1987): 1–10.

Böhme, Jacob. *Die Seele und das Ich im Homerischen Epos.* Leipzig: Teubner, 1929.

Brelich, Angelo. *Paides e Parthenoi.* Vol. 1. Rome: Ateneo, 1969.

Bremmer, Jan. *The Early Greek Concept of the Soul.* Princeton: Princeton University Press, 1983.

Brock, Nadia van. "Substitution rituelle." *Revue hittite et asianique* 65 (1959): 117–46.

Burke, Edmund. *A Philosophical Enquiry into the Origin of Our Ideas of the Sublime and Beautiful.* 1759. Reprint, Oxford: Oxford University Press, 1990.

Burkert, Walter, *Greek Religion.* Translated by John Raffan. Cambridge: Harvard University Press, 1985.

Burkert, Walter. *Structure and History in Greek Mythology and Ritual.* Berkeley: University of California Press, 1979.

Burkert, Walter. "Zum Altgriechischen Mitleidsbegriff." Inaugural diss., Friedrich-Alexander-Universität, Erlangen, 1955.

Bushnell, Rebecca W. "Reading 'Winged Words': Homeric Bird Signs, Similes, and Epiphanies." *Helios,* n.s., 9 (1982): 1–13.

Buxton, R. G. A. "Blindness and Limits: Sophokles and the Logic of Myth." *Journal of Hellenic Studies* 100 (1980): 22–37.

Calame, Claude. *Les choeurs de jeunes filles en Grece archaïque.* Rome: Ateneo, 1977.

Cheyns, A. "Sens et valuer du mot *Aidōs* dans les contextes homériques." *Recherches de philologie et de linguistique* 1 (1967): 3–33.

Clarke, W. M. "Achilles and Patroclus in Love." *Hermes* 106 (1978): 381–96.

Claus, David B. "*Aidōs* in the Language of Achilles." *Transactions of the American Philological Association* 105 (1975): 13–28.

Claus, David B. *Toward the Soul.* New Haven: Yale University Press, 1981.

Clay, Jenny Strauss. *The Wrath of Athena: Gods and Men in the "Odyssey."* Princeton: Princeton University Press, 1983.

Cole, Thomas. "Archaic Truth." *Quaderni Urbinati di Cultura Classica* 13 (1983): 7–28.

Cooper, John M. "Aristotle on Friendship." In *Essays on Aristotle's "Ethics,"* edited by Amélie Oksenberg Rorty, pp. 301–40. Berkeley: University of California Press, 1980.

Crotty, Kevin. *Song and Action: The Victory Odes of Pindar.* Baltimore: Johns Hopkins University Press, 1982.

D'Arms, Edward F., and Karl K. Hulley. "The Oresteia Story in the *Odyssey*." *Transactions of the American Philological Association* 76 (1946): 207–13.

Detienne, Marcel, and Jean-Pierre Vernant, eds. *The Cuisine of Sacrifice among the Greeks.* Translated by Paula Wissing. Chicago: University of Chicago Press, 1989.

Detienne, Marcel, and Jean-Pierre Vernant. *Les ruses de l'intelligence: La metis des Grecs.* Paris: Flammarion, 1974.

Devereux, Georges. "Penelope's Character." *Psychoanalytic Quarterly* 26 (1957): 378–86.

Dimock, George E. *The Unity of the "Odyssey."* Amherst: University of Massachusetts Press, 1989.

Dodds, E. R. *The Greeks and the Irrational.* Berkeley: University of California Press, 1951.

Dover, K. J. *Greek Homosexuality.* Cambridge: Harvard University Press, 1978.

Edwards, A. T. *Achilles in the "Odyssey": Ideologies of Heroism in the Homeric Epic.* Beiträge zur Klassischen Philologie 171. Königstein/Ts.: Hain, 1985.

Edwards, Mark W. *The "Iliad": A Commentary, Volume V: Books 17–20.* Cambridge: Cambridge University Press, 1991.

Eisenberger, Herbert. *Studien zur "Odyssee."* Wiesbaden: Steiner, 1973.

Eliade, Mircea. *Zalmoxis: The Vanishing God.* Translated by Willard R. Trask. Chicago: University of Chicago Press, 1972.

Fenik, Bernard. *Studies in the "Odyssey."* Hermes Einzelschriften 30. Wiesbaden: Steiner, 1974.

Fenik, Bernard. *Typical Battle Scenes in the "Iliad": Studies in the Narrative Techniques of Homeric Battle Descriptions.* Hermes Einzelschriften 21. Wiesbaden: Steiner, 1968.

Finley, John H., Jr. *Homer's "Odyssey."* Cambridge: Harvard University Press, 1978.

Finley, M. I. *The World of Odysseus.* Rev. ed. New York: Viking Press, 1977.

Finley, Robert. "Patroklos, Achilleus, and Peleus." *Classical World* 73 (1980): 267–73.

Foley, Helene P. "'Reverse Similes' and Sex Roles in the *Odyssey.*" *Arethusa* 11 (1978): 7–26.

Foley, Helene P. *Ritual Irony: Poetry and Sacrifice in Euripides.* Ithaca: Cornell University Press, 1985.

Ford, Andrew. *Homer: The Poetry of the Past.* Ithaca: Cornell University Press, 1992.

Fortenbaugh, W. W. *Aristotle on Emotion.* London: Duckworth, 1975.

Fränkel, Hermann. *Early Greek Poetry and Philosophy.* Translated by Moses Hadas and James Willis. New York: Harcourt Brace Jovanovich, 1973.

Frontisi-Ducroux, Françoise. *La cithare d'Achille: Essai sur la poétique de "l'Iliade."* Rome: Ateneo, 1986.

Geertz, Clifford. "Notes on the Balinese Cockfight." In *The Interpretation of Cultures,* pp. 412–53. New York: Basic Books, 1973.

Gentili, Bruno. *Poetry and Its Public in Ancient Greece.* Translated by A. Thomas Cole. Baltimore: Johns Hopkins University Press, 1988.

Glenn, Justin. "The Polyphemus Folktale and Homer's Kyklōpeia." *Transactions of the American Philological Association* 102 (1971): 133–81.

Golden, Leon. "Catharsis." *Transactions of the American Philological Association* 93 (1962): 51–60.

Goldhill, Simon. *The Poet's Voice: Essays on Poetics and Greek Literature.* Cambridge: Cambridge University Press, 1991.

Goody, Esther. "'Greeting,' 'Begging,' and the Presentation of Respect." In *The Interpretation of Ritual: Essays in Honor of A. I. Richards,* edited by J. S. LaFontaine. London: Tavistock, 1972.

Gould, John. "Hiketeia." *Journal of Hellenic Studies* 93 (1973): 74–103.

Griffin, Jasper. *Homer on Life and Death.* Oxford: Clarendon Press, 1980.

Halliwell, Stephen. *Aristotle's "Poetics."* London: Duckworth, 1986.

Halliwell, Stephen. "Pleasure, Understanding, and Emotion in Aristotle's *Poetics.*" In *Essays on Aristotle's "Poetics,"* edited by Amélie Oksenberg Rorty, pp. 241–60. Princeton: Princeton University Press, 1992.

Harsh, Phillip. "Penelope and Odysseus in *Odyssey* XIX." *American Journal of Philology* 71 (1950): 1–21.

Havelock, Eric A. *Preface to Plato.* Cambridge: Harvard University Press, 1963.

Heubeck, Alfred, Stephanie West, and J. B. Hainsworth. *A Commentary on Homer's "Odyssey." Volume 1: Introduction and Books I–VIII.* Oxford: Oxford University Press, 1988.

Hölscher, Uvo. "Die Atridensage in der *Odyssee.*" In *Festschrift für Richard Alewyn,* edited by H. Singer and B. von Weise. Cologne: Böhlau, 1967.

Howald, E. *Der Dichter der "Ilias."* Zurich: Rentsch, 1946.

Huizinga, Johan. *Homo Ludens.* Boston: Beacon, 1950.

Hurwit, Jeffrey M. *The Art and Culture of Early Greece, 1100–480 B.C.* Ithaca: Cornell University Press, 1985.

Janko, Richard. *Aristotle on Comedy: Towards a Reconstruction of "Poetics II."* London: Duckworth, 1984.

Janko, Richard. *Aristotle: "Poetics I."* Indianapolis: Hackett, 1987.

Janko, Richard. "From Catharsis to the Aristotelian Mean." In *Essays on Aristotle's "Poetics,"* edited by Amélie Oksenberg Rorty, pp. 341–58. Princeton: Princeton University Press, 1992.

Jeanmaire, Henri. *Couroi et courètes: Essai sur l'education spartiate et les rites d'adolescence dans l'antiquité hellénique.* Lille: Bibliotheque Universitaire, 1939.

Jeanmaire, Henri. "Le substantif *Hosia* et sa signification comme terme technique dans le vocabulaire religieux." *Revue des études grecques* 58 (1945): 66–89.

Jones, Peter V. "The *Kleos* of Telemachus: *Odyssey* 1.95." *American Journal of Philology* 109 (1988): 496–506.

Kakridis, Johannes Th. *Homeric Researches.* Lund: Gleerup, 1949.

Katz, Marylin A. *Penelope's Renown: Meaning and Indeterminacy in the "Odyssey."* Princeton: Princeton University Press, 1991.

Kaufman-Bühler, Dieter. "Hesiod und die Tisis in der *Odyssee.*" *Hermes* 84 (1956–57): 267–95.

Kessels, A. H. M. *Studies in the Dream in Greek Literature.* Utrecht: HES Publishers, 1973.

King, Katherine Callen. *Achilles: Paradigms of the War Hero from Homer to the Middle Ages.* Berkeley: University of California Press, 1987.

Kirk, G. S. *The "Iliad": A Commentary. Volume 1: Books 1–4.* Cambridge: Cambridge University Press, 1985.

Kirk, G. S., ed. *The Language and Background of Homer.* Cambridge: Cambridge University Press, 1964.

Kosman, L. A. "Being Properly Affected: Virtues and Feelings in Aristotle's *Ethics.*" In *Essays on Aristotle's "Ethics,"* edited by Amélie Oksenberg Rorty, pp. 103–16. Berkeley: University of California Press, 1980.

LaFontaine, J. S., ed. *The Interpretation of Ritual: Essays in Honor of A. I. Richards.* London: Tavistock, 1972.

Latacz, Joachim. *Zum Wortfeld 'Freude' in der Sprache Homers.* Heidelberg: Winter, 1966.

Lear, Jonathan. "Katharsis." In *Essays on Aristotle's "Poetics,"* edited by Amélie Oksenberg Rorty, pp. 315–40. Princeton: Princeton University Press, 1992.

Lesky, Albin. "Göttliche und Menschliche Motivation im Homerischen Epos." *Sitzungsberichte der Heidelberger Akademie der Wissenschaften, Phil.-Hist. Kl.* 4 (1961): 1–52.

Lloyd-Jones, Hugh. *The Justice of Zeus.* Berkeley: University of California Press, 1971.

Lohmann, Dieter. *Die Komposition der Reden in der Ilias.* Berlin: de Gruyter, 1970.

Long, A. A. "Morals and Values in Homer." *Journal of Hellenic Studies* 90 (1970): 121–39.

Lonsdale, Steven H. *Creatures of Speech: Lion, Herding, and Hunting Similes in the "Iliad."* Stuttgart: Teubner, 1990.

Lord, A. B. *The Singer of Tales.* Cambridge: Harvard University Press, 1960.

Lord, Mary Louise. "Withdrawal and Return: An Epic Story Pattern in the Homeric Hymn to Demeter and in the Homeric Poems." *Classical Journal* 62 (1967): 241–48.

Lowenstam, Steven. *The Death of Patroclus: A Study in Typology.* Beiträge zur Klassischen Philologie 133. Königstein/Ts.: Hain, 1981.

Lynn-George, Michael. *Epos: Word, Narrative, and the "Iliad."* Houndmills, U.K.: Macmillan, 1988.

MacCary, W. Thomas. *Childlike Achilles: Ontogeny and Phylogeny in the "Iliad."* New York: Columbia University Press, 1982.

Macleod, C. W. *Homer: "Iliad," Book XXIV.* Cambridge: Cambridge University Press, 1982.

Makarius, Laura. "Le mythe du 'Trickster.'" *Revue de l'histoire des religions* 175 (1969): 17–46.

Marg, Walter. *Homer über die Dichtung.* Munster: Aschendorffsche Verlagsbuchhandlung, 1957.

Marquardt, Patricia. "Penelope *Polutropos.*" *American Journal of Philology* 106 (1985): 32–48.

Martin, Richard P. *The Language of Heroes: Speech and Performance in the "Iliad."* Ithaca: Cornell University Press, 1989.

Mattes, Wilhelm. *Odysseus bei den Phäaken.* Würzburg: Trilsch, 1958.

Monro, D. B. *Homer's "Odyssey": Books XIII–XXIV.* Oxford: Clarendon Press, 1901.

Monsacré, Hélène. *Les larmes d'Achille.* Paris: Albin Michel, 1984.

Moore, Sally F., and Barbara G. Myerhoff, eds. *Secular Ritual.* Assen: van Gorcum, 1977.

Moran, William Stephen. "*Mimnēskomai* and 'Remembering' Epic Stories in Homer and the Hymns." *Quaderni urbinati di cultura classica* 20 (1975): 195–215.

Motto, A. L., and J. R. Clark. "Isē Dais: The Honor of Achilles." *Arethusa* 2 (1969): 109–25.

Mülder, Dietrich. "Götteranrufungen in *Ilias* und *Odyssee.*" *Rheinisches Museum* 78 (1929): 35–53.

Murnaghan, Sheila. *Disguise and Recognition in the "Odyssey."* Princeton: Princeton University Press, 1987.

Murray, Penelope. "Poetic Inspiration in Early Greece." *Journal of Hellenic Studies* 101 (1981): 87–100.

Nagler, Michael N. "Odysseus: The Proem and the Problem." *Classical Antiquity* 9 (1990): 335–56.

Nagler, Michael N. *Spontaneity and Tradition: A Study in the Oral Art of Homer.* Berkeley: University of California Press, 1974.

Nagy, Gregory. *The Best of the Achaeans: Concepts of the Hero in Archaic Greek Poetry.* Baltimore: Johns Hopkins University Press, 1979.

Nagy, Gregory. *Comparative Studies in Greek and Indic Meter.* Cambridge: Harvard University Press, 1974.

Nietzsche, Friedrich. *Beyond Good and Evil.* Translated by R. J. Hollingdale. London: Penguin, 1990.

Nietzsche, Friedrich. *"On the Genealogy of Morals" and "Ecce Homo."* Translated by Walter Kaufmann and R. J. Hollingdale. New York: Vintage, 1969.

Notopoulos, J. A. "Mnemosune in Oral Literature." *Transactions of the American Philological Association* 69 (1938): 465–93.

Nussbaum, Martha C. *The Fragility of Goodness: Luck and Ethics in Greek Tragedy and Philosophy.* Cambridge: Cambridge University Press, 1986.

Nussbaum, Martha C. "Tragedy and Self-Sufficiency: Plato and Aristotle on Fear and Pity." In *Essays on Aristotle's "Poetics,"* edited Amélie Oksenberg Rorty, pp. 261–90. Princeton: Princeton University Press, 1992.

Olson, S. Douglas. "The Stories of Agamemnon in Homer's *Odyssey.*" *Transactions of the American Philological Association* 120 (1990): 57–71.

Onians, R. B. *The Origins of European Thought.* Cambridge: Cambridge University Press, 1951.

Page, Denys. *The Homeric "Odyssey."* Oxford: Clarendon Press, 1955.

Parry, Adam. "The Language of Achilles." *Transactions of the American Philological Association* 87 (1956): 1–7. Reprinted in *The Language and Background of Homer,* edited by G. S. Kirk. Cambridge: Cambridge University Press, 1964.

Parry, Milman. *The Making of Homeric Verse: The Collected Papers of Milman Parry.* Oxford: Clarendon Press, 1971.

Pedrick, Victoria. "The Hospitality of Noble Women in the *Odyssey.*" *Helios* 15 (1988): 85–101.

Pedrick, Victoria. "Supplication in the *Iliad* and the *Odyssey.*" *Transactions of the American Philological Association* 112 (1982): 125–40.

Pelton, Robert D. *The Trickster in West Africa.* Berkeley: University of California Press, 1980.

Peradotto, John. *Man in the Middle Voice: Name and Narration in the "Odyssey."* Princeton: Princeton University Press, 1990.

Pohlenz, Max. "Furcht und Mitleid? Ein Nachwort." *Hermes* 84 (1956): 49–74.

Pucci, Pietro. "The Language of the Muses." In *Classical Mythology in Twentieth-Century Thought,* edited by W. M. Aycock and T. M. Klein. Proceedings of the Comparative Literature Symposium 11. Lubbock: Texas Tech Press, 1980.

Pucci, Pietro. *Odysseus Polutropos: Intertextual Readings in the "Odyssey" and the "Iliad."* Ithaca: Cornell University Press, 1987.

Pucci, Pietro. "The Proem of the *Odyssey.*" *Arethusa* 15 (1982): 39–62.

Pucci, Pietro. "The Song of the Sirens." *Arethusa* 12 (1979): 121–32.

Pucci, Pietro. *The Violence of Pity in Euripides' "Medea."* Ithaca: Cornell University Press, 1980.

Radermacher, L. "Die Erzählungen der *Odyssee.*" *Sitzungsberichte der Kais. Akademie der Wissenschaften in Wien.* Phil.-Hist. Kl. 178 (1915): 1–59.

Radin, Paul. *The Trickster: A Study in American Indian Mythology.* New York: Greenwood Press, 1956.

Rankin, Anne Vannan. "Penelope's Dreams in Book XIX and XX of the *Odyssey.*" *Helikon* 2 (1962): 617–24.

Redfield, James M. "The Economic Man." In *Approaches to Homer,* edited by Carl A. Rubino and Cynthia W. Shelmerdine, pp. 218–47. Austin: University of Texas Press, 1983.

Redfield, James M. *Nature and Culture in the "Iliad."* Chicago: University of Chicago Press, 1975.

Redfield, James M. "The Proem of the Iliad: Homer's Art." *Classical Philology* 74 (1979): 95–110.

Richardson, Nicholas. *The "Iliad": A Commentary. Volume VI: Books 21–24.* Cambridge: Cambridge University Press, 1993.

Roisman, Hannah M. "*Kerdion* in the *Iliad:* Profit and Trickiness." *Transactions of the American Philological Association* 120 (1990): 23–35.

Rorty, Amélie Oksenberg, ed. *Essays on Aristotle's "Ethics."* Berkeley: University of California Press, 1980.

Rorty, Amélie Oksenberg, ed. *Essays on Aristotle's "Poetics."* Princeton: Princeton University Press, 1992.

Rosner, Judith A. "The speech of Phoenix: *Iliad* 9.434–605." *Phoenix* 30 (1976): 314–27.

Rousseau, Jean-Jacques. *"The Social Contract" and "Discourse on the Origin of Inequality."* New York: Washington Square Press, 1967.

Rubino, Carl A., and Cynthia W. Shelmerdine, eds. *Approaches to Homer.* Austin: University of Texas Press, 1983.

Russo, Joseph. "Interview and Aftermath: Dream, Fantasy, and Intuition in *Odyssey* 19 and 20." *American Journal of Philology* 103 (1982): 4–18.

Russo, Joseph, Manuel Fernández-Galiano, and Alfred Heubeck. *A Commentary on Homer's Odyssey.* Vol. III. Oxford: Clarendon Press, 1992.

Rutherford, R. B. "The Philosophy of the *Odyssey.*" *Journal of Hellenic Studies* 106 (1986): 145–62.

Saïd, Suzanne. "Les crimes des pretendants, la maison d'Ulysse et les festins de l'*Odyssée.*" In *Etudes de littérature ancienne,* 9–49. Paris: Presses de l'Ecole Normale Supérieure, 1979.

Schadewaldt, Wolfgang. "Furcht und Mitleid?" *Hermes* 83 (1955): 129–71.

Schein, Seth L. *The Mortal Hero.* Berkeley: University of California Press, 1984.

Schlunk, Robin R. "The Theme of the Suppliant-Exile in the *Iliad.*" *American Journal of Philology* 97 (1976): 199–209.

Schouler, Bernard. "Dépasser le père." *Revue des études grecques* 93 (1980): 1–24.

Schwenn, F. *Gebet und Opfer.* Heidelberg: C. Winter, 1927.

Scodel, Ruth. "The Autobiography of Phoenix: *Iliad* 9.444–95." *American Journal of Philology* 103 (1982): 128–36.

Scott, Mary. "Pity and Pathos in Homer." *Acta Classica* 22 (1979): 1–14.

Segal, Charles. "*Kleos* and Its Ironies in the *Odyssey.*" *L'Antiquité classique* 52 (1983): 22–47.

Segal, Charles. *The Theme of the Mutilation of the Corpse in the "Iliad."* Mnemosyne Supplement 17. Leiden: Brill, 1971.

Sergent, Bernard. *Homosexuality in Greek Myth.* Translated by Arthur Goldhammer. Boston: Beacon Press, 1984.

Servais, Jean. "Les suppliants dans la 'Loi sacré' de Cyrène." *Bulletin de correspondance hellénique* 84 (1960): 112–47.

Simon, Bennett. *Mind and Madness in Ancient Greece.* Ithaca: Cornell University Press, 1978.

Sinos, Dale. *Achilles, Patroklos, and the Meaning of "Philos."* Innsbrücker Beiträge zur Sprachwissenschaft 29. Innsbruck: Institut für Sprachwissenschaft der Universität Innsbruck, 1980.

Slatkin, Laura M. *The Power of Thetis: Allusion and Interpretation in the "Iliad."* Berkeley: University of California Press, 1991.

Slatkin, Laura M. "The Wrath of Thetis." *Transactions of the American Philological Association* 116 (1986): 1–24.

Smith, Adam. *The Theory of Moral Sentiments.* 1853. Reprint, New York: Augustus M. Kelley, 1966.

Snell, Bruno. *The Discovery of the Mind.* Translated by T. G. Rosenmeyer. 1953. Reprint, New York: Dover, 1982.

Solmsen, Friedrich. *Hesiodi Theogonia, Opera et Dies, Scutum.* Oxford: Clarendon Press, 1970.

Stanford, W. B. *Greek Tragedy and the Emotions: An Introductory Study.* London: Routledge & Kegan Paul, 1983.

Stanford, W. B. *The "Odyssey" of Homer.* 2 vols. Houndmills, U.K.: Macmillan, 1974.

Svenbro, Jasper. *La parole et le marbre: Aux origines de la poëtique grecque.* Lund: Studentlitteratur, 1976.

Tambiah, Stanley Jeyaraja. *Culture, Thought, and Social Action: An Anthropological Perspective.* Cambridge: Harvard University Press, 1985.

Taylor, Charles H., Jr. *Essays on the "Odyssey."* Bloomington: Indiana University Press, 1963.

Thalmann, W. G. *Conventions of Form and Thought in Early Greek Epic Poetry.* Baltimore: Johns Hopkins University Press, 1984.

Thornton, Agathe. *Homer's "Iliad": Its Composition and the Motif of Supplication.* Hypomnemata 81. Gottingen: Vandenhoeck & Ruprecht, 1984.

Thornton, Agathe. *People and Themes in Homer's "Odyssey."* London: Methuen, 1970.

Turner, Victor. *The Ritual Process.* 1969. Reprint, Ithaca: Cornell University Press, 1977.

Ulf, Christof. *Die Homerische Gesellschaft: Materialen zur Analytischen Beschreibung und Historischen Lokalisierung.* Munich: Beck'sche Verlagsbuchhandlung, 1990.

van der Valk, M. H. A. L. H. "Quelques remarques sur le sens du nom Hosia." *Revue des études grecques* 64 (1951): 417–22.

van Gennep, Arnold. *Rites of Passage.* Translated by Monika B. Vizedon and Gabriel L. Caffee. Chicago: University of Chicago Press, 1961.

van Groningen, B. A. "The Proems of the *Iliad* and the *Odyssey.*" *Mededeelingen der Koninklijke Nederlandse Akademie van Wetenschappen.* Afd. Letterkunde, n.s., 9 (1946): 279–94.

Vernant, Jean-Pierre. "At Man's Table." In *The Cuisine of Sacrifice among the Greeks,* edited by Marcel Detienne and Jean-Pierre Vernant, translated by Paula Wissing. Chicago: University of Chicago Press, 1989.

Vernant, Jean-Pierre. "Hestia-Hermes: The Religious Expression of Space and Movement among the Greeks." *Social Science Information* 8 (1969): 131–68.

Vernant, Jean-Pierre. *Mortals and Immortals: Collected Essays.* Translated by Froma Zeitlin. Princeton: Princeton University Press, 1991.

Vernant, Jean-Pierre. *Mythe et pensée chez les Grecs.* Paris: Maspéro, 1965.

Vickers, Brian. *Towards Greek Tragedy.* London: Longman, 1979.

Vidal-Naquet, Pierre. *The Black Hunter: Forms of Thought and Forms of Society in the Greek World.* Translated by Andrew Szegedy-Maszak. Baltimore: Johns Hopkins University Press, 1983.

von der Mühll, Peter. *Kritisches Hypomnema zur "Ilias."* Schweizer Beiträge zur Altertumswissenschaft 4. Basel: Reinhardt, 1952.

von Erffa, Carl Eduard Frhr. *"Aidōs" und Verwandte Begriffe in Ihrer Entwicklung von Homer bis Demokrit.* Philologus Supplementband 30, Fasc. 2. Leipzig: Dieterich'sche Verlagsbuchhandlung, 1937.

von Fritz, Kurt. "Greek Prayer." *Review of Religions* 10 (1945–46): 5–39.

von Wilamowitz-Moellendorff, Ulrich. *Die "Ilias" und Homer.* 2nd ed. Berlin: Weidmann, 1920.

Walcot, P. "Odysseus and the Art of Lying." *Ancient Society* 8 (1977): 1–19.

Walsh, George B. *The Varieties of Enchantment.* Chapel Hill: University of North Carolina Press, 1984.

Webber, Alice. "The Hero Tells His Name: Formula and Variation in the Phaeacian Episode of the *Odyssey.*" *Transactions of the American Philological Association* 119 (1989): 1–13.

Wender, Dorothea. *The Last Scenes of the "Odyssey."* Mnemosyne Supplement 52. Leiden: Brill, 1978.

West, Stephanie. "Laertes Revisited." *Proceedings of the Cambridge Philological Society,* n.s., 35 (1989): 113–43.

Whitfield, Guy Kevin. "The Restored Relation: The Supplication Theme in the 'Iliad.'" Ph.D. diss., Columbia University, 1967.

Whitman, Cedric H. *Homer and the Heroic Tradition.* Cambridge: Harvard University Press, 1958.

Winkler, John J. *The Constraints of Desire.* New York: Routledge, 1990.

Ziegler, K. "De precationum apud Graecos formis Questiones Selectae." Diss., Breslau, 1905.

Index Locorum

General Index

Achilles, 44, 45, 103, 112, 127, 138, 183
  and absence of Peleus, 113–14
  abuse of Hector's body, 6
  and Agamemnon's breach of shame,
    34–35, 92
  delight in sight of Priam, 101–2
  and destructive wrath, 158–59
  on evils sent by gods, 130, 131
  and friendship with Priam, 5, 23, 83–
    84, 86, 87, 88, 130, 177, 182, 199
  and gods' absence, 97
  and gods' participation in Priam's sup-
    plication, 70–72
  Hector's dying plea to, 4, 5, 9–10, 14,
    152
  and Hector's imagined supplication, 85–
    87
  insight of, 78–80, 89, 93, 98–99, 167,
    168
  lament for Patroclus, 39, 40, 48–49
  and Lycaon's supplication, 84–85
  memory of grief for Patroclus, 69, 71,
    72, 73, 74, 75, 76–77, 102
  and memory of Peleus, 24, 39–40, 75–
    76, 89
  Odysseus' advice to, 50, 59–64, 65–69,
    80, 137
  and parable of jars, 77–78, 80–81, 137
  passion of, 140–41
  Patroclus' plea to, 46, 50, 54–59
  Peleus' advice to, 26–28, 35
  and Phoenix, 26
  and pity as *katharsis*, 15
  and pity for Peleus, 37
  reconciliation with Agamemnon, 59,
    61, 62, 157

  return of Hector's body to Priam, 81–
    82
  and Thetis' supplication to Zeus, 94,
    96–97
  and warrior society values, 7–8, 30, 33,
    36, 211
Adkins, Arthur, 28–30
Aegisthus, 113, 131, 133, 145, 153
Aeneas, 25–26, 138–39
Agamemnon, 184
  Antimachus' sons' supplication to, 9
  and Chryses, 21–22, 34, 56, 87, 88, 92,
    111
  and Clytaemnestra, 213
  murder of, 113, 145, 153
  offer of reparation to Achilles, 33, 39,
    51, 53, 72
  reconciliation with Achilles, 59, 61, 62,
    157
Agathos, 28–29
Aidōs. See Shame
Ajax, 33, 72, 149
Alcinous, 116, 162, 164, 208–9
  and Demodocus' song, 124, 126, 130
  invitation to Odysseus, 160, 161
  on Odysseus as a god, 135, 142
  and Odysseus' supplication to Arete,
    134
Althaea, 211
Amphimedon, 184, 197n.32
Amphinomus, 150, 154, 156
Amyntor, 52–53, 54, 212
Andromache, 29, 31, 32, 74, 86
  grief for Hector, 73
  plea to Hector for pity, 46, 47–48, 49–
    51, 124

234

MYTH AND POETICS

A series edited by
GREGORY NAGY